RUN!

RUN!

My Story of
LGBTQ+ Political Power,
Equality, and Acceptance
in Silicon Valley

Ken Yeager, PhD

atmosphere press

Published by Atmosphere Press

Cover design by Dan DiVittorio

Atmospherepress.com

To Michael Haberecht, for his love and support for this project and all our years together

TABLE OF CONTENTS

INTRODUCTION

There were two main reasons why I wrote *Run!* The first was to record the progression of the LGBTQ+ movement from political outcasts to integral community members in San Jose/Silicon Valley. Having lived and breathed queer activism for almost 40 years, I felt uniquely positioned to tell this story.

Further, San Jose/Silicon Valley has a unique story—separate from San Francisco's—that illustrates how queer people in a large suburban city went about bringing dramatic social change. The lessons learned and the strategies used may serve as a guide for activists elsewhere when organizing to counter the current uptick of anti-gay and anti-trans hostilities in their communities.

I am keenly aware that the history in San Jose/Silicon Valley could be overlooked or forgotten by others, resulting in the next generation believing no gay activism happened here. Nothing could be further from the truth. That is why I have tried to recount as much of this crucial history as I could, both in this book and in my history project *Queer Silicon Valley*.

I hope *Run!* will inspire queer people to write about their own histories so they are not lost. This can be done through a website, podcasts, short essays, or video recordings. From such beginnings, a full-scale history project can be born.

The second reason for writing *Run!* is to serve as a roadmap for people thinking of pursuing public office. As I hope to show from my own experience, serving as an elected official is one of the most effective ways to improve the lives of everyone in our communities, especially LGBTQ+ residents whose issues have often been ignored by the government.

As I look back on my almost three decades in office, I know many of my legislative achievements only happened because I was in the room when decisions were being made. This is true for small victories like raising the Rainbow flag for the first time at City Hall, as well as for bigger things like creating the nation's first county Office of LGBTQ+ Affairs and opening a Gender Health Clinic.

Most cities—and certainly counties—have never elected an LGBTQ+ person to their councils or boards. This was true for me. No LGBTQ+ person had been elected to the San Jose City Council or any city council in the county until I won a seat in 2000. This was significant because San Jose is the third most populous city in California and the 12th largest in the U.S. In 2006, when I was elected to the Santa Clara County Board of Supervisors, I was the first gay person elected to that body as well.

The election of a queer person makes a statement far beyond that of the winning candidate. It sends a strong signal to the business sector, the political class, party activists, and the larger community that support for a queer candidate demonstrates backing for the LGBTQ+ community at large. Residents often care more about who represents them in their city and county than at higher levels of government because people's quality of life is much more closely tied to local services. That is why it is so meaningful when they select someone who is LGBTQ+ to make decisions on behalf of the whole community, overcoming the false narrative that gays are "one-issue" candidates.

The thread that weaves both themes together is my personal story. When I was a political science student at San Jose State University in the early to mid-1970s, the idea of running for office never occurred to me. Why would it? I had never heard of any gay person being elected before. Harvey Milk would accomplish it in 1977, but that was San Francisco, not San Jose. As a queer person, I felt that I had better odds of walking on the moon than I did of being elected to office.

4

As I transitioned from staff aide to gay activist, to neighborhood leader, I saw a path slowly being cleared by my own hands and the hands of others. I ran down that path in 1992 when I filed papers for a seat on the community college board and stopped in 2018 when I was termed out of my third elective office.

I hope society is getting closer to the day when anyone—regardless of sexual orientation or gender identity—feels they can pursue their dreams, including seeking office at the local, state, or federal level. That is part of the legacy I want to leave behind. I hope my story moves us closer to that goal.

CHAPTER 1

Do You Know the Way to San Jose?

My interest in politics began at an early age. Two weeks after starting seventh grade, I ran for class president and won. I don't know what possessed me to run or, more accurately, what possessed my mother to encourage me to run. Surely it was her idea; I had never been so much as a room monitor in elementary school. I remember sitting around the kitchen table with my family making campaign buttons out of construction paper and writing clever political slogans that Mom made up as we went along. I continued serving in student body offices for five of my six years in junior and high school. Holding office gave me a great deal of confidence and helped me establish my own identity. Little did I know it would help me on my path to elected office.[1]

My mother, while never a political activist, always had a sense of fairness and high moral standards. It was from her that I inherited my interest in politics. She was against war, poverty, bigotry, and racism, and by the time I was a teenager, I was against these things, too. After joining the school newspaper staff in the eighth grade, I wrote editorials against the Vietnam

---

1   Note: Sections about my early life, the founding of BAYMEC, and my campaigns for community college board and assembly were published in *Trailblazers: Profiles of America's Gay and Lesbian Elected Officials.* Ken Yeager. "The Making of a Candidate: A Personal Memoir." Haworth Press. 1999.

War and in support of the student protests. In the ninth grade, I was named editor and elected student body president. Looking back, I have no idea where I found the wherewithal to do either, much less both. As a teenager, I was on autopilot, full of energy and free of the self-doubts that plagued me as an adult.

I inherited several traits from my father. First would be my work ethics and work habits. He ran a heavy construction company in our hometown of Riverside, California, which is 60 miles southeast of Los Angeles and is part of the Inland Empire. The family business was started and named for my grandfather, E.L. Yeager Company. People in town knew the Yeager name because it was painted on all the trucks and heavy equipment that traveled to construction sites. People I met would often ask if I was part of *the* Yeager family. Years later, I would laugh when I saw my name on lawn signs throughout my district and wonder if this always was to be my destiny.

My father was highly competent and successful at what he did. Observing him, I learned that for any endeavor to succeed, you must devote a large amount of time and energy to it. He would spend workdays and weekends putting together multi-million-dollar bids for large engineering contracts. Throughout my childhood, I would see him leave for work in the morning and come home late in the day, six days a week. He never complained, seldom was cross, and was practically never home. By the time I was 12 and gaining a sense of who I was, I already found myself enjoying working on projects away from home, like student government and the newspaper, rather than being with my family. This would be a pattern I would follow in my adult life: working late into the evening on political activities I loved.

Ever since I can remember, I knew I was gay. As I grew older, I knew that all the demeaning stereotypes about gay men weren't true about me, so I never felt any shame or sinfulness about who I was. As a young teenager, I thought I was the only gay person in the entire town. I didn't know any out students in high school, but then I hid my gayness pretty well, preventing any other gay person from revealing themselves to me. I was popular in school and had a platonic relationship with a smart and wonderful girl for three years, so I was never suspected of being gay or called names.

Because people knew of the Yeager name, I worried that I would bring shame to my family if people discovered the truth about me. That is why I knew I could never be gay in my hometown and why I needed to leave as soon as I could. So, on one hot, smoggy day after I graduated high school in 1971, I left Riverside for good, driving 400 miles to San Jose State University (SJSU).

Looking back on why I had to leave and what I missed out on, I wonder if the religious right and social conservatives realize how their lies about LGBTQ+ people separate families, for we queer youth leave our hometowns in more significant numbers than non-queer teenagers. Our absence means we do not have the opportunity to get to know our parents, siblings, nieces, and nephews as well as we would have if the climate allowed us to stay. I became part of the gay diaspora, where we are transported to towns where no one knows us and where we must create a new identity by ourselves.

A New Life in San Jose

There was always something about San Jose that kept me there long after I graduated in 1976. Even as a newly enrolled undergraduate, I knew I could create the kind of life I imagined for myself and explore my sexuality in ways I couldn't in Riverside. In addition, I sensed that I could use my political idealism to bring about social change in San Jose, where it was needed more than in cities like Los Angeles or San Francisco. In the 1970s, San Jose was still governed by conservative Republican white men. Still, I felt that was about to change with the explosive population growth it was undergoing.

It was my good fortune that SJSU had an excellent political science department, particularly in the study of local government. This allowed me to get involved in city politics early on. As a senior, I interned at San Jose City Hall for Susanne (Susie) Wilson, a councilwoman with whom I would have a long association. I remember spending more than the required hours in her office, almost pleading that she gives me as much work as possible so I could prove myself competent.

Politically, minorities and women were beginning to be elected to local office. Hometown hero Norm Mineta—future congressman, secretary of transportation under Bill Clinton, and commerce secretary under George W. Bush—was elected mayor of San Jose in 1971, the first Asian-American mayor of a large U.S. city. He was followed by Janet Gray Hayes in 1974, the first female mayor of a U.S. city of over 500,000 people.

My willingness to put in long hours at City Hall led me to be asked to be Susie Wilson's campaign precinct coordinator for her re-election in 1976. Her campaign took place before district elections were adopted, which meant candidates had to run citywide. I knew the campus area pretty well, but little of the growing city where orchards were being plowed under to make way for miles of new residential neighborhoods. It was an overwhelming job for a 22-year-old who had never worked on a political campaign. Nevertheless, I lived and breathed it, barely attending my classes. Through the experience, I met people I still have contact with nearly five decades later, many of whom helped me when I ran for public office. It also taught me how to be a campaign manager, a skill I would use my entire adult life, especially in my own campaigns.

As exhilarating as this was, I had always harbored thoughts of being a writer. I had given politics a try so, at the age of 25, I decided now was the time to try writing. From 1978 to 1979, I lived in Chicago, reading American novelists and writing hopelessly incoherent short stories, all the while working various demeaning jobs to make enough money to live in my studio apartment. As months of bitter cold and oppressive humidity passed, I grew pretty miserable and depressed, slowly concluding that I would be a total failure as a fiction writer. By this time, as luck would have it, Wilson was elected to the Board of Supervisors. She asked me if I wanted to work as one of her aides: I took the next plane out.

Except for the two years in Chicago, the years between college graduation in 1976 and when I came out publicly as a gay man were filled with politics. Throughout this period, I was resolved to be a behind-the-scenes person. It never once occurred to me that I would run for public office. How could I run? I was gay. Except for Harvey Milk, I wasn't aware of any gay politicians.

More concerning, there was an anti-gay backlash sweeping the country. In the late 1970s and early 1980s, gay civil rights laws were being repealed, starting in Dade County, Florida. In this homophobic atmosphere, the best I could do was wait quietly in the background. In most cases, I worked for women candidates because I felt that having women in leadership positions would begin to change the rigid roles that society dictated for men and women. The ability to break down barriers—be they for women, gays, lesbians, bisexuals, transgender people, or any minority group member—is the primary reason why I became involved in politics.

In 1982, while working for Supervisor Wilson, I was told by a good friend that our much revered local congressman, Don Edwards, was looking for someone to run his re-election campaign. I thought it would be a good career opportunity for me, so I applied and was hired. After the successful campaign, Edwards asked if I wanted to work in his DC office as his press secretary. After telling him I was gay—something he had no problem with—I said yes. So off I went to Washington, dreaming my rapid ascent in national politics had begun.

I found DC an exciting place to work. There was always

something to do, something to see, someone to meet. It was non-stop, and I loved it. But slowly, I began to look around, and what I saw were carbon copies of myself—an army of young, educated go-getters competing with each other to claw to the next level on the congressional staff ladder. Maybe if you were exceptionally gifted and aggressive, you could climb the rungs—that is, until 20 years later, when you find yourself as an assistant to a cabinet official. It would be worth the effort for many, but not for me.

I knew one limiting factor would be my sexual orientation. In 1983, there was only a handful of gay DC staffers. The National Gay and Lesbian Task Force (NGLTF) existed, but it was a relatively small operation. It was run by Steve Endean, whom I got to know. He tried to get LGBTQ+ staffers together, but there just weren't enough of us to keep it going. Coincidentally in the late 1990s when I was writing my book on openly gay and lesbian officials across the country, I learned more about his previous history after interviewing Minnesota State Senator Allan Spear. Endean ran the campaign to stop a gay rights ordinance from being overturned in St. Paul, similar to a campaign in San Jose shortly after. I have fond memories of him. He was a real pioneer. Sadly, he died of AIDS in 1992.

So, in 1984, back to San Jose I went, coordinating press outreach from the congressional district office. I did so believing that I could bring about more significant change at the grassroots level rather than the federal level. My only hesitancy was that I'd be a little bored. If I wanted the same adrenaline rush I got from DC, I'd have to create it myself. I didn't know how to accomplish that, but I was determined to try.

Destiny revealed itself on a sunny March 18, 1984, morning when I picked up the Friday *Mercury News* and read an opinion piece urging then-Governor George Deukmejian to veto AB 1, the law passed by the legislature that would make it illegal to discriminate based on sexual orientation. The assembly member, with the unfortunate rhyming name of Alister McAlister, believed that signing the bill would give the "wrongful" practice of homosexuality legal, social, and political legitimacy, resulting in LGBTQ+ people becoming a legitimate class deserving of legal protection.[2]

The statement stunned me.

San Jose was still reeling from the 1980 repeal ordinances that would have given LGBTQ+ people protections in housing and employment, so McAlister probably felt there would not be any outcry against his views.

I was a 31-year-old gay man, out to friends but not to others. I was well aware of the hatred and persecution faced by queer people, but McAlister's condemnation was the first time I had seen someone express their view so bluntly: You, Kenneth Eugene Yeager, are so despicable that you are undeserving of any benefits provided to others by society.

I was angry that an elected official thought I had forfeited my civil rights simply because I was gay. Putting the paper down, I said to myself: *Ken, if you don't fight for your rights to be a part of this community, then no one else will.* I realized that if I were to have equality in San Jose, I would have to fight for it. I decided to challenge the assemblyman by using his weapon of choice: an op-ed in the *Mercury News*.

There was a minor hiccup: I wasn't completely out. My byline in the *Mercury News* meant I would come out to the newspaper's entire Bay Area readership. I knew that the publicity might cause me problems. I wondered if my political friends would distance themselves because I was too out or if I would ever be hired to manage another political campaign.

I told Congressman Edwards of my plans, realizing he might not think it a plus to have a press secretary who was openly gay. But he didn't bat an eye. He said, "Do it." And I did.

I came out publicly a week later, authoring an opinion piece that denounced McAlister and argued for accepting gays and

---

2 Alister McAlister. "Deukmejian Should Veto the Gay Employment Bill." *San Jose Mercury News*. March 9, 1984.

lesbians as full participants in society. I mentioned LGBTQ+ friends who were working to make San Jose a better place for everybody, arguing that their efforts should be embraced, not disregarded.[3]

I came to learn that the circumstances of my coming out were not unique. It is often the case when LGBTQ+ people are pushed beyond their limits, like being fired from a job, kicked out of their home, or told they are worthless pieces of garbage. They view it as the final straw and bravely come out.

One positive consequence of coming out is that I could now get involved in LGBTQ+ politics. Equally important, it allowed me to be myself, no longer hiding who I was. In 1991, I wrote about how my life changed because of the McAlister opinion piece, aptly titled, "A Thank-You Note to a Homophobic Politician."[4]

I voiced similar sentiments when quoted in a lengthy 1985 article in the community newspaper *San Jose Metro*. The writer, a straight male, was trying to understand more about being gay. Looking back on what I said many years ago, I think I stated the importance of coming out as well as I could:

"It took me a long time to know how much a part of me was being gay. When I tried to hide it, I wasn't able to express myself, be comfortable with who I was, or be relaxed with people. Before, I thought that it didn't matter or that there wasn't really a connection, that I could be in the closet and there was no harm done to my psychology or with the people I related to. You learn after a while that isn't true."[5]

By 1985, I didn't want to wake up one day as an unemployed political staffer. I was always interested in education and knew

----

3   Ken Yeager. "Tolerance Will Allow Gays to Help Build Our Land." *San Jose Mercury News*. March 18, 1984.

4   Ken Yeager. "A Thank-You Note to a Homophobic Politician." *Our Paper/ Your Paper*. September 11, 1991.

5   Craig Carter. "Gay in the South Bay. A Straight Look." *San Jose Metro*. July 25, 1985.

Stanford's School of Education had a well-regarded education studies department. I applied and was accepted. When I finished my master's degree, I was accepted into the Ph.D. program with a full scholarship. I was fortunate to have the esteemed feminist economist Dr. Myra Strober as my dissertation advisor. She helped set me on an academic career path that changed the trajectory of my life.[6]

The years of graduate school were hectic. I was as busy as ever with politics, running the LGBTQ+ political committee I co-founded in 1984, chairing the County AIDS Task Force, and managing two regional campaigns against Lyndon LaRouche's AIDS quarantine initiatives. So why not throw in graduate school? Somehow, I fit in attending class, studying, and doing research.

In November 1990, after I turned in my dissertation, I traveled to Atlanta with a friend, Ira Greene, a dermatologist.[7] He was attending a conference, and he invited me to go along. In the hotel room, he noticed a blemish on the back of my right upper arm and asked how long it had been there. I said I wasn't sure but thought it was a large freckle. He expressed concern and said I should have a biopsy done as soon as we returned. What an intervention of fate.

As he suspected, I had a form of skin cancer called malignant melanoma. It is believed to be caused when ultraviolet rays damage a cell, usually when a person is a child. For reasons oncologists do not fully understand, this genetically altered cell can evolve into melanoma, often many years later. If removed early, the cancer is not fatal but is deadly if allowed to spread. Mine was a Clark Level III melanoma, which meant I

---

6   Note: To read more about this extraordinary woman and her groundbreaking career, see Myra Strober, *Sharing the Work: What My Family and Career Taught Me about Breaking Through (and Holding the Door Open for Others)*. Massachusetts Institute of Technology Press, Cambridge, Massachusetts. 2016.

7   Note: To learn more about Dr. Greene and his work in the early days of the AIDS epidemic, go to queersiliconvalley.org/ira-greene.

was probably okay, but they would not know for several years if it had spread to the lymph nodes. In December, I had an operation to remove the tumor. Since then, there has not been a reoccurrence, and my doctor is optimistic that the melanoma will not reappear.

At the time, I felt that if I was going to die, I wanted to do two things. The first was to run a marathon. This became a goal when, in 1989, I quit smoking and started long-distance running. Second, I wanted to run for public office. That would prove harder than the 33 marathons I ultimately ran.

The big unknown was if San Jose was ready to elect an openly gay person. The outlook was not promising. By 1992, neither San Jose nor any other of the 14 cities in the county had ever elected an out LGBTQ+ person to any office at any level. To make matters worse, in 1980, two-thirds of local voters rejected ordinances giving legal protections to LGBTQ+ people, signaling to elected officials that the public was decisively anti-gay. And lastly, the religious right still had a chokehold on electoral politics, making it difficult for LGBTQ+ candidates to get mainstream political support.

Over the next 10 years, I discovered that it would take everything I had to fight these forces, but sometimes even *that* was not enough to win a campaign.

CHAPTER 2

Swept Away
by an Anti-Gay Tide

After the Stonewall Riots in 1969, the 1970s began with great exuberance for the LGBTQ+ movement. As LGBTQ+ people became free to be themselves and no longer felt shame for who they were, "gay pride" became the celebratory anthem. There were gay pride festivals, gay pride parades, and gay pride proclamations. On a more substantive note, some cities began to pass ordinances protecting LGBTQ+ people from discrimination in housing and employment. There was great optimism that life would finally get better for queer people. This was very much the case in San Jose.

But much like today, optimism soon turned to pessimism as religious right politicians found an issue they could use to build their base, raise money, and set the political, social, and moral agenda in towns like San Jose. "Save our children from gays" became the battle cry of Anita Bryant in Miami in 1977. "Homosexuals can't reproduce so they must recruit." These messages were very effective, just as it remains today when right-wing politicians accuse people who don't oppose anti-gay legislation of secretly being pedophiles.

Slowly, the religious right began getting a foothold in San Jose politics, first with issues around the pride proclamation, then with anti-discrimination ordinances. Any thoughts I might have had of running were quickly dashed.

Can You Have a Gay Pride Proclamation Without the Words Gay or Pride?

It was not until 1975 that leaders in San Jose's LGBTQ+ community first asked Mayor Janet Gray Hayes and the city council for a pride proclamation. It would take three years, but on February 21, 1978, Hayes, along with Councilmembers Susie Wilson, Al Garza, and Jim Self, approved a resolution that declared the week of June 18, 1978, as "Gay Pride Week." However, conservative Councilman David Runyan, who was absent from the meeting, requested a reconsideration of the vote, which was approved. This gave opponents time to organize.

The LGBTQ+ community made a valiant effort to mobilize support for the proclamation with a telephone campaign, and more than 200 supporters attended the council meeting. But unfortunately, it proved nothing compared to the sheer number of opponents.

In his 2002 book *From Closet to Community*, Ted Sahl reported that some 800 evangelical Christians protested at the meeting. Opposition was led by Rick Harrington, chair of the Citizen's Committee Against Gay Pride Week, who claimed to represent 60 church organizations.[8] Years later, Councilwoman Wilson remembered how the second-floor council chambers were packed with people, with the overflow crowd stretching down the winding staircase into the cafeteria below, where sound monitors were placed.[9]

This may have been the first time the local Christian right was so well organized, but it wouldn't be the last.

When the item came up for discussion, Runyan made the motion to rescind it altogether. This was approved on a 4-3 vote. Hayes then recommended that the council consider calling it Gay Human Rights Week, thus keeping the word "gay" but leaving out "pride." Runyon then moved to remove the word

----

8   Ted Sahl. *From Closet to Community*. Ted Sahl Gallery. 2002. Page 23.

9   Valley Politics: Measures A & B. CreaTV. July 2017.

"gay" and "week" and simply call it "Human Rights Day." That failed on a 3-4 vote. Hayes finally called for a vote with the wording of "Gay Human Rights Week," which passed 4-3.

It turned out that this was not the end of the matter. At the April 4 meeting, the issue came up again. According to council minutes, Garza moved for the council to reconsider the vote on the proclamation, which passed 5-2, with Councilmembers Self and Wilson voting no. Next, Garza made the motion to rescind it altogether. The resolution passed with the same 5-2 vote.

The adoption of February's original ordinance created a firestorm. According to the San Francisco *Sentinel*, a City Hall official said it started "the most terrific and hateful pressure" he had ever seen. An aide to Hayes said of the phone calls, "they were horrible, just horrible." Following the vote, Hayes issued a statement explaining her change in position, saying the resolution "caused more division in the community than I had originally anticipated. We must get on with the business of running the city."

The vote played a minor role in the upcoming mayoral election. The Concerned Citizens for Morality in Government placed an ad in the *Mercury News* with the headline, "Gay Issue is Not Dead." One paragraph read: "The recent Gay Pride Week initiated by Mayor Janet Gray Hayes is a perfect example of moral insensitivity and weak leadership." It then endorsed Garza for mayor and the re-election of two councilmembers "based on their proven commitment to higher morality in government." [10]

On a more humorous note, on the Saturday before the November 7, 1978, election, a small aircraft flew over parts of South San Jose for three hours carrying a banner saying "South Bay Gays for Hayes." The intent was to damage Hayes

---

10 Note: Advertisement found in papers of Mayor Janet Gray Hayes in Special Collections at San Jose State University. No date or page number known.

by making it seem to appear that gays were showcasing their support for her. According to a *Mercury News* article, Hayes had not received an endorsement from a gay group and accused Garza of a dirty trick to discredit her. Garza claimed he did not hire the plane. The *Mercury News* reported that the plane was contracted out by R.C. Ackerman, a San Jose attorney listed as a $20 contributor to Garza's campaign.[11] I grew fond of Hayes and her husband over the years. When I was at their house, she often showed me a picture of the airplane with the banner. She'd laugh and say she still believed Garza had done it. She was always a big supporter of mine in all my campaigns, which proved valuable as her popularity remained high.

To complete this saga, it wouldn't be until nine years later, in 1987, that the first proclamation related to gay pride would be issued. This was when Mayor Tom McEnery agreed to do it, well after his re-election in 1986, and safe from any political blowback. This was after two months of lobbying by the Bay Area Municipal Elections Committee, or BAYMEC, the LGBTQ+ political group I co-founded in 1984. Because of BAYMEC's work with various councilmembers, I felt we had the six votes necessary for passage and was prepared to proceed with a council-issued proclamation had the mayor not acted. However, bringing the issue before the council could have been risky. Despite their previous commitments to BAYMEC, councilmembers might switch votes if 500 fundamentalists filled City Hall for the hearing.

As mayor, McEnery had the authority to issue the proclamation by himself. In a four-paragraph statement beginning with words affirming that San Jose exists to serve all people and that all citizens have equal protection under the law, it then ends with "Therefore, I hereby proclaim June 10, 1987, as Gay and Lesbian Human Rights Day." Once again, the highly

----

11　"Candidates Denies Ties to Plane Towing 'Gays for Hayes' Sign." *San Jose Mercury News*. November 6, 1978.

charged word "pride" was absent.

Susan Hammer, who succeeded McEnery as mayor in 1990 and was elected with considerable LGBTQ+ support, included "pride" in her proclamations. However, it would not be until 2001, when I was elected as the first openly gay person to the San Jose City Council, that the council itself—not just the mayor—would proclaim Gay and Lesbian Pride Week.

I believe that the disaster resulting from the organized opposition to the 1978 proclamation was the harbinger of an all-out assault on the local LGBTQ+ community by the Religious Right two years later. They were well organized, showed up in large numbers at the council meetings, flooded the telephones with messages of opposition, and wrote postal trays of letters. Elected leaders hadn't seen that type of public disapproval before. On the other hand, the gay community did not have a central gathering place like churches on a Sunday morning to rally around. This made it hard to muster the crowds or the phone calls to make a counterattack.

But another intervening political battle arose that seemed to give local activists false hope that the Religious Right's influence was of little concern.

Emerging Pro-LGBTQ+ Protections

The first major push for LGBTQ+ anti-discrimination laws occurred not at the state or federal levels but at the city level, particularly in liberal college towns. While Stonewall in 1969 marked a major step forward for gay rights, it took many years for progress to begin to reach other parts of the country, where overwhelming opposition to LGBTQ+ rights continued.

In 1972, East Lansing, Michigan, became the first city to pass an ordinance forbidding discrimination based on "affectional or sexual preference." Ann Arbor, Michigan, followed a few months later. Larger jurisdictions passing similar laws included Boulder, Colorado; Miami-Dade, Florida; St. Paul, Minnesota;

Wichita, Kansas; Eugene, Oregon; and Seattle, Washington.[12]
Just when the gay rights movement was gaining steam, with
people coming out of the closet and gay pride parades being
held across the country, Anita Bryant, a Miss America runner-
up and Florida orange juice pitchwoman, entered the scene.
In 1977, building on her friend Phyllis Schlafly's anti-Equal
Rights Amendment work, Bryant founded an anti-gay group,
Save Our Children, Inc., which led a highly publicized campaign
to repeal Miami-Dade's ordinance.

The campaign was based on conservative Christian beliefs about the sinfulness of homosexuality and the perceived
threat of homosexual recruitment of children and child moles-
tation. Bryant stated, "What these people really want, hidden
behind obscure legal phrases, is the legal right to propose to
our children that theirs is an acceptable alternate way of life. I
will lead such a crusade to stop it as this country has not seen
before." [13]

As the number of jurisdictions that outlawed discrimination based on sexual orientation grew, Bryant began traveling
across the country, spreading her anti-gay message. "As a mother,
I know that homosexuals cannot biologically reproduce children; therefore, they must recruit our children," she stated.[14]

Indeed, the campaign she initiated resulted in a conservative backlash, setting the tone of gay rights battles for years
to come and turning the tide against the advancement made
to destigmatize homosexuality. It also launched the careers of
evangelists Jerry Falwell, Pat Robertson, and Jim and Tammy
Bakker, among others.

Years later, I would quip that the three people who had the

----

12 Note: Some of this material appears in a booklet I wrote: "The Long
Struggle for LGBTQ+ Equality in Santa Clara County." It can be found at
queersiliconvalley.org/measures-a-and-b.

13 Anita Bryant, Bob Green. *At Any Cost*. Fleming H. Revel, Co. Grand
Rapids, Michigan. 1978.

14 Ibid.

greatest impact on my life were my father, my mother, and Anita Bryant.

The political capital the anti-gay rhetoric created did not escape California State Senator John Briggs of Fullerton. In 1977, he campaigned with Bryant in Florida. When he returned to California, he introduced a ballot measure, Proposition 6, to deny gays and lesbians the right to be employed as teachers. Playing the card of gay recruitment, Briggs was quoted as saying the proposition was needed since "Homosexuals want your children. They don't have any children of their own. If they didn't recruit children or very young people, they'd all die away. They have no way of replenishing. That's why they want to be teachers...." [15]

Set for a November 1978 election, the Briggs Initiative galvanized the LGBTQ+ community into action statewide. Recently elected San Francisco Supervisor Harvey Milk, the first openly gay person elected to public office in California, worked hard to defeat it, traveling the state and out-debating Briggs at every turn. The film, *The Times of Harvey Milk*, has extensive footage of some of these debates. [16]

In San Jose, the LGBTQ+ community began to organize against the initiative. It was reported that 250 to 300 people showed up at a July meeting with a total of $1,500 pledged. It also led to the formation of the Santa Clara Valley Coalition for Human Rights, which would play a pivotal role in an upcoming campaign. [17]

After widespread statewide opposition by newspapers and politicians—including former California Governor Ronald Reagan and President Jimmy Carter—the measure was defeated by a 60 percent vote.

Although the momentum for passing local non-discrimination ordinances was waning across the country, San Jose

----

15   Randy Shilts. *The Mayor of Castro Street*. St Martin's Griffen. New York, New York. 1982.

16   Rob Epstein, Director. *The Times of Harvey Milk*. 1984.

17   Sahl. Page 20.

activists were bolstered by the Prop. 6 campaign win. As a result, they began pushing for such City and County ordinances. The backlash to this was so severe that I have wondered how City leaders could have missed—not once but twice—political cues and whether something different could have been done to avoid political expulsion of the LGBTQ+ community.[18]

Local LGBTQ+ Anti-Discrimination Ordinances Enacted

In an April 2017 interview I had with Johnie Staggs[19]—a pioneering lesbian activist in San Jose—she said that support for the anti-discrimination ordinances began when the community wanted a gay pride proclamation. However, Mayor Hayes believed that an anti-discrimination bill would be easier to pass than a proclamation. Staggs told me, "She reasoned that a gay pride proclamation was too in your face for the public, but who could be against basic rights?"

As it turned out, just about everyone.

Staggs went on to say, "We were in a kind of euphoria on the heels of the Briggs defeat. We knew we were right and wanted to live our lives openly. But, unfortunately, many of us were kind of pie in the sky."

From the outset, the idea was to have the City pass the ordinance, but according to Staggs, it became bogged down in the 1978 race for mayor and the continuing debate over a gay pride proclamation. Thus, the attention turned to the Santa Clara County Board of Supervisors. They took up the issue and passed an ordinance before the City did.

Staggs gives credit to Jim McEntee, director of the Santa Clara County Office of Human Relations, for bringing the ordinance forward. Others credit Steward from the Human Rights

----

18   Ken Yeager. "Silicon Valley Was Anti-Gay? Yes, Not So Long Ago." _San Jose Mercury News_. June 9, 2017.

19   Note: To learn more about Johnie Staggs go to queersiliconvalley.org/johnie-staggs.

Commission as spearheading the effort. Steward was the first openly gay person to serve on the commission. It is probably safe to say that Steward and McEntee worked side by side to get the ordinance in front of the supervisors.

It should be noted that the County's ordinance applied only to rural pockets of the county that were outside the jurisdictions of any city. Thus, it could be viewed as largely symbolic because almost all residents and businesses were within a city boundary. Since the ordinance only applied to the unincorporated areas, there was a need for the San Jose City Council to pass it as well.

Even from the beginning, it seemed that many in the LGBTQ+ community were ambivalent about moving forward. In a *Lambda News* article, Steward stated that only one letter and one phone call were received from the commission in support of an ordinance. "I am not going to carry the fight for protective legislation by myself," Steward said. He went on to lament that gays and lesbians must let their elected officials know of the support in the community. "Our mandate is clear," he said. "But time is not on our side if apathy toward protective legislation prevails."[20]

Nevertheless, on April 24, 1979, the Human Relations Commission voted to adopt the ordinance and asked the Board of Supervisors to enact it. Early comments by Board members interviewed by *Mercury News* reporter Scott Herhold seemed to indicate at least three votes in favor.[21]

The supervisors first heard the proposed anti-discrimination ordinance on June 12. There would be six hearings before the final adoption, with more than 25 hours of public testimony.

The first meeting provided a good indication of what was to follow. According to official transcripts of the meeting, speakers

20 "Apathy Reigns Supreme – Gay Rights Ordinance Floundering." *Lambda News*. April 4, 1979.

21 Scott Herhold. "Gay Ordinance Finds Support on County Board." *San Jose Mercury News*. May 2, 1979.

who opposed the measure included Rick Harrington, a 28-year-old Mormon who led the group Concerned Citizens Against the Sexual Orientation Ordinance and Rev. Marvin Rickard of the Los Gatos Christian Church. Rickard is quoted at the hearing as saying he was "against the ordinance because it protects homosexuality, which is an immoral practice." Another speaker said the ordinance denies his rights because, if it passes, he must hire gays, who may offend his customers.

Forty-five years later, these remain the dual arguments used by religious conservatives against granting LGBTQ+ people the same protections against discrimination as others. They were key arguments in the 2018 U.S. Supreme Court's decision in the Masterpiece Cakeshop ruling that allowed a business to not serve customers based on claims of free speech and free exercise of religion.

After the first reading of the ordinance on July 30, Supervisors Dan McCorquodale, Rod Diridon, Gerry Steinberg, and Susie Wilson expressed support. Opposing the ordinance was Supervisor Dominic Cortese, who felt it was inappropriate because it involved lifestyles and personal preferences. He commented that it was a moral issue that should be resolved in the religious community, not by legislation.[22]

Perhaps as a premonition of things to come, activist Dan Relic, writing in *Lambda News*, said he was "filled with dread and anxiety" over the lack of support given to the four supervisors who favored the ordinance.[23]

As with the City of San Jose proclamation a few years earlier, opponents were getting their people to the Board chambers in far greater numbers than supporters. Relic was pleading for the gay community to attend the hearings to counter the claim by fundamentalists that they—not the gays—represented the public's view on the issue. Relic said, "Is it any wonder that a politician will believe them when they look out at an audience

----

22 Minutes of the July 30, 1979, Board of Supervisors meeting.

23 Dan Relic. *Lambda News*. July 1979.

of 800 badge-wearing, bible-thumping fanatics who surround 150 vocal activists?"[24]

The final hearing on August 6, 1979, is mainly remembered for the hundreds of religious protestors in attendance, the disruption of a 6.0 Richter scale earthquake, and the scores of opponents who broke out in song when the jolt occurred, singing "Onward Christian Soldiers" and "Amazing Grace." [25]

As reported in the *Mercury News*, one ordinance opponent who addressed the Board said, "That earthquake we had is just an example of what will happen in Santa Clara County if this ordinance is passed." [26]

On August 6, 1979, nearly two months after it was first considered, the supervisors adopted the ordinance. Following the 4-1 vote for passage, Rev. Rickard held an impromptu press conference and said an attempt would be made to place the issue on the ballot to overturn the decision.

With far less fanfare, the San Jose City Council approved the ordinance on a 6-1 vote on August 28 after only two hearings.

Retaliation from the Religious Right

Opponents of the LGBTQ+ anti-discrimination ordinances wasted no time collecting signatures supporting repeal. An *East San Jose Sun* article discussed how the Concerned Citizens Against the Gay Rights Ordinance planned to send 2,500 persons to collect 37,000 signatures to stop the ordinance from taking effect. They got 57,000. For San Jose, they needed 18,000 and got 27,000.[27]

----

24   Ibid.

25   Scott Herhold. "Gay Rights Wins Despite Mass Protest." *San Jose Mercury News*. August 7, 1979.

26   Ibid.

27   Bruce Alderman. "Group Plans Drive to Repeal Gay Ordinance." *East San Jose Sun*. August 18, 1979.

Under California law, once the required signatures are validated, the Board of Supervisors and City Council have the right to rescind the ordinance or place it on the ballot.

The four supervisors who supported the ordinance stated they were in favor of placing the measure on the ballot. Perhaps reflecting the hope of most of the gay community, McCorquodale said, "I think on a county-wide vote, the ordinance would be sustained. Prop. 6 was defeated in my district by over 60 percent."

The measures—Measure A for the county and Measure B for the city—were placed on the June 1980 ballot by the Registrar of Voters. A "yes" vote meant you favored the ordinances; a "no" vote signified you were against them and wanted them repealed.

From all indications, the local gay and lesbian community struggled to organize. LGBTQ+ leaders worried that community members were not contacting their elected officials. Staggs said to me that although proponents of the ballot measures raised $100,000, much of the support came from out of the area. Likewise, she said, "busloads of people came up from Los Angeles on the weekends to walk precincts, but we had enormous difficulty getting local people to do it."

Staggs commented that the gay community in San Jose was still largely closeted back then. "In general, there was a feeling that many local gay people cringed when we held rallies or other public events. They were afraid some of the spotlight would splash on them."

From all accounts, the campaign was riddled with organizational problems. According to Sahl, the public relations firm Salem and Associates was hired to run the "Yes on A and B" campaign but was dismissed in January 1980 after it finished the preliminary work. Coalition members did not feel that the campaign was moving as quickly as needed.[28]

Included in Sahl's book was an interview with Michael

----

28   Sahl. Page 25

Morris, one of the few high-tech executives who was out and involved. He brought a level of management skill to the campaign, which had been lacking. Morris spoke candidly about the disorganization of the initial campaign committee, with meetings lasting long into the night with no resolution, infighting, and members storming out or threatening to resign unless demands were met.

According to an interview Sahl had with Morris, "The problems were further exacerbated when the ballot argument was delivered to the Registrar's Office five minutes past the legal deadline. The County Clerk refused to open the door, and the campaign had to file a suit of mandate. Had a judge not agreed to hear the complaint, only the 'no' argument would have appeared on the ballot. Finally, Staggs was appointed campaign manager, which provided more focused leadership."

Although high-tech companies have a well-deserved reputation for being progressive on LGBTQ+ issues, that was not always the case, especially in 1979. A high-tech trade association named the Santa Clara County Manufacturing Group—the precursor to the highly influential Silicon Valley Leadership Group—initially opposed both measures. In a letter to Cortese, President Peter Giles wrote of the group's concerns over the legal and economic implications of the ordinance, stressing the cost to companies to defend themselves. He noted, "Please understand that our opposition to this ordinance is based on the sincere interest we share with you—that of promoting the continued prosperity and well-being of Santa Clara County."

Morris, who was general counsel to ROLM Corporation, wrote a memo to co-founder Ken Oshman, arguing, among other points, that concerns over affirmative action were groundless and that human costs of prejudice could affect employee productivity. Oshman sent the memo to the board of the Manufacturing Group. Afterward, the Manufacturing Group took a neutral position.

Anita Bryant's aide and campaign manager in the Dade

County campaign, Mike Thompson, arrived to help run the Santa Clara County campaigns. When asked by a *Mercury News* reporter why he was coming to San Jose, Thompson said, "It's an important issue. The encouragement of homosexual activity is a detriment to society. They [homosexuals] should be treated humanely, but also should be made to realize their lifestyle is not desirable." [29]

The "No on A and B" campaign used the same playbook as in Miami: "Vote NO for the sake of our children." Literature headlines read: "Enough is Enough," "Don't Let it Spread," and "Keep it Private."

Their main mail piece, when fully opened, made their position very clear. Under a capitalized, enlarged headline of "WHAT'S AT STAKE" were pictures of partially clad men. Dispersed throughout were eight sub-headlines: Children, Freedom, Moral Values, Property Rights, Privacy, Health, Civil Rights, and Money. Each emphasized a particular stereotype of gay men as sexual deviants and child molesters who wanted their behavior legitimized. Repulsively, they even managed to cite the slayings by John Wayne Gacy, Patrick Kierney, and Elmer Wayne Henley.

In one section, the opponents claim that gays argue that "all they want is privacy." But then they counter that by saying, "[gays] have the compulsion to flaunt their sex in public. A public washroom is frequently their stage for sex in public. Bus stations, parks, and bowling alleys are haunted by gay guys. Random and reckless selection of partners is the trademark. The fact that the stranger is likely to be a policeman, sadomasochist, or syphilitic never seems to occur to them. This is the core of homosexuality."

Under the money section, it says that gays claim the measure will not cost money but then say the contrary is true: "It costs the taxpayers of California approximately $20 million

----

29 Barbara French. "Gay Rights Opponents Disagree on Campaign." *San Jose Mercury News.* March 30, 1980.

per year to treat homosexuals for V.D." In addition, "passage of the ordinance would undoubtedly increase the local homosexual population and, therefore, law enforcement costs. Both male and female homosexuals had been arrested more often than heterosexuals."

All the other sections were just as bad.

Backers of the ordinances were overwhelmed by the damaging assault. Their tagline for the "Yes on A and B" campaign was "Live and Let Live." Their ballot statement stayed away from gay rights and focused on the principles of religious freedom, privacy, and equal protection of the law. "If you believe as we do, in privacy, fair play, and live and let live, please join us to vote YES." It was a valiant attempt but not a strong enough argument to refute all the lies and misconceptions about gay people.

The *Mercury News* came out in favor of the measures. Their strong editorial began: "A homosexual who is denied a job or housing because he or she is homosexual presently has no legal recourse in this community," and ended with: "If the voters vote 'no,' they will be saying, explicitly, that homosexuals in this community do not have legal recourse when they suffer discrimination. In our opinion, that would be illogical and unfair. We recommend a 'yes' vote on Measures A and B." [30]

To me, this is what the campaign arguments should have been. However, with the opponents focusing so heavily on recruiting children, illicit behavior, and religious freedom, the supporters felt forced to counter those claims instead of discussing the lack of protections for LGBTQ+ people Final campaign reports show the two anti-gay forces—Moral Majority of Santa Clara County and Concerned Citizens Against the Sexual Orientation Ordinance—spent a combined $153,000.

The Santa Clara Valley Coalition for Human Rights spent

---

30   Editorial Board. "Yes on Measures A and B." *San Jose Mercury News.* May 29, 1980.

$102,00.[31] In the LGBTQ+ community, a portion was raised through a controversial "10 for 10" program. All bars, bathhouses, and establishments catering to the gay community were to raise their drinks or admission prices by 10 percent and donate the money monthly until the June election. The plan was met with immediate opposition by some bar owners. One owner is quoted as saying in the *Mercury News*, "Once we open our doors to this type of activity, you're dead." Resentment by campaign organizers toward the six bars that did not participate lasted for many years.[32]

The conservative ministers were effective in organizing their congregations. Supervisor Diridon would later reflect on how he always knew when opposition to the measures was part of the Sunday sermon because his office would be flooded with calls on Monday.

I recall how Supervisor Wilson asked me and another staff member, Sarah Janigian, to attend one of the church services as a couple to see firsthand what was being preached. I remember walking into the massive church filled to the brim with worshippers and thinking, "Wow, what an army." At the end, campaign forms were handed out for people to volunteer. As I left, I worried someone would point at me and shout, "He's gay!" and I'd have to run for my life.

The election result was devastating. In a mean-spirited and homophobic campaign, fundamentalists defeated Measures A and B by a three-to-one vote. With 70 percent opposing in San Jose and 65 percent in the county, this wasn't just a loss—it was a slaughter.[33]

----

31   Rosalie Nichols. "Bigots Outspent Gays 3:2." *Lambda News*. September, 1980.

32   Barbara French. "Gay Rights Advocates Outspending Opponents." *San Jose Mercury News*. May 8, 1980.

33   To read a 2018 short interview of the four Santa Clara County supervisors who voted on the measures and their recollection of those turbulent times, please see Appendix B.

The repercussions were immediate. The nascent LGBTQ+ rights movement vanished. Gay activism came to a dead stop. Most local political leaders backed away from gay rights issues. It would be five years before members of the LGBTQ+ organization I co-founded would appear before the Board of Supervisors.

Adding insult to injury, two conservative San Jose council candidates backed by the Moral Majority won election.

A final note about the religious right's entry into local politics came in June 1988 when the pastor of the Los Gatos Christian Church, Marvin Rickard, resigned after confessing to his congregation that he conducted a liaison with a woman who was not his wife. Rickard called the relationship "a friendship that became an infatuation that lasted about 11 months, and that shouldn't have happened."

According to the *Mercury News*, Rickard had made headlines locally and nationally for his conservative political views, including anti-gay and pro-South African government stances.

I was quoted in the article as saying, "What a hypocrite; I'm glad to see him go. He has let loose so much bigotry in the past that the valley is well rid of him." [34]

---

34   Brad Kava. "Los Gatos TV Preacher Confesses, Quits." *San Jose Mercury News*. June 20, 1988.

CHAPTER 3

Rising from the Rubble

After I had come out publicly in 1984 with my opinion piece in the newspaper, I was chomping at the bit to see what political talents I had. I had been active in local politics for 10 years, had worked for a number of elected officials, had gone to Washington, DC, and, like so many young people who have not yet found their career path, was ready to find the right opportunity to make a difference. But when? Where? One goal that I believe all LGBTQ+ people share is the wish to make the world better for the next generation of queer people than it was for themselves. I sensed that my calling was to help the LGBTQ+ community gain a political foothold so we could be full participants in government. But how? Or more specifically, how in San Jose, which was not particularly a hotbed of political activism?

Having run campaigns, I knew about political action committees or PACs. Under California law, candidates running for office and committees that raise and spend money for candidates need to file reports to the California Secretary of State Office. Having created PACs for candidates, I was knowledgeable of all the paperwork that needed to be done to form that type of group.

In addition, I was aware of the success of a powerful LGBTQ+ PAC in Los Angeles that held big political dinners and had great clout with straight politicians. Named MECLA (the Municipal Elections Committee of Los Angeles), I wondered if

San Jose could ever pull off something similar.

There were several reasons why I went the route of PACs over a Democratic club. PACs, for instance, can contribute funds to candidates, while clubs cannot. I also knew it was necessary to be non-partisan because, in the 1980s and 1990s, there were still a number of moderate Republicans running in heavily Republican districts, and I wanted the opportunity to support them under the right conditions. Lastly, I had seen some clubs being overrun by one faction or the other, alienating many of the original members. For me, a PAC seemed more stable. This has turned out to be true as the group I co-founded will celebrate its 40th-year anniversary in 2024.

The spark that made me believe a political group could succeed was when I attended a meeting of a new group that formed in 1983 called High Tech Gays.[35] It was an offshoot of a San Francisco organization called Lesbian and Gay Associated Engineers and Scientists. They began meeting at the old San Jose Billy DeFrank Center on Keyes in San Jose but soon outgrew the small lounge area. By the spring of 1984, their membership had swelled to the point that they were gathering in people's homes, filling the living rooms and backyard patios with young tech workers. At my first meeting, I met the host for the evening, Ron Taylor, along with their president, Rick Rudy. I left that evening thinking there might be enough civic-minded LGBTQ+ people who would be interested in joining a political organization. I was jazzed.

In the days when there was just the L and the G in the LGBTQ+ banner, I always knew that lesbians needed to be included in any group in order to be representative. Luckily, I knew of the perfect person to fit the bill.

Enter Wiggsy Sivertsen.[36]

----

35   https://www.queersiliconvalley.org/organizations/org-high-tech-gays/

36   Note: An hourlong interview I conducted with Wiggsy can be seen at youtube.com/results?search_query=Evening+with+Wiggsy+and+Pals

Born Aimee Devereaux Sivertsen in Southern California, she would go by Wiggsy from early childhood after her sister mispronounced "wiggles" to describe her rambunctiousness. Most people mispronounce her last name, but she is universally known just as Wiggsy.[37]

Having graduated from San Jose State University in 1962 and received her master's degree in social work from Tulane University in New Orleans, she began her career as an activist and community leader before she was outed and then fired while working as a counselor at the Peninsula Children's Center in Palo Alto. "The whole process of losing my job was a nightmare," she told the *Mercury News* in 1998. "I was damaged goods. I could have lost my therapy license. I didn't know if anyone would ever hire me again. I made up my mind right then that I was never again going to hide who I am." [38]

She had already been working part-time at San Jose State's counseling center, so she was able to join the university's staff full-time in 1968. She was SJSU's first openly LGBTQ+ employee. Although Wiggsy was out at San Jose State, she was not active politically until 1977, when state Senator John Briggs authored an initiative that would have banned gays and lesbians from teaching in California public schools. She took an active part in the campaign to defeat the Briggs Initiative, which was on the November 1978 ballot as Proposition 6, making appearances on both radio and television.

As a result of the defeat of the Briggs Initiative, Wiggsy's public profile began to rise steadily. Over the next four decades, she would become one of the most visible members of Silicon Valley's LGBTQ+ community.

I didn't know her well. Our connection was through Dr. Terry Christensen, a political science professor at SJSU who was my local politics instructor and mentor. I soaked up his

----

37   Ken Yeager. "Wiggsy Sivertsen." queersiliconvalley.org/wiggsy-sivertsen/

38   Trace Cone. "Out Where." *West* Magazine. *San Jose Mercury News.* May 17, 1998.

class lectures on city government as much as I could, trying to impress him with my capabilities. I might note that Christensen, as a relatively new professor, was seemingly 10 to 20 years younger than most tenured male professor. He was also, at the age of 31, by far the best-looking professor on campus. In ways I didn't totally understand at the time, he became my first adult relationship, separate from the student-teacher role. We have remained close friends ever since.

From there, I took the internship class that he facilitated, which led to a highly rewarding placement with Councilwoman Wilson. The following semester, with Christensen and Cari Beauchamp as Wilson's re-election campaign managers, I was hired as the precinct coordinator, a heady position for someone who really didn't know what he was doing.

Fast forward to 1984. Christensen knew of my interest in starting a group and had mentioned it to Wiggsy. That led to having drinks with her at the Toyon bar in San Jose. We both knew of the 1980 defeats of the two non-discrimination measures A and B and how that had stopped any political activism that had begun a few years before. We knew no one was going before the city council or board of supervisors saying that our issues weren't being addressed. The idea was to create a proactive political action group that would go before elected governing bodies and advocate for supportive services and non-discrimination protections.

She and her former partner lived in the Santa Cruz mountains. I remember driving up winding, narrow roads to get to her house. It was the first of many discussions we would have on how to proceed in turbulent times without making things worse for the LGBTQ+ community or the politicians we supported.

The first order of business was a name. Joining us in this discussion was another longtime activist, Dot James. Wiggsy agreed that we needed to be multi-county, which restricted any reference to San Jose or Santa Clara County. (The ubiquitous "Silicon Valley" was yet to come.) There was no good name that incorporated all three counties we wanted to represent: Santa Clara, San Mateo, and Santa Cruz. So, in the end, we settled on "Bay Area."

Next was how to indicate we were a lesbian and gay group. The actual words themselves would be too self-identifying on an envelope and bound to make closeted suburban members nervous. We were still living in an era when people were receiving most of their communications through letters in the mail, so we needed a somewhat nondescript name. In the end, and out of exhaustion, we took the rest of MECLA's name, "Municipal Elections Committee," which gave us the syllable "MEC," and we ended up with the two-syllable name "BAY-MEC." Not perfect, but a name that has become very identifiable, even though few know what all the letters stand for.

Although few people would know of the MECLA connection, we thought it might demonstrate an association with statewide PACs. Later that year, Wiggsy and I, along with Rich Gordon, attended a meeting in San Francisco by the Non-Partisan Alliance of Gay and Lesbian Political Action Committees. PACs were present from San Diego, Los Angeles, Oregon, East Bay, and California NOW. Most of the day-long meeting was spent sharing information about the organization, purpose, fundraising, and endorsement proceedings of the various PACs. It was decided to meet again in May in Los Angeles in order to have a training session on fundraising. MECLA would host the meeting.

The next step was to create a board.

This was tricky. I knew I wanted people already involved in politics who believed that social change could come from working inside the political system. I also sought people who had a track record in politics and were well thought of. The hope was that their good reputation would help give BAYMEC credibility from the beginning.

I was fortunate to be able to handpick the people to serve

on the board. From Santa Clara County, I knew having people from High Tech Gays would be invaluable, so I asked Ron Taylor[39] and Rick Rudy,[40] who both agreed. Rosalie Nichols,[41] who owned a print shop and published *Our Paper/Your Paper* with her partner Johnie Staggs, said yes. From Santa Cruz County, it was a no-brainer to invite one of the first openly gay councilmembers in the country, John Laird, from the City of Santa Cruz.[42] After accepting, he suggested Wanda House, who was involved in Santa Cruz Democratic politics. From San Mateo County, a friend recommended political strategist Doug DeYoung, who, in turn, introduced me to Rich Gordon,[43] who was active in the Peninsula Business Group.

Most of us didn't know the other members, but the one trait we all shared was the desire to actively work for LGBTQ+ civil rights through political activism. Waiting around for something to happen wasn't an option. With little to go on, we all hoped that BAYMEC would be the conduit to start bringing about change.

I knew of the importance of group affiliations, particularly when it comes to members of a board. Just using names provided no context for who people were. That is why I always used an affiliation with each board member. I held no elected office and had no official title, but I did work for a highly regarded member of Congress who allowed me to use his name.

----

39   Note: To learn more about Ron Taylor, go to queersiliconvalley.org/ron-taylor

40   Note: To learn more about Rick Rudy, go to queersiliconvalley.org/rick-rudy and queersiliconvalley.org/organizations/org-high-tech-gays

41   Note: To learn more about Rosalie Nichols, go to queersiliconvalley.org/nikki-nichols

42   Note: To learn more about John Laird, go to queersiliconvalley.org/john-laird and Valley Politics. "Hear Our Voices, South Bay Politics, and the Founding of BAYMEC."

43   Note: To learn more about Rich Gordon, go to queersiliconvalley.org/rich-gordon and to Valley Politics. "Hear Our Voices, South Bay Politics, and the Founding of BAYMEC."

Thus, I was listed as press secretary to U.S. Representative Don Edwards.

Once we held our first meeting, I knew I could finally send out a press release announcing our existence. I was heartened by the favorable coverage we received in the straight and gay press. At the time, newspapers were the only way to communicate to a larger audience, especially to LGBTQ+ members who didn't go to bars or read gay publications.

The *Mercury News* headline above the fold on the front page of the local section announced, "Gays enter local political campaigns." The article was straightforward, mainly mentioning the names and occupations of the board and the races which we endorsed.[44]

The San Francisco *Bay Area Reporter* (B.A.R.), in its September 13 issue, gave us a good, if long, headline: "South Bay Activists Form Political Fund. Board is 'Who's Who of Gay Leaders, Supporters in the Area." [45]

As far as informing local LGBTQ+ people that we existed, it was the San Jose-based *Our Paper/Your Paper* that mattered most. They ran the large headline "BAYMEC is Born" and included nice quotes from Nichols and myself. "We lick our wounds while the Moral Majority licks their chops," I was quoted as saying. "We want politicians to finally recognize our community as voters, financial contributors to political campaigns, and as politically active citizens." [46]

First Meeting

The first meeting of the board was, appropriately enough, at Taylor's house on August 13, 1984. Years later, the BAYMEC

----

44   Harry Farrell. "Gays enter local political campaigns." *San Jose Mercury News*. October 8, 1984.

45   "South Bay Activists Form Political Fund. Board is 'Who's Who' of Gay Leaders, Supporters in the Area." *Bay Area Reporter*. September 13, 1984.

46   "BAYMEC is Born." *Our Paper/Your Paper*. August 29, 1994.

Board decided it was as good of an anniversary date as any for our founding. The purpose of the gathering was to meet each other and discuss the general philosophy and guidelines under which BAYMEC would operate.

When it came to our endorsement process, we thought it best not to over-extend ourselves and to concentrate on key races. In what was clearly a sign of the political times and our pragmatic outlook, we needed to make sure our endorsement did not hurt the candidates we were trying to help.

We discussed our first fundraising piece, which ended up being 3½ by 8½ cards with information about BAYMEC and a response section. I wrote the piece, and my friend, Dan Di-Vittorio, a great graphic artist, designed it. The BAYMEC logo he created is still used today: a large triangle made up of three inner triangles, which form an upside-down triangle inside. The outside triangles are not wholly colored in, signifying that equality has not yet been achieved. Under the triangle is the word "BAYMEC."

As was the case with everything BAYMEC did in the early years, all the work was done by volunteers: myself, the rest of the board, and ex-boyfriends who helped along the way. At the end of the meeting, each of us donated $500 to fund our efforts. We were on our way.

Having a seasoned group of lesbian and gay activists created a lively debate on what issues to stress on our candidate questionnaire. Part of BAYMEC's DNA has always been to include issues important to other groups, just as we appreciate when they include several of ours. One often overlooked advantage of having an LGBTQ+-focused political organization is that it can be part of a network where all liberal-leaning groups can share information and answers to questionnaires. That is why we included questions about supporting equal pay for equal work, the Equal Rights Amendment, and programs to expand child care.

One of the first big issues that BAYMEC took on was AB 1,

so named because it was the first bill introduced in the new assembly session by San Francisco Assemblymember Art Agnos. The bill would prohibit discrimination based on sexual orientation in housing and employment. If passed, California would be one of a handful of states with such legislation. This was always the first question we asked candidates because it was, without a doubt, the "Are you with us or against us" piece of legislation. Little to no hope lay at the local or federal level for such a law; If any legal protections were to exist, they would come from the state. This was our first question.

In 1984, the issue wasn't marriage equality, but we asked whether candidates would support governmental agencies providing health insurance for domestic partners, just as they did for married partners of straight employees.

LGBTQ+ people were still routinely harassed by police officers, and we wanted to know if endorsed candidates supported guidelines for police behavior.

We asked if candidates would nominate and support qualified gay and lesbian appointments to commissions and staff positions. This was necessary because there were no openly queer commissioners or staff serving at the City of San Jose or County of Santa Clara level. In fact, the only out commissioner who had been appointed was David Steward on the Human Relations Commission. It would take seven years before another gay person was appointed to any commission.

Fifteen years after Stonewall, we were still having to ask candidates and elected officials to support proclamations for LGBTQ+ Pride Day or Month. As discussed in the previous chapter, what seems routine now was literally impossible to achieve for many years, all surrounding the controversial word "pride."

Some candidates' answers were a little disingenuous. Republican Assemblyman (and later Congressman for one term) Ernie Konnyu responded that he meant "no disrespect' when he told us frankly, "I am not seeking the endorsement of your group."

We chose to endorse his supportive Democratic challenger, Gloria Rose Ott, who unfortunately lost.

Democratic Assemblyman Rusty Areias, who voted for AB 1, filled out the questionnaire, earned our endorsement, and was sent a $100 check. Subsequently, we received the check back with a short letter. After thanking us for our support, he wrote, "Unfortunately, because of the sensitive nature and emotionalism surrounding AB 1 and similar issues in my district, I do not feel that I am in a position to accept your contribution at this time." He concluded that he wanted to reassure us that he appreciated our support and would continue to work in our interest in the future.

I remember laughing, thinking there we were, a political action committee with hardly any candidates who wanted our endorsements or even our money. We had a steep hill to climb.

We decided to make recommendations in 13 races: two state senate races, eight state assembly races, and three local races. We gave our support to the four members of the assembly who voted for AB 1: Lou Papan, Byron Sher, John Vasconcellos, and Rusty Areias. Besides McAlister, we opposed Bob Naylor, Ernie Konnyu, and Dominic Cortese, all of whom voted no.

The state senate vote for AB 1 was also razor close, with just one vote to spare. There was the "yes" vote from long-time supporter Dan McCorquodale but not from Al Alquist. As described in the next chapter, BAYMEC worked hard to get Alquist to finally support the bill when it was really needed, in 1991.

Our Paper/Your Paper ran our candidate recommendations as their banner headline in their October 24, 1984, edition, along with what I wrote in the BAYMEC newsletter. In part, this is what I said:

"Candidates interviewed realized BAYMEC was not asking for anything other than what other segments of the population have come to take for granted: healthcare, equal rights, and non-discriminatory government and business practices. Lesbians and gays have never asked for special treatment, just equal treatment.

"Contrary to what the Moral Majority would want people to believe, the general public does not condone bigotry and oppression toward lesbians and gays. Our issues and concerns are not out of step with mainstream America. While most people do not understand the repression many lesbians and gays must confront and overcome in society, few would deny us the constitutional rights that some say we cannot have." [47]

As with other minority groups, LGBTQ+ people are eager to know where candidates stand on their issues. Because of this, BAYMEC has continued to endorse candidates in every race since 1984, and we still get emails from people wanting to know where to see our candidate slate and whom to vote for.

Looking back on that first endorsement process reminds me that, unlike now, South Bay counties were political swing counties with moderate to conservative Democratic legislators. From our area, four of our state legislators voted against AB 1. Four brave souls voted in favor.

To the surprise of no one, in 1984 Republican Governor George Deukmejian vetoed AB 1. Humorously, I said that my "coming out" editorial in the *Mercury News* obviously had no impact on him.

To deliver more votes from our legislative delegation meant BAYMEC still had a lot of work to do. Challenges were numerous throughout BAYMEC's first decade—conflict with law enforcement, the onslaught of HIV/AIDS, multiple political attempts to exclude queer people from the rest of society, and homophobic politicians who thought we needed to change our behavior or that we could be cured of homosexuality. The significant role BAYMEC played in these issues was a testament to its board and volunteers' dedication and hard work throughout the years.

----
47   Ken Yeager. "BAYMEC Candidate Recommendations." *Our Paper/Your Paper.* October 24, 1984.

CHAPTER 4

Not the Lepers Politicians Thought We Were

It was important from the outset that BAYMEC be professional. Wiggsy, who is one of the most dynamic and articulate people I have ever met, did the speaking, helped plan strategy, and used her impressive network of friends to open doors and raise money. Moreover, she made sure that lesbians were welcomed into BAYMEC, an accomplishment of which not all LGBTQ+ organizations can boast.[48]

Wiggsy and I made a good team. Each of us brought something to the relationship that the other lacked. I believe I provided Wiggsy with more discipline and organization, and she gave me more confidence and assertiveness. We often joke that we should have gotten married, given how much time we spent with each other. It is remarkable to us both that after all these years we have never grown bored or impatient with each other.

My role was more behind the scenes, doing all the work that keeps an organization going. I am a much better writer than speaker, so I wrote the brochures and newsletters, in addition to doing the media work. I also brought my campaign

----

48   Ken Yeager. "The Making of a Candidate: A Personal Memoir." *Trailblazers: Profiles of America's Gay and Lesbian Elected Officials*. Note: The chapter is posted on "The Making of a Candidate: A Personal Memoir" – *Queer Silicon Valley*

and fundraising skills to the group, which I used when I managed the local Stop LaRouche/AIDS Quarantine campaigns in 1986. Together, Wiggsy and I walked the corridors of city halls, county buildings, and boards of education, lobbying our elected officials on numerous issues and serving on a variety of task forces and committees.

Early on in our formation, we began inviting elected officials to have breakfast meetings to talk about our issues. Wiggsy and I knew most of them well enough to contact their offices and set up arrangements. These breakfasts were a great way for all board members—and later advisory board members, too—to get to know our elected officials and for them to know us. We felt we needed to tell them directly how better organized our community was since the defeats of Measures A and B. Much of this was in preparation for asking for their support on matters such as proclamations for Gay Pride. Many hesitated, referencing the defeat of those measures as a sign that the public was not yet with us. We never pushed, always agreeing to meet again. As time passed, we got more politicians to support us, which made others feel comfortable adding their names. The strategy we used was to change hearts and minds one person at a time until we had support from everyone.

This was accomplished by listening and responding to concerns rather than using a divisive approach. Granted, this worked best for politicians who were already in support of civil and human rights but nervous about the political consequences of supporting a gay and lesbian group. One great example was Norman Y. Mineta, who was a mayor and congressman from San Jose before getting tapped to be commerce secretary under President Clinton and secretary of transportation under President Bush. A great civil rights champion, he led the fight for reparations for Japanese-Americans who were interned during World War II. Mineta himself was sent to an internment camp as a child.

We knew of Mineta's overall support of our issues when

we had breakfast with him in 1989. He received an "A" from the National Gay and Lesbian Task Force on his voting record, sponsored the BAYMEC dinner, and opposed the three AIDS quarantine state initiatives. The main issue of discussion was his reluctance to co-sponsor the federal Gay and Lesbian Civil Rights Bill, a law that would add sexual orientation to the language of the 1964 Civil Rights Act.

He had been a co-sponsor of the bill in the 1976-77 and 1978-79 sessions but withdrew his support after the overwhelming defeats of Measures A and B in 1980, which is discussed in an earlier chapter. Of no small matter, his district included the Almaden Valley, which many people referred to as the "Bible Belt" of Santa Clara County.

After thanking him for his strong support on a variety of issues of concern to the LGBTQ+ community, we discussed at length why it was so important for Mineta to be a co-sponsor. We thought the viewpoints of many of his constituents had changed since 1980. As a way to demonstrate support in the community, we told Mineta we would ask our members to circulate petitions asking him to support the bill. Over a thousand signatures were collected, and Mineta staff aides credited our efforts in helping to convince him to sponsor the legislation.

Perhaps most critical was Mineta's relationship with Wiggsy. They had worked together on a number of issues over the years and had become close friends who enjoyed each other's company immensely. Whenever appropriate, Wiggsy would bring up the topic of the Civil Rights Bill to monitor Mineta's evolution in his thinking. Finally, in 1991 he agreed to be a co-signer.

Mineta was the fourth of our five members of Congress in our three-county BAYMEC area to sponsor the bill. Congressman Don Edwards was unwavering in his support and was always a co-sponsor. We met with Congressmen Tom Campbell and Tom Lantos and won their support, too.

It was a similar progression with Congressman Leon Panetta. Former Santa Cruz Mayor John Laird tells the story of how before Panetta served in the Clinton and Obama administrations, he was still a congressman from the Monterey Bay area. Throughout the 1980s, Laird would make a point of sitting down with him at the beginning of every session to see if he would be a co-sponsor of the federal non-discrimination bill. "The key thing was to get more sponsors every session than you had in the previous session," Laird said in a television interview with four founding members of BAYMEC. "There was one time when we crossed 50 co-sponsors, and we thought we had arrived. I would go and sit down with Leon and say, 'We want you to be a co-sponsor.' I remember he would say things like, 'I really don't want to move until there's critical mass.' After I and all of us asked, he finally became a co-sponsor, and he would go on every year and be really helpful." [49]

Laird said he had to smile when, 10 years later, that investment paid off when Panetta presided over the end of Don't Ask, Don't Tell as secretary of defense. "It's a tribute to when you're doing all of these things, that over time they get you somewhere."

These stories reinforce the importance of the long haul, which is often overlooked or undervalued in politics. Yes, protests are needed to gain immediate attention, but often repetitive efforts are required to win the trust and ultimately votes with reasonable people. That is probably my strongest piece of advice for queer people trying to change minds in their communities. I have to believe that a number of Republican legislators in red states would prefer not to vote on anti-gay, anti-trans bills, but the political climate is so toxic that they feel they have no other choice. They are the politicians to target.

BAYMEC's first fundraiser was at the Toyon bar on October 10, 1984, with San Francisco Assemblymember and later Mayor Art Agnos as the guest speaker. Agnos was the champion sponsor of AB 1, the state LGBTQ+ non-discrimination bill.

---

49 Valley Politics. "Hear Our Voices, South Bay Politics, and the Founding of BAYMEC." queersiliconvalley.org/organizations/org-baymec

The price of the event was a whopping $15 a person. Attend-ees were grateful to Agnos for driving down. Unfortunately, in San Francisco, Agnos had received death threats against himself and his children. He arrived with security protection and kept his comments short, which we totally understood. He vented his frustration over the attacks he was getting from fundamentalists. "The only kind of people the Christians think ought to exist on Earth are those who think like them and act like them," he said. "Anybody else is a deviant in their Chris-tian frame of reference."

Five years after the defeats of Measures A and B we were not done with the Moral Majority, nor were they with us. A new group called the Coalition for Christians in Government had been formed to elect fundamentalist Christians to public of-fice. At their meetings, they mentioned that there was a school superintendent who was a homosexual, which was a reference to Jim Baughman, the superintendent of the San Jose Unified School District. They also included a guidance counselor who was gay and several teachers who were lesbian. It seemed like Proposition 6, or the Briggs Initiative, was being proposed all over again: Ban gay and lesbian teachers in schools.

Moreover, a friend of mine who worked for a state leg-islator mentioned that a letter-writing campaign against the reintroduction of AB 1 had started. He said that whereas for months there was no mention of the bill, suddenly letters and phone calls in opposition to it were being received. It was clear that we needed to increase our outreach to elected officials.

Elizabeth Birch, who was a BAYMEC board member, a gen-eral counsel at Apple in the late 1980s and early 1990s, and who would go on to be the executive director of the Human Rights Campaign, said in an interview that BAYMEC was an organization that was totally relatable to elected officials. "They could understand how BAYMEC operated, what it wanted, how it went about things, and what defined success," she said in the documentary film *Queer Silicon Valley*. "There were lots of reasons in those days to be rageful and radical and to throw blood and be angry, but there is also a political technique and style that needs to be used in a place like Silicon Valley that frankly was an agricultural area at the time." [50]

Birch also added that BAYMEC "was incredibly clever in that Silicon Valley was one of the few places where a national organization didn't swoop in and put their footprint on top of the local groups like BAYMEC."

Wiggsy echoed the same sentiments. She mentioned in an interview that "Ken and I attended more rubber chicken dinners than I can remember. Elected officials got to know us and realized we weren't so weird. Our tactic was to hold their hands as we crossed the river rather than throwing mud at them. We wanted them to be more knowledgeable and educated about what the gay community was about." [51] This approach to politics has served BAYMEC well over the years.

Longtime board member and past president, James Gonzales, shared with me that one reason for BAYMEC's longevity is the minimal infighting within the organization. "While any board involved in politics will inevitably face disagreements, we have managed to prevent these issues from consuming us or breaking us down," he explained. "Overall, board members have treated one another with respect, a principle we strive to integrate into our political endeavors."

"For four decades, BAYMEC has maintained an almost unblemished reputation for firm yet fair politics," he continued. "As a leader who inherited this culture, I felt a profound obligation to ensure BAYMEC's civility did not waver in the heat of the moment, as can easily occur."

----

50   Bob Gliner and Ken Yeager, Producers. *Queer Silicon Valley*. 2022. youtube. com/results?search_query=queer+silicon+valley+documentary

51   Valley Politics. "Hear Our Voices, South Bay Politics, and the Founding of BAYMEC."

The Killing of Melvin Truss

Thirty-five years before the murder of George Floyd by Minneapolis police in 2020 was the 1985 killing of Melvin Truss, a 17-year-old Black teen who was shot at close range by a San Jose police officer. It was the most controversial issue facing the LGBTQ+ community that year.

Truss's fatal shooting sparked public outcry as many called into question the conduct of the officer responsible for Truss' death and the handling of the case by the grand jury, law enforcement, and city officials.[52]

The San Jose Police Department's version of events was that Officer Paul Ewing was on duty in the Street Crimes Unit on May 4, wearing civilian clothes and driving an unmarked police car. Around 6:45 p.m., Ewing claimed he saw Truss dressed in women's clothes and jewelry, soliciting drivers at Second and San Carlos streets, according to a city memo authored by San Jose Police Chief Joseph McNamara.[53]

Truss approached Ewing's car and asked if he was looking for a date, the memo continued. Ewing drove Truss first to a Highway 280 overpass, then to San Jose Bible College, and finally to Olinder School.

According to McNamara's memo, Truss then began to act agitated and took a steak knife out of a rolled-up windbreaker on his lap, demanding Ewing's money. Ewing said he distracted Truss and drew his .357 magnum service revolver, pointing it at Truss in hopes that he would retreat. As Truss came toward him, Ewing fired five rounds and jumped out of the car without any injuries.

Truss was transported to San Jose Hospital, where he died at 9:05 p.m. the same night, according to records from the Human Relations Commission of the County of Santa Clara.

It should be noted that Truss weighed 115 pounds, while

----

52   Ken Yeager. "Fatal Police Shooting of Melvin Truss Sparked Public Outcry." https://www.queersiliconvalley.org/melvin-truss-story

53   Joseph McNamara. "Memo to Mayor and Council." May 31, 1985.

Ewing was 6'1" and weighed 200 pounds.

Public uproar followed as community members and Truss's family disputed police accounts. The family believed that trying to portray Truss as a "despicable character" was an attempt to justify the murder.[54]

During the council meeting, police in full uniform lined the walls of City Hall, opposing the proposed independent investigation. It was at that meeting that Assistant Police Chief Stan Horton angered the LGBTQ+ community with his remark that "it was not Officer Ewing that killed Truss. It was Melvin Truss' lifestyle that killed him." [55]

"No one will ever know what really happened at the time of the shooting," I stated at the hearing, "but it isn't difficult to imagine the circumstances that created the situation in the first place, nor the attitudes of the policeman involved. This is what we find very frightening." [56]

Sivertsen stated that "Our focus now is to call attention to the fact that police in San Jose seem to believe anyone who might be lesbian or gay is a criminal or in the process of committing a crime, notably solicitation or prostitution. The ramifications of this are enormous."

Three of Truss' classmates at James Lick High School testified that Truss would never hurt anyone, "especially someone older than him and a lot bigger than him." [57]

At a subsequent city council meeting to discuss police conduct toward the gay community, BAYMEC presented a five-point program to deal with police attitudes. On a 9-2 vote, the San Jose City Council approved the following measures:

----

54   "Hung Jury in Melvin Truss Case." *Our Paper/Your Paper*. August 12, 1987.

55   Jim Dickey. "Class on Gay Lifestyle Upsets S.J. Police." *San Jose Mercury News*. April 22, 1986.

56   "Gay Pac Protests Police Shooting." *Our Paper/Your Paper*. June 15, 1985.

57   Michael Rezendes. "S.J. Won't Form a Panel to Probe Teen's Death." *San Jose Mercury News*. June 5, 1985.

- Police officers would receive training in the area of gender and sexuality issues.

- Have the police chief meet with LGBTQ+ leaders to resolve any concerns that arise from police conduct or attitudes.

- The police will not make assumptions about an individual's sexual orientation in statements issued to the media.

- The police will not prejudge an individual merely because of their sexual orientation.

- A person's sexual orientation is not a criminal activity.

The San Jose Police Officers Association opposed the training. At the hearing, the president of the association stated, "I am against the training program, which could be interpreted as an admission that police officers could have some kind of bias against the gay and lesbian community, which I think is inappropriate and incorrect." [58]

Gosh, I thought, how could the gay community be so wrong, especially given all the bar raids, harassment, and meaningless arrests over the decades?

No one was better suited to do the training than Wiggsy, who did it every week for a year. In 2018, she reflected that parts of it were wonderful. "One guy came up to me and tapped me on the shoulder and whispered, 'Thank you for doing this. It is so important.' I realized that a number of officers were really scared to come out. You could feel the strain of being worried about being identified and not being able to be free about who you are." [59]

----

58   "BAYMEC Wins Change in Police Practices." *Our Paper/Your Paper.* July 10, 1985.

59   Valley Politics. "Hear Our Voices, South Bay Politics, and the Founding of BAYMEC."

Responding to community concerns, the Santa Clara County Human Relations Commission held a public hearing in August.

"Melvin was the kind of person anyone could read like a book. By that I mean he did not carry any false pretenses," said Sharon Youngblood in a statement to Santa Clara County's Human Relations Commission. Youngblood, a business instructor at James Lick High School who knew Truss for over two years, also noted: "You could look into his eyes and read his soul."

Youngblood, an advisor for James Lick's Black Student Union, recalled the time when Truss participated in the group's fall fashion show. "He was scared to death on that stage, and it was written all over his face, but he knew it was for a worthwhile cause, and it was exciting for him, too," Youngblood told the commission. "Melvin was not capable of violence."

A grand jury voted in May 1985 not to indict Ewing for fatally shooting Truss. Ewing returned to regular duty.[60] Despite calls for an independent citizens committee to investigate the shooting, in June the San Jose City Council voted against the proposal. In 1989, a federal jury cleared Ewing of violating Truss' civil rights in a civil suit brought by Truss's mother.

It is important that we remember Melvin Truss as another victim of police violence.

Responding to the AIDS Crisis[61]

As HIV/AIDS numbers began to rise in 1984, the disease became an issue BAYMEC discussed with politicians and public health officials. By 1985, there were 148 new HIV diagnoses and 33 new deaths. It was the year when the first HIV test became available, and the Public Health Department opened an

----

60   Betty Barnacle. "Grand Jury Won't Indict Cop for Shooting Teenager." *San Jose Mercury News*. May 22, 1985.

61   Note: Some parts of this section come from my booklet, "Battle Against AIDS. A Look at the First Decades of the Santa Clara County Experience." Ken Yeager. It is Appendix D. It can also be found at queersiliconvalley.org/battle-hiv-aids

HIV testing site.

AIDS hit home for BAYMEC and me personally in the late summer of 1985 when founding board member Doug DeYoung, who had been diagnosed the year before, grew steadily weaker. My sorrow and concern for him led me to write an op-ed in the *Mercury News* that was published on September 30.[62]

"Local officials perceive it to be political suicide to support any issue concerning AIDS. To be on the record as favoring AIDS education or patient care might categorize them as 'sympathetic' to the gay community and hand an opponent a weapon to be used at election time. Because gays and lesbians have been discouraged or made to feel unwelcome by city hall—much as women and minorities before them—the awareness by officials of the disease is minimal."

I also directly linked the slow government response to the political atmosphere that had led to the defeats of Measures A and B in 1980: "Gays and lesbians have no choice in their sexual orientation, but they do have a choice in whom they tell. Many in Santa Clara County choose to remain silent. Fear of repercussions by employers, landlords, and co-workers makes them conceal their identities. Added to the low visibility is a lack of political power."

"The clout of the Moral Majority may be real or imagined, but local politicians believe in it," I continued. "Only a handful of politicians are courageous enough to speak out against the bigotry and hatred aimed toward homosexuals. Anti-gay rhetoric is increasing in velocity and voracity as fundamentalist preachers learn of its fundraising potential. Since few non-gays demand that the tactic be stopped, the religious right has become more powerful as coins drop in the coffers."

At the time I was writing the op-ed, the only public funding being spent on AIDS in Santa Clara County was the state grant that partially paid the salaries of the nurse and health

----

62 Ken Yeager. "Politicians Can't Keep AIDS at Arm's Length." *San Jose Mercury News*. September 30, 1985.

educators. Local nonprofits such as the AIDS/KS Foundation and the Aris Project, which provided counseling and support programs to AIDS patients, did not receive any funds at that time from either the County or local cities. There was no health-care facility where AIDS patients with chronic cases could receive ongoing treatment. Santa Clara Valley Medical Center only treat-ed acute patients who were gravely ill. As I noted in my op-ed, this was "irresponsible and inhumane."

DeYoung died in the summer of 1986. As a political con-sultant who was an early specialist in using data management for voter outreach and targeting, he played a key role in the electoral successes of San Mateo Supervisor Tom Nolan and future Congresswomen Anna Eshoo and Jackie Speier. He also mentored Doug Winslow, who took over DeYoung's business and went on to help elect Democratic candidates throughout the Bay Area and country.

As 1985 drew to a close, the AIDS crisis continued to be full of despair. In my conversations with medical health pro-fessionals, it was clear that the County Health Department did not know how to respond. That led Wiggsy, Ron Taylor, and myself to draw up a list of actions we wanted to take before the Board of Supervisors. On January 17, 1986, we presented our nine-point proposal. Joining us was Dr. Ira Greene, a chief dermatologist at Valley Medical Center.

Our request to the Board was to:

- Provide the Aris Project with $180,000 in funding over the ensuing 18 months.

- Allocate funds to establish a residential care facili-ty for chronically ill AIDS patients.

- Establish a program to educate County employees who may work with AIDS patients, including dep-uty sheriffs, probation officers, social workers, and health department staff.

- Create a Board-sponsored task force to assess needs and develop a comprehensive AIDS program for the County.

- Allocate additional funds for education and educational materials targeted to high-risk groups.

- Increase staff levels of the AIDS Project in order to provide more proactive outreach to community groups.

- Publicize the County's ability to care for AIDS patients at Valley Medical Center.

- Direct the Mental Health Department to establish a working relationship with the Aris Project to coordinate mental and emotional support for AIDS patients.

As nervous as I was, you can imagine the comfort I felt from having my former boss and now good friend, Supervisor Susie Wilson, as the Board president. If you've never spoken before a government body, it can be quite intimidating. You are never sure if they are paying attention, despising you, or supporting you. You learn to keep on talking for your full two minutes and hope for the best. But I knew I was talking to a receptive audience.

The supervisors responded positively to our proposal, embracing the recommendations. At the following meeting, along with other actions, the Board approved the expenditure of $60,000 for AIDS support services, with more funds to follow. The supervisors also established an AIDS Task Force, to which Wilson appointed me as chair.

As part of our lobbying efforts, BAYMEC asked its members to send postcards and letters to the supervisors. More than 25 percent of our members responded within three days to show their support and appreciation.

Progress was finally being made, albeit in small steps.

I have often wondered if BAYMEC would have used more violent methods had the supervisors denied our request. We were aware of protests conducted by ACT UP and other groups that involved such actions as people chaining themselves to government buildings, blocking highways, and splattering red paint to represent someone's HIV blood. I give thanks to the Larry Kramers of the world for their demonstrations because they brought about desperately needed change. I think we would have done whatever was necessary to get the funding, but we were fortunate to have receptive County supervisors who listened to our needs.

My Brush with HIV

On a personal level, it was in March 1986 that I learned a friend of mine had died of AIDS. I was saddened by his death, and because of a brief encounter we had a year earlier, there was the possibility I might have become infected.

I was fortunate to know Dr. Denny McShane, a gay physician who was one of the few doctors on the San Mateo Peninsula who worked with AIDS patients. I met him through his partner, Rich Gordon, who was president of BAYMEC at the time. McShane and his medical partner, Dr. Bill Lipple, started a private practice that included AIDS patients, the only one between San Francisco and Los Angeles. They were very involved in getting their patients into medical trials.

We discussed the pros and cons of getting tested. Because there were no medications available, the results weren't all that useful. There was also the risk that a person's HIV status could be used to deny them medical coverage or be subject to discrimination. "It was damned if you do, damned if you don't," he laughed when I interviewed him in 2015.

I decided to get tested, mainly because I had started dating someone and was frantic that I might have passed on the virus to him. He and I talked extensively about our options, and we both decided to get tested.

At the time, it took two agonizing weeks to get the results. I was in my last quarter of graduate school at Stanford, and I was all but immobilized. The anxiety and self-reflection that occurred over those 14 days were grueling. It was with relief that we both heard from McShane that we were negative. Thankfully, today the rapid HIV test takes 20 minutes.

I tell this story because it is reflective of the thousands of frightening experiences of gay men in the 1980s and early 1990s. Testing was terrifying because a positive result was analogous to a death sentence. The odds seemed great that any sexually active gay man would encounter someone who carried the virus, creating a prevailing atmosphere of fear that we all may become HIV positive.

I think back on all the people who died of AIDS; their lives cut short, and their potential never reached. Testing negative has given me 37-plus years so far to have a wonderful career and life—37 extra years that so many others did not get. It's one reason I have worked so hard on the Getting to Zero campaign in Santa Clara County: Zero Infections, Zero Deaths, Zero Stigma.

Proposition 64[63]

The early to mid-1980s was a time of widespread misinformation and hysteria about AIDS. There were public fears that AIDS could be transmitted through the air like the common cold or by mosquitoes.

Into this atmosphere stepped Lyndon LaRouche, a onetime Marxist who by 1986 had become a far-right reactionary, calling Henry Kissinger a communist and accusing Great Britain's Queen Elizabeth of conspiring to get the U.S. population

----

63　Note: Parts of this section were included in my *The Long Struggle for LGBTQ+ Equality in Santa Clara County*. The booklet can be found at queersiliconvalley.org/measures-a-and-b/

hooked on drugs. His followers exploited the misinformation and public fears about the AIDS epidemic to secure the 500,000 voter signatures necessary to get Proposition 64 on the November 1986 ballot. It would have allowed public health officials to make AIDS testing mandatory, required the public disclosure of anyone who tested positive for HIV, and prohibited anyone with HIV from attending or teaching school, as well as restricting their ability to travel.

When Proposition 64 qualified for the ballot, many Californians had a negative or hostile attitude toward both the AIDS epidemic and the LGBTQ+ community. A *Los Angeles Times* poll published that summer found that half of the public favored quarantining AIDS victims, and a quarter believed "AIDS is a punishment God has given homosexuals for the way they lived."

On July 1, BAYMEC's board voted to put the organization's full resources into defeating Proposition 64. The South Bay's LGBTQ+ community, which had been demoralized by the passage of Measures A and B and the subsequent arrival of the AIDS epidemic, acquired a renewed sense of activism. The next few months would see a dramatic transformation in the community's profile and relevance.

BAYMEC knew we had a lot of work to do in educating voters about both the realities of the epidemic and just how dangerous and disruptive Prop. 64 would be if it were approved.

The statewide "No on 64" campaign initially planned to open offices only in San Francisco and Los Angeles. BAYMEC board members thought this was short-sighted. I feared that the San Francisco and Los Angeles-based campaign leadership would ignore the South Bay and put little or no effort or outreach into the region.

BAYMEC was eager to run the local campaign for two reasons. First, even though we were a fledgling organization, I felt we had the capabilities to run a professional campaign. Second and equally important, we believed that South Bay needed a strong LGBTQ+ organization to lead all the subsequent fights we knew would surely come over the years. Having an outside group run the campaign would have been a lost opportunity for a local group to build relationships that would last far beyond when the campaign ended. Though there was no universal agreement on BAYMEC's leadership role by all activists, over time almost everyone got on board. As I learned over the years, bringing everyone along for the ride is not easy.

Sivertsen agreed to serve as our local "No on 64" campaign chair, Paul Wysocki as our finance chair, and I became the campaign manager for Santa Clara and San Mateo Counties. Sivertsen, Wysocki, and Rich Gordon served on the statewide campaign committee.

There was never any question that the headquarters would be at the Billy DeFrank LGBTQ+ Community Center, located at the time on Park Avenue. In 1986, it was not only the hub of South Bay LGBTQ+ political and social activity but also a landlord who was willing to rent us space for the incredibly low rate of $200 a month.

Financially, the South Bay stepped up in a big way. State organizers only expected BAYMEC to raise $20,000. We raised $73,000, which is the equivalent of $189,000 in 2022 dollars. Santa Clara County donors actually contributed more to the campaign than those in the much larger San Diego County. All this occurred in less than 14 weeks. Our first fundraising letter was mailed out on July 30. The kickoff fundraiser took place on September 7, with more than 200 people attending and over $7,000 raised.

The fundraising campaign was the definition of grassroots. More than 1,200 small contributors wrote checks of $10, $50, or other similar amounts. The average contribution was $60. There were no corporations or wealthy individuals writing us big checks. Fundraisers were held at bars and nightclubs stretching from San Jose to the Peninsula to Santa Cruz. In all, there were 23 house parties in Santa Clara and San Mateo Counties.

On election night, November 4, 1986, a large crowd of supporters watched the returns at the Billy DeFrank Center. The mood of happiness and relief mounted as it became clear that the people of California listened to the message of reason and understanding that had been so much a part of the "No on 64" campaign.[64]

The next day, BAYMEC immediately began to plan for a celebration party. Ron Taylor had a connection to Archbishop Mitty High School in San Jose, so we decided to have the event there. Rebecca Obryan organized volunteers who cooked spaghetti for approximately 400 people. We charged $5.

Because so many people deserved to be recognized for their work, during the program I asked people to stand up and be acknowledged for their contribution: voter registration, speakers' bureau, fundraising, house parties, voter outreach, or being a Billy DeFrank board member. Lastly, when I asked who had donated their hard-earned dollars, everyone in the cafeteria stood up. There was a roar of applause, creating a sense of community that was palpable.

I often note that San Jose Councilwoman Iola Williams was the only elected official who came to the dinner. This speaks volumes about Williams' longtime and public support of the LGBTQ+ community. I had met her when I was working on Councilwoman Wilson's re-election campaign. We became good friends, and I ran her re-election campaign to a local school board, my first job as a manager. She would later be appointed to the San Jose City Council in 1979 and then elected in 1980, becoming the city's first African American member. After her short speech, she received a prolonged standing ovation. We then presented her with our first Friend of BAYMEC award and 12 long-stemmed roses.

When I told this story in an interview for *Valley Politics*

----

64   Note: I recount more about the Proposition 64 campaign and other issues occurring in 1986 in my opinion piece, "Recalling the 1986's AIDS-phobic Prop. 64." *Bay Area Reporter*. November 10, 2016.

with other founding BAYMEC board members, John Laird was quick to add that, as a then-Santa Cruz city councilman, he also attended the dinner, thus resulting in *two* elected officials being there. We all laughed at my undercounting. Whatever the number, it was an indication of how far we still had to go to get widespread support from local politicians.[65]

The decision to run our own "No on 64" campaign served BAYMEC well. We were able to establish our own relationships with the press and elected officials, raise and spend money locally, and mentor new leaders.

The turning point for the LGBTQ+ community in the South Bay political mainstream was the 1988 dinner. After the success of the spaghetti dinner, I knew we were ready for the big time—a splashy gala where people wore tuxedos and evening gowns. We weren't quite sure our bravado translated into charging $100 per ticket, so we decided that because it was 1988, we'd go with $88.

The *Mercury News* took an interesting twist on the story. Jim Dickey, a gay reporter who once told me he seldom was given gay stories by the newspaper because he might not be objective, was given the assignment. He made the lead story about Assemblyman Dominic Cortese, who, when a county supervisor, was one of the 50,000 petition signers in calling for the repeal of the 1980 Measure A pro-gay rights ordinance.[66]

Further, Dickey said that Cortese "had called for an investigation of the County's Human Relations Commission, which had proposed the ordinance recognizing gay rights."

But—get ready for it—here was Dickey's tagline: "When the three-county political group holds its first fundraising dinner May 21, Cortese will be among the sponsors."

In so many ways, that summed up what BAYMEC was able

----

65   Valley Politics. "Hear Our Voices, South Bay Politics, and the Founding of BAYMEC."

66   Jim Dickey. "Gay Rights Group Finds New Clout." *San Jose Mercury News*. May 9, 1988.

to achieve. Those who voted against us were now voting with us. As Wiggsy often said, it was never the strategy of BAYMEC to vilify those politicians who did not support us but to walk with them to a better understanding unless it was utterly impossible.

Dickey's article then listed the most prominent political sponsors of the dinner. It included Senator Alan Cranston, Representatives Don Edwards, Norman Mineta, Leon Panetta, San Jose Mayor Tom McEnery, numerous city councilmembers, county supervisors, and elected officials from nearby cities. Our longtime friend, San Jose Assemblyman and Chair of the Assembly Ways and Means Committee, John Vasconcellos, gave the keynote address.

Dickey got to the heart of the matter when he wrote, "Until recent years, many of them would have considered an endorsement of such an event as political suicide."

As BAYMEC's treasurer, I was quoted as saying that the dinner's popularity was the result of four years of talking with elected officials at breakfasts, luncheons, and group meetings. "I think they've realized we're not the lepers they thought we were. Times have changed, and there is no longer that outcry by bigots against politicians who support non-discrimination ordinance issues for lesbians and gay men," I stated.

BAYMEC board member and Santa Cruz Mayor Laird reflected how four years ago political people in Santa Clara Valley were very nervous about lesbian and gay issues. "Today, for many, that nervousness has gone away. They now understand the justice of gay issues, and gay people are now very difficult for politicians to ignore."

Baby steps continued to be taken throughout 1988, slowly chipping away at the entrenched attitudes that Measures A and B represented. Making appointments to city or county commissions was still seen as politically dangerous, which may explain why there weren't any open queer commissioners at either the city or county levels and still only one known county gay commissioner ever. So rare was this species of "homosexual" commissioner that when spotted, a headline in the *Mercury News* blasted out, "Two homosexuals appointed to city, county commissions." [67]

The two homosexuals were Richard Nichols, who was appointed to the County Human Relations Commission, and Arthur Morris, appointed to the San Jose Civil Service Commission. Both were active in BAYMEC and reflected our growing influence in local politics.

Morris commented that the appointments indicated that public officials were beginning to support gay causes for the first time since the San Jose and Santa Clara County gay rights measures were defeated eight years ago. "Since 1980, elected officials have been shy in addressing the agenda of the gay community," he said, "and our appointments indicate a turnaround." That said, Morris still squeaked by with the minimum six votes he needed from the council for appointment.

It was Supervisor Dianne McKenna who appointed Nichols to the county commission. She said, "Richard is the type of person I would have appointed if he were purple."

Gay. Purple. What's the difference?

Well-Known Gay Activist Runs for Council

In June 1989, Paul Wysocki, a well-known community activist and BAYMEC's president, announced he was running for San Jose City Council from the downtown area. Although not the first gay candidate to run in San Jose, he was the most prominent.

Wysocki, 42, was a 20-year resident of San Jose, having moved here in 1969. During that time, he was involved with the San Jose State Gay Liberation Front, where he collaborated with Wiggsy. He worked for several real estate firms before

---

67 Jim Dickey. "Two Homosexuals Appointed to City, County Commissions." *San Jose Mercury News.* March 5, 1988."

becoming a broker and opening his own firm, Goosetown Realty, in 1981.

A seasoned political veteran at a young age, Wysocki was a campaign worker for the 1978 No on the Briggs Initiative, followed by the local No on 64 campaign in 1986, where he served as the county's fundraising chair. In 1986 and 1987, he chaired the political action committee for High Tech Gays.

There was no incumbent in the race, so optimism was high that Wysocki would be able to break through the lavender ceiling. His campaign theme was "A New Voice for the Heart of San Jose." Beneath his name on the campaign literature were the words "Rhymes with ice hockey," a good example of his ability to laugh at himself.

Although Wysocki was seen as credible, campaigns aren't just about one candidate; they're about who else is running and whether you are the first choice of important constituency groups that get involved in local campaigns. Unfortunately, being everyone's second choice results in few contributions or volunteers. I think that is what happened with Wysocki. He was only the first choice of the LGBTQ+ community, and that simply wasn't enough.

The first-place finisher in the primary with 31.6 percent of the vote was David Pandori, who had the support of the city establishment and the *Mercury News*; next was Pete Carrillo with 30.3 percent, who had the backing of labor and voters in the heavily Latino parts of the district; he was followed by Scott Strickland with 18.7 percent who had the Chamber of Commerce endorsement and several of the smaller neighborhoods in the district. Wysocki was fifth out of six candidates, with 6.5 percent of the vote.

Several years later I asked him how he took his defeat. His answer was one of the funniest political lines I've heard. "I was so bitter afterward," he said, "that I didn't have sex for a year." Now *that's* bitter.

In an opinion piece published in the *Mercury News* after

the election, Wysocki wrote, "My campaign was not about gay rights, but rather about the right of one gay man to be taken seriously as a political leader. I certainly didn't expect to be welcomed overnight—few newcomers are—but I did expect to make new inroads in a society where a campaign such as this would have been unheard of in the 1980s.

"There are clear implications here for the gay community. A look at the civil rights movement of the 60s shows that while the more radical segment, e.g., Black Panthers, sped up an ongoing process, it was the less volatile people, e.g., Martin Luther King, who succeeded in gaining power.

"In the same manner, the gay community will succeed not as radicalized political gadflies, but rather by becoming part of the mainstream." [68]

That sentiment reflects the political philosophy and strategy that always guided BAYMEC and to which I credit my own electoral success.

Wysocki passed away in 2017 at the age of 69.

"I Won't Vote for it Until You Guys Stop Having Sex in Public Bathrooms."

There were a number of local legislators that ended up supporting us after years of voting against us, but one of the most notable was state Senator Al Alquist, who represented Santa Clara Valley from 1963 to 1996. As mentioned in the previous chapter, Alquist was the only one of our state senators who voted against AB 1, the non-discrimination law to include sexual orientation, which had passed by a narrow margin. As was BAYMEC's way of conducting business, we decided to try to work with him in a respectful manner, knowing that he was a solid union-supporting Democrat who needed education on our issues. We soon learned it was more than education that

------

68   Paul Wysocki, "Opening Up Politics in San Jose and Elsewhere." *San Jose Mercury News*. June 25, 1990.

was needed. We needed to play hardball.

When Deukmejian vetoed AB 1 in 1984, it did not come back for another vote in the legislature until 1991 because legislators knew there was no chance of him signing it. With Governor Pete Wilson newly elected, it was felt that he might be more amenable to supporting it. The bill was now known as AB 101. The push was on to secure legislators' support.

At a Women's Fund event that Wiggsy and I attended, we began talking with Alquist in the relaxed manner you do during the cocktail hour. We thought it might be a good opportunity to bring up the issue of AB 101 to get a sense if there had been any movement in his position. In remarks I'll never forget, he said he had too many other issues on his mind to be worried about AB 101.

Fair enough. But then he stunned us when he added that he didn't think that people who participated in filthy acts in public restrooms should be given special rights. "I won't vote for it until you guys stop having sex in public bathrooms," he said.

Hmm, I thought. *Does that mean never? Let me get the word out to my bros.*

The publication of his statements in my *Our Paper/Your Paper* column created an uproar loud enough for the gay-deaf straight press to hear. As I mentioned, many of Alquist's liberal supporters were angry enough to lobby him directly. Many LGBTQ+ people wrote letters telling him what they thought of him.[69]

Compounding the pushback was a group called Queer Nation, which took its playbook from ACT-UP, a more militant group of AIDS activists angry at the U.S. government's slow response to the epidemic. According to the *Mercury News,*[70] Alquist

----

69   Ken Yeager. "Alquist Votes in Favor of AB 101 in Committee." *Our Paper/ Your Paper.* August 21, 1991.

70   Gary Webb. "Controversial Gay Rights Measure Survives Because of Vote Switch." *San Jose Mercury News.* August 20, 1991.

had "vowed not to support the measure, saying he had been insulted by the militant group. The group had threatened to send a letter to some of his contributors, attacking Alquist for what it called 'his bigotry and hatred of gays and lesbians.'"

Despite gays still having sex in bathrooms, in the end, Alquist said his change of heart came after meeting with Senate President David Roberti, enabling the bill to pass a committee and go to the full Senate. Had Alquist not changed his mind, the bill would have died. So certain were the fundamentalists that Alquist was a "no" vote that they were dancing in the Capitol hallway when they got word that the bill had actually passed.

The *Mercury News* political gossip column, *The Insider*, mentioned that some long-time Democrats like Consuelo Killins played a role in the conversion. I was quoted as saying, "I'm not quite sure what road to Damascus Alquist took, but we're certainly glad he took it." [71]

The lone assembly member who voted "no" from our area was Republican Chuck Quackenbush. A staunch conservative, he had never been a supporter of LGBTQ+ issues or of AIDS programs. Because he was a Republican, BAYMEC—as a nonpartisan political action committee—sent its Republican board members to speak to him. All the members left shaking their heads, wondering what planet Quackenbush had been on for the last decade.

What the group found particularly disturbing was that Quackenbush stated he had heard there was "a cure for people like you." He saw homosexuality as something people freely choose. He wondered if there was any need for the law because gays and lesbians may not need to be victims of discrimination if they simply left that lifestyle. When he said he needed proof that discrimination does occur, members told him that information would be supplied to him.

So, what had happened locally in the seven years after the

----

71 Political Insider. "Today's Question: Who's on First?" *San Jose Mercury News*. September 22, 1991.

initial state vote in 1984 for AB 1, the non-discrimination law? On the state level, McAlister was long gone, replaced by Delaine Eastin, a great champion of civil rights. Two legislators who had voted against the bill in 1994—Cortese and Alquist—voted for it in 1991, along with Areias, Vasconcellos, Sam Farr, Ted Lempert, Byron Sher, Jackie Speier, and Dan McCorquodale and Rebecca Morgan in the senate.

Optimism was high that Wilson would sign the bill. In an April 17 *San Francisco Chronicle* editorial, the sub-headline read: "Governor says it is 'very likely' he will sign legislation to outlaw discrimination in jobs and housing." [72]

The piece talked about the big difference between Wilson and Deukmejian, adding that in a meeting with editorial page editors across the state, "Wilson all but committed himself to sign the gay rights bill, saying that there was no reason not to sign it."

Furthermore, the editorial ended by saying what great courage Wilson was showing "in recognizing the right of all people to protections regardless of their sexual orientation. This bill's time has come."

But trouble was brewing. In a *Mercury News* editorial five days later, it mentioned that Wilson had said earlier that he would support the bill but was now wavering. Wilson's aides have asked Republicans not to vote for the bill. [73]

Apparently, its time had not come. On September 29, 1991, Wilson vetoed the bill, saying it would bring a flood of meritless lawsuits against businesses. He was quickly denounced by those who supported the bill. Demonstrations took place in San Francisco, Los Angeles, and Sacramento, accusing the governor of bowing to political pressure.

Interestingly, Wilson's veto came right before a California

---

72   Editorial Board. "Wilson and Gay Rights." *San Francisco Chronicle.* April 17, 1991.

73   Editorial Board. "Basic Civil Rights for Gays." *San Jose Mercury News.* August 22, 1991.

Poll was to be released on whether people thought Wilson should sign or veto the bill. Fearing that the poll would show opposition, his staff worried if he waited to veto the bill that people would think he was responding to the poll.[74]

As it turned out, 62 percent of the respondents said Wilson should sign it, with 29 percent saying no and 9 percent undecided. Supporters of the bill would try again the following year.

With significant changes that included only anti-discrimination statutes that covered sexual orientation and provided penalties that were civil rather than criminal, the bill, now called AB 2106, was passed and signed by Wilson in 1992.

1991 BAYMEC Dinner – the Biggest Yet

The BAYMEC dinners continued to grow in size and popularity. For the 1991 event, we had an all-time high of 95 elected officials being sponsors, up from the 33 who agreed to be sponsors at the 1988 inaugural dinner. For the first time, we had the mayor and all 10 San Jose councilmembers as sponsors—11 out of 11. This occurred because arch-fundamentalist Councilwoman Lu Ryden was replaced on the council by BAYMEC-endorsed Trixie Johnson, who readily agreed to be listed. Moreover, it was the first year that Senator Alquist was a sponsor, along with all our state legislative delegation—minus Quackenbush—our congressional delegation, and five county supervisors. We had a little over 500 attendees, each paying $100 a plate.

Each year we would have more attendees and more elected officials as sponsors, but for me, the 1991 dinner was the culmination of a decade of hard, methodical work that told me we were doing things the right way.

By far, the big announcement regarding the dinner was our keynote speaker: recently elected San Jose Mayor Susan Hammer. We were swooning with delight. She had won a tough

---

74   Roberts, Gerry, and Burress, Charles. "More Timed To Beat Release of Poll Today." *San Francisco Chronicle*. September 30, 1991.

campaign in November 1990, and BAYMEC made her race its top priority. Yes, gay groups in LA and SF might be able to get big movie stars or national leaders, but for us, getting the newly minted mayor whom we adored was tops.

Having taken office only a few months earlier, Hammer was in high demand as a speaker, so BAYMEC was thrilled she accepted our invitation. In and of itself, that demonstrated our influence and political resurrection.

There was a tremendous difference between Hammer and McEnery. BAYMEC had to fight McEnery for everything, but this was not the case with Hammer. She didn't hesitate in issuing the proclamation for Gay Pride, supporting AB 101, or participating in Gay Pride events. She had ushered in a new day for the San Jose LGBTQ+ community.

The evening was magical. Held at the glitzy San Jose Fairmont Hotel, everyone was in tuxedos and gowns. Spirits were high. After everyone was seated, all the elected officials were introduced, each to a nice applause. After dinner was finished, Hammer was introduced.

Her speech was so eloquent. She began talking about the early days of the gay rights movement, referencing the Mattachine Society, the Stonewall Riots, and Harvey Milk, adding that "gays and lesbians deserve a place in the spotlight of America's civil rights movement."

Next, she proposed that there are three essential elements necessary in shaping any political agenda, all of which BAYMEC embodies. "Number one: Break the silence. Number two: Organize. Number three: Keep the faith. I believe BAYMEC has achieved these three commitments, without wavering, since it first began in 1984." Hammer then gave examples of the political battles that had been fought, along with mentioning individuals who had done the fighting.

One point she forcefully emphasized was being alert to hate crimes against LGBTQ+ people or anybody. "I have said it before, and I say it again. Hate crimes of any kind will simply not be tolerated in the City of San Jose...I have pledged to provide the leadership to make San Jose a place where we thrive on diversity instead of fearing each other." This received one of her several standing ovations.

Hammer's conclusion also brought people to their feet. "I know BAYMEC will keep the faith, and you will continue to educate and lobby. You and I will work to elect gays and lesbians to office, fight to end discrimination, and celebrate with the entire community your contributions and your presence in this city. I know that in the next decade your influence will continue to grow in our community. I welcome that and the opportunity to continue to work with you."

Tears and applause. After all that our community had been through, it was a new day, and it was glorious. We were proud to honor her with the Friend of BAYMEC Award.

The success of the dinner and the LGBTQ+ movement in general caught the attention of the *Mercury News.* "Gays and lesbians gain strength in S.J. politics," read the front-page headline.[75] After mentioning the support of all the council and supervisors, reporter Nick Anderson went on to write that at the dinner, "Hammer backed gay rights more forcefully than any of her predecessors. Most gay activists appraise former mayors Tom McEnery and Janet Gray Hayes with caution and sometimes skepticism, but they are positively effusive about Hammer."

Anderson included numerous passages from Hammer's speech in his article. One was especially moving: "You deserve a place in the political agendas of the 90s—in the high-tech world of Silicon Valley, in the suburbs of Almaden and Evergreen, in the galleries of the best museums, on the shelves of our libraries, in the life beat of the community where you toil and play."

Amen.

Anderson did mention that getting to that place was a matter

----

75   Nick Anderson. "Gays use savvy, money, to move into the mainstream." *San Jose Mercury News.* August 16, 1991.

of groups like BAYMEC "using savvy manipulation of endorsements, moral persuasion, and money to get what they wanted. They've been smart enough to know when not to push a
politician too hard, taking half a loaf when they can get it and
coming back later for more and more."

"Maybe things have changed," I am quoted as saying, "and
it might be time to ask for the whole loaf."

I want to mention that one of my staunchest supporters
was Mayor Hammer. She endorsed me when I ran for community college board, state assembly, city council, and board of
supervisors. There weren't any questions or hemming and hawing, as can be the case if there is a perceived risk involved.
Right away it was always a yes. She remained very popular
after she left office, and her support carried a lot of weight. In
my brochures, I always included her photo with a nice quote.
I owe her a great deal.

Bigoted, Racist, and Homophobic
All Rolled Into One

In a case of remarks almost too bigoted, racist, and homophobic
to be true, the political newcomer and San Jose Councilwoman
Kathy Cole gave a speech early in her term in 1993 intended
to motivate Black activists. In a transcript of the speech, she
jumped right in at the start by talking about the lack of power
Black people have, although "we have been here the longest
in the sense of people fighting for civil rights, for equality." In
City Hall, she said, "We have less respect than anybody, and
we have the least empowerment from them in the political
system. It is atrocious."[76]

So, who has the most empowerment? Cole started off with
Hispanics. "I am getting sick and tired of everything that comes
in here that has a Hispanic name on it. They got buildings,

----

76 "What Cole Said." Transcripts of Cole's Speech. *San Jose Mercury
News*. May 30, 1993.

they got youth centers coming, they got money that the city has given them for everything because they went after it."

The gays: "Now, if you really want to be something, then be Black and gay. You might really get something out of the deal."

Moreover: "[City Hall] doesn't actually like [Hispanics]. They like the Asians and the gays better than the Hispanics, but the Hispanics have persevered; they are like little pit bulls."

The Asians: "If you get up and slant your eyes, you might get something out of the deal." As she said this, she pulled her eyes into a slant.

It is true that Blacks were not getting the services due to them, but denigrating other minority groups was clearly not the way to make her point.

Denouncement came quickly when a video of her remarks was given to the press. Criticized from all sides by those offended, she apologized as a way to save her infant political career.

I was having none of it. In a *Mercury News* article about her remarks, I mentioned how the LGBTQ+ community had difficulty getting her to meet or talk with us, which I interpreted as hostility. "I don't live in her district," I said. "If I did, I'd lead a recall." [77]

It was nice to get the agreement in the article from a well-known Black leader, Tommy Fulcher. He called Cole "an obvious bigot—a homophobic racist. There is no place for someone like that on the council." [78]

From the onset, BAYMEC was part of the multiracial, multiethnic coalition that was formed, demanding that she resign.

In an example of how aggressive Cole could be in responding to her critics, when San Jose Congressman Norm Mineta called her remarks "outrageous" and urged her to resign, Cole said she had not turned against him when "he made a mistake

----

77   Marilyn Lewis. "San Jose Councilwoman Apologizes for Remarks." *San Jose Mercury News*. May 20, 1993.

78   Ibid.

and chose to do something in public that embarrassed his family," referring to his divorce. "In my community, in the Christian community, divorce is a mistake."[79]

She specifically mentioned BAYMEC. She complained that we disliked her because she did not initially seek the group's endorsement and would not support two city council resolutions: One condemning Colorado's Amendment 2, which prevented cities from enacting gay rights measures; the other in favor of gays serving in the military.

Holding fast in the eye of almost universal condemnation, she refused to resign, even though a poll in April showed 55 percent of voters in her district said she should. That left a recall as the only option.

There was something about BAYMEC that was in her craw. She had filled out our questionnaire and given measured answers to our nine questions. Reading them over now makes it clear she did not write the answers and maybe did not review them either. For example, when asked if she'd be willing to attend any gay and lesbian event, such as the BAYMEC dinner or Pride Celebration, she answered that "It's important to ensure that I am both visible and accessible, both within City Hall and in community forums and events, to all aspects of our local community. Every request for my personal participation will be treated fairly and with the thought of enhancing my personal understanding and effectiveness in representing the diverse interests of our citizens."

Well, that was hogwash. After we ended up supporting her opponent, the Cole campaign issued a remarkable press release that I had never seen before. It stated that Cole was releasing her response to the "highly controversial BAYMEC Questionnaire," stating that the public should have access to answers to these questionnaires and encouraged her opponent to do the same.

----

79 Brandon Bailey. "Cole Strikes Back at Mineta, Vows to Keep Council Seat." *San Jose Mercury News.* May 25, 1993.

The press release took direct aim at her opponent in the council race, Patricia Martinez-Roach, saying, "By trying to make gay and lesbian rights a major issue in her campaign, Ms. Roach demonstrates a typical political activist's shallow understanding of the primary neighborhood concerns of area residents in this election."

So, it was whether to work on potholes or homosexual rights. Clearly, no room for both.

The baiting of BAYMEC was not over yet. In a full-page ad in the June 1993 edition of the *Evergreen Times,* Cole implied that voting for her removal from office would lead to the gay community controlling the council district. "Under the city charter, the Mayor and City Council would pick Evergreen's new Council representative if the recall passes. BAYMEC has won City Hall support on all of its issues. That's one reason they're working really hard to force Kathy Cole out of local government. They know they're one of the 'special interests' who will finally get to determine the kind of leadership who will represent the Evergreen community."

In the April 1994 special election, 59.2 percent of voters favored a recall, making her the first council member to be recalled in San Jose history.

Electing Zoe Lofgren to Congress

Santa Clara County Supervisor Zoe Lofgren stunned the political community in June 1994 by defeating former San Jose Mayor Tom McEnery in a primary race to replace retiring Congressman Don Edwards. BAYMEC had endorsed Lofgren, who, as a supervisor, was a strong ally who had fought to maintain adequate funding for AIDS service along with other LGBTQ+ services.

It was a bold endorsement for us, one which I remember well. McEnery, a popular mayor who was termed out of office, was seen, by far, as the heir apparent. Ahead in the polls, he had the downtown business and chamber support. If we had wanted to play it safe, BAYMEC's endorsement of McEnery could have served us well. It might have been enough to turn a reluctant supporter into an ally. Wiggsy and I had been in politics long enough to know that opposing a candidate who ultimately wins leaves wounds that are difficult, if not impossible, to heal.

But McEnery had always rubbed us the wrong way. As noted earlier, he only issued a gay pride proclamation after his re-election. Perhaps his lukewarm support was because he was around in 1980 for the overwhelming anti-gay vote. Ultimately, we believed he was never going to see eye to eye with us. In principle, win or lose, Lofgren deserved our support. Thankfully, she won in a close race.

We have been blessed to have Lofgren in office since 1995. She has tirelessly climbed up the ranks of Congress for the last 28 years, being a staunch supporter of immigration reform, being chosen as one of the House managers for the impeachment of Donald Trump, and serving on the special congressional panel investigating the January 6, 2019, insurrection.

Years later, when interviewed by Terry Christensen in *Valley Politics*, McEnery conceded that it would have been a disaster if he had won; that he would have had little interest in the tedious work of Congress. Lofgren, as we have seen, has been a star.[80]

The Boy Scouts Are Out; the Girl Scouts Are In

In 1991, the trustees of the Alum Rock Elementary School District in East San Jose voted to sever ties with the Boy Scouts of America because of the Scouts' discrimination policies. The 5-0 vote came after BAYMEC members and Scout supporters spoke at an October 10 meeting.

At issue was if the school district would enter into a $12,000

---

80   Valley Politics History Interviews: Tom McEnery. CreaTVSJ 2017.

contract with the Scouts to provide an in-school Scouting program. The program had existed in the district since 1983 and included teaching science once a week to elementary school students.

Prior to the school hearing, Wiggsy, Paul Wysocki, and I had met with members of the Santa Clara County chapter of the Boy Scouts to discuss their policy.

It was then that Scout officials told BAYMEC that college-age students were hired to teach the classes. When we asked if the Scouts would hire someone who disclosed that he or she was LGBTQ+, a Scout official said no, they would not hire that person. Further, Scout officials said if students openly said they were gay, they may not be allowed to attend the classes.

I asked if the local chapter would issue a statement declaring that they would not follow the national policy.

Scout officials stated they had no flexibility in the matter, and they might lose their charter if they went against the national organization. When I suggested that they defy the national policy and see what would happen, Scout officials became silent.

At the end of the meeting, Wiggsy stated that the Scouts needed to know that it was not the gay and lesbian community that was denying students the classes but the Scouts themselves. "You have the choice between offering the program or sticking by your discriminatory policy, and you've chosen the policy over the program," she said.

Wysocki added that it was unfortunate that the Scouts were taking the position they were. "It sends a bad signal on two accounts. First, it says that it's okay to discriminate, and second, it perpetuates the myth that gay men can't be trusted around children."

I offered to meet again if they felt there was room for negotiations. They said no, that they wanted to go forward with the school board hearing. This was fine with us. The Boy Scouts of America were on our turf now. We had contacted school trustees the day before and were reasonably certain the votes were there for the cancellation of the project.

BAYMEC had a good relationship with most of the trustees, having endorsed several of them over the years. One reason why BAYMEC endorses candidates at all levels is that you never know when you will need someone's help. Coincidentally, I was the campaign manager for one of the trustees, Gary Serda, when he ran for trustee in 1985.

At the school board meeting, Wysocki and BAYMEC board member Don Nelson spoke against the Scouts. Also attending was Ron Schmidt, a member of the Bay Area Network of Gay and Lesbian Educators or BANGLE. He said the Scouts were telling the district's LGBTQ+ students that they weren't fit as human beings.

Scout officials argued that the science program was important to district children and that the contract should be signed.

When public testimony was over, each of the five trustees spoke. Serda said the district would be doing a great disservice to children by teaching that discrimination is something that only happens in school books. This is because discrimination still occurs and it must be stopped. Trustee Pat Martinez-Roach said that this was the 1990s and that things needed to change. "If we discriminate against gays and lesbians, it could be Asians, Blacks, and Hispanics next week." Trustee Alex Salazar asked how staff could bring the Boy Scout contract to the board, knowing that they discriminate. Trustees Esau Herrera and Joaquin Luna also spoke against the contract on the basis that the Scouts didn't treat people equally or fairly.

After the 5-0 vote not to renew the contract, trustees asked district staff to report back in a month to find another organization to teach the classes.

This was relatively big news. The action was the first in Santa Clara County and the second in the nation to end a contract with local Scouts over their discriminatory positions. "We see it as a precedent," I was quoted as saying in the *Mercury News*. "It's a really great victory. Everybody saw it as a message to

Dallas [Scouting headquarters] as saying we don't tolerate this type of discrimination in San Jose."[81]

As it turned out, the Scouts' loss was the Girl Scouts' and everyone else's gain. About a month after the trustees' vote, the district hired the Girl Scouts of Santa Clara County to teach science enrichment classes at 12 schools in the district. The district's curriculum coordinator stated in the *Mercury News*, "The Girl Scouts don't have any kind of discriminatory practice that we have a problem with. They don't investigate or intrude into personal matters, including sexual preference." [82]

This had a fortunate cascading effect with funding of the Scouts by the various Bay Area United Ways. For the first time, there was a focus on the thousands of dollars given to the Boy Scouts who violated United Way's policies of non-discrimination. Certainly, the Boy Scouts of America have fallen from grace over the years, but at the time, the United Way was politically, socially, and financially a major force in the community. United Way chapters were worried that criticizing or defunding the Scouts would result in a dramatic loss of revenues, mainly from the conservative business community. Local Boy Scout chapters tried to say they didn't discriminate but were hapless in the face of national policies that they couldn't override.

It seems a little incomprehensible now, but for decades United Ways across America was the sole powerhouse of charitable fundraising. Companies would agree to have the local United Way distribute a list of nonprofit member agencies that had met their criteria for funding. Employees could then choose which organization they wanted to contribute to. Being a designated member agency often resulted in tens, if not hundreds, of thousands of dollars and would be the primary source of

81   Scott Herhold. "Boy Scouts Program Expelled Over Gay Ban." *San Jose Mercury News*. October 11, 1991.

82   Jim Dickey. "Scouting: Boys' Loss. Girls' Gain." *San Jose Mercury News*. October 31, 1991.

funds for eligible nonprofits. Companies would sponsor am-
bitious United Way fundraising drives with the goal of raising
more money than they had the year before. There would be a
big company celebration with congratulations going all around
when the fundraising drive was over and goals were met or
surpassed.

Issues surrounding the funding of the Boy Scouts led to
discussions of the level of support for the LGBTQ+ community
in general. As it turned out, the United Way of Santa Clara
County had never given any funding to an LGBTQ+ organization
or designated one as a member agency. A United Way Ad Hoc
Committee on Services for the Gay/Lesbian/Bisexual Communities was created in October 1991 to research the current
service needs of the LGBTQ+ community.

The committee found that there was a significant need for
youth services, support groups, mental health counseling, legal services, and substance abuse services. This led the United
Way to give $122,000 to the Billy DeFrank LGBTQ+ Commu-
nity Center[83] to fund special programs, a major breakthrough
for the LGBTQ+ community. Shortly thereafter, the DeFrank
Center was declared "eligible" to become a United Way agency,
allowing it to receive desperately needed financial resources.

While I was gratified by all the positive outcomes of my work
with defunding the Boy Scouts based on their discriminatory
practices, it was used against me in an anti-gay hit piece when
I ran for assembly in 1996. As I discuss in Chapter 6, one example used to show that I was against traditional families was
related to the Scouts. Under a photo of a young boy in a Scouts'
uniform were the enlarged words "Outlaw the Boy Scouts."
The corresponding paragraph stated, "As founder and leader
of BAYMEC, the gay and lesbian political action committee,
Yeager took personal pride in leading the fight to outlaw Boy
Scouts from San Jose Schools—and vowed to 'keep on battling'

----

83   Note: To learn more about the Billy DeFrank LGBTQ+ Community
Center go to queersiliconvalley.org/organizations/org-billy-defrank/

to block a major source of funding for local Boy Scouts."

It was perhaps those words that caused me to lose the state assembly race and prevented me from being the first openly gay man elected to the California state legislature.

CHAPTER 5

Making of a Candidate[84]

A local political office that is often overlooked by those interested in serving as a public officeholder is that of a community college trustee. In California, these elected officials have real authority, making policy on issues dealing with curriculum, vocational education, academic standards, collective bargaining, and so on. In the community college district where I live—the San Jose/Evergreen Community College District—there are two colleges with a combined student population of 25,000.

As soon as I had the idea of running for the college board, I knew the position was the right office at the right time. There were five reasons why it was a good fit.

First, I had paid my dues. For almost 20 years, I helped elect scores of people to office. I donated hundreds of dollars of my own money to candidates, political organizations, and minority groups. Through my work with BAYMEC, I helped hundreds of other candidates with endorsements and contributions. I joined marches and testified at hearings in support of other groups' causes. I worked to build coalitions with women's groups, unions, Democratic Party groups, Hispanic groups, Asian groups, and African-American groups. I knew the political players, and they knew me.

Second, I was a good match for the district. Trustees run in specific areas rather than at large, making the campaign less costly and easier to manage. This allowed me, as an LGBTQ+

---

84   Ken Yeager. "The Making of a Candidate: A Personal Memoir." Op. cit.

candidate, to run a competitive campaign. Although my area contained 110,000 people—42,000 of whom were registered voters—its boundaries included the older section of San Jose. This is where I spent most of my time in San Jose and where the highest concentration of liberal Democrats and LGBTQ+ people were. Also, there was no incumbent, which meant I could spend my time establishing my own credibility rather than criticizing a sitting politician.

Third, I had academic and professional credentials. Because of my Ph.D. in education and my M.A. in sociology, I knew a great deal about educational policy and educational organizations. Professionally, I was teaching at San Jose State University, where I was hired after I finished my dissertation. This gave me classroom experience at the college level and added to my credibility as a candidate. It also provided me with an image that I could use in my literature. The main photo was of me lecturing to students in a classroom, reinforcing the message that I was an educator and knowledgeable about higher education. I never allowed myself to be defined as "the gay candidate," which could have happened if I had not promoted myself as the candidate who was a San Jose State University lecturer.

Fourth, I knew how to run campaigns. I had worked for a national campaign consulting firm that was located in San Jose. Through managing school bond campaigns and overseeing the production of mail pieces for congressional candidates across the country, I learned the latest techniques in campaign management. I used much of this knowledge in my own campaign.

Fifth, I would be the first openly LGBTQ+ person ever elected to public office in Santa Clara County, a relatively liberal area with a population of two million people. I knew it was important for qualified queer people to run for office so voters would know that we could represent the interests of the entire community. Given my skills, connections, and resolve, I believed I would be a strong candidate.

For these reasons and more, I felt confident about my decision to run for the college board. My main concern was whether I would be a good candidate and how well I would interact with voters. From past experience, I knew I was a good campaign manager, but I was unsure if I had what it took to be the person on center stage.

I was aware that it would be difficult to know how to balance my gayness and my qualifications for the job. It was fortunate that anybody who knew me in San Jose was aware I was gay because of how often I was quoted in the newspaper and appeared on local television. Setting aside the gay issue, I was a candidate like anybody else. When my consultants and I were designing my brochure, we saw my being gay as a non-issue because I was already out. Thus, we assumed being gay would either be a big problem or no problem at all. If it were a big problem, then we would deal with it when it came up; otherwise, it was to be downplayed.

When the filing period closed, there were six of us running, all men. It was fortunate for me that no women had entered the race because women candidates were expected to do well in the 1992 election. One candidate had a Spanish surname, which would help him in Hispanic neighborhoods. Only one of my opponents had strong community ties, and he proved to be my main competitor. He was a lawyer and a former ESL teacher at the community colleges.

After consulting with my political friends, I finalized the campaign strategy and budget. Once I was able to form a mental picture of the entire campaign from start to finish, my stress level went down. No longer was the campaign a nebulous concept, but a sense of tasks that needed to be completed, one by one, day by day.

The budget was set at $15,000, which is about $32,000 in today's dollars. I had no idea if I would be able to raise that amount, given that this was a down-ballot race that wouldn't attract much special interest money. I loaned the campaign $500 to do the initial printing of literature. Fortunately, money came in steadily, mostly from people I had known over the years. Without these prior contacts, I would never have found 200 people to donate between $25 and $100. At first, it was hard to ask for money, but I knew that if I didn't have the grit to do it, then I was no good to myself or the issues I represented. Furthermore, as my campaign coordinator kept telling me, people will not give what they do not have. Amazingly, the more I asked for money, the easier it became.

Endorsements from elected officials and community leaders are crucial in any race, but even more so in low-profile ones where voters have not heard of the candidates. Because of the work I had done with many politicians on a variety of issues, securing endorsements was not hard. All I did was pick up the phone and talk to the person or his or her top aide. I usually got an answer the same day. My long list of endorsements helped to establish my credibility early, to raise funds, to get volunteers, and win the support of other organizations. I also knew it took some wind out of the sails of my opponents when they contacted elected officials only to be told they already had endorsed me.

The main strategy for the campaign was to contact voters through the mail. There was a total of three mailings: a four-page brochure, a personalized letter, and a jumbo postcard, all of which were to be mailed the final week. The selection of which voters would receive the pieces was determined by a longtime friend, Doug Winslow, who owned a political database management company that handled lists of registered voters.

The second way to contact voters was through a field and volunteer operation. The field operation included walking precincts, putting up signs on supporters' lawns, and passing out literature. The volunteer operation mainly consisted of addressing envelopes. All the work was run out of my garage, which the previous homeowner had turned into a recreation room, complete with an AstroTurf, telephone, toilet, and sink. Volunteers were there Monday through Friday from 6:00 to 10:00 p.m. and all-day Saturday and Sunday, writing the names of voters on envelopes. On average, there were five people working in the garage each day. One regular volunteer, Arlene Rusche, would bring her 14-year-old daughter because she felt it was part of her responsibility as a parent to teach her how the government worked. Most of the volunteers were people I had known from my work with BAYMEC.

The volunteer operation was the aspect of the campaign with which I had the least involvement. For one thing, I was too busy raising money and meeting people; for another, I was not good at handling volunteers. I was blessed to have my good friend Leslee Hamilton as my campaign coordinator. She had worked for many years as the canvass supervisor for a political organization and knew how to deal with different personality types. Throughout the campaign, I never once had to worry about whether the volunteers were happy or had enough to do. There was no sniping, no backstabbing, no rebellions, a feat which many political campaigns—gay or straight—cannot claim.

One of the primary volunteer efforts was the production of mailing neighbor-to-neighbor letters. These were one-page letters that detailed my qualifications and goals targeted by the neighborhood. I broke down my area into 16 different neighborhoods, then asked a friend living in each one if I could use his or her name. Next, our computer programmer printed the person's name and address on letterhead. Each letter was the same, except that the first sentence differed by neighborhood. Then, volunteers hand-addressed the envelopes. One glorious night, the last of 12,000 letters were folded, sealed, stamped, and ready to go. They were mailed six days before the election and arrived in people's mailboxes the next day.

As it turned out, the neighbor-to-neighbor letters were enormously effective, mainly because they looked like personalized mail from a neighbor, not campaign literature. People must have read them because when I was walking precincts many people said, "I got a letter from someone down the street telling me about you."

Another successful aspect of the campaign was the lawn and street signs. The colors we chose were lavender and white—lavender being the color identified with gay pride. About 150 people agreed to put signs on their lawns, which was a high number for any campaign. Even San Jose Mayor Susan Hammer put a sign in front of her house. Every now and then, I would be driving and see a wave of lavender with my name on it and think, "You're really out there with being gay, Ken." Sometimes this would make me nervous, believing I could be a victim of a hate crime. Only once since I was elected was my house a target in a poorly executed toilet paper and egg attack.

The campaign was a three-month endurance race, not unlike a marathon. In the afternoons, when I came back from teaching, I would either walk a precinct, write thank-you letters, or answer a group's questionnaire. There were always two or three events to attend in the evenings. Late at night, I would grade papers or prepare my lectures for the next day.

As a child, I had a severe stuttering problem, so I didn't talk much in school until I began to overcome the speech impediment in the fourth grade. That is why I was always more comfortable with writing than talking. As a consequence, I was never a good public speaker. I think this is one reason why I, along with the millions of people who stuttered as children and adults, were moved to tears when 13-year-old Brayden Harrington spoke at the 2020 Democratic Convention. As he stuttered on words for what seemed like an eternity, he said he and Joe Biden belonged to the same club. Hearing Brayden speak made me remember all the times I would get stuck on words, not knowing how to finally break through to get to the next word, especially in a classroom with other kids. People who stutter, like Biden, learn which words and consonants to avoid. Today, it is rare that when speaking in public or a college classroom I will stutter on a word, but it does happen. When it does, I often wonder how students are reacting.

Despite the impediment, giving speeches is part of the job description for a politician, so I had to learn how to be more effective at it. By asking friends what they thought of my talks, I figured out what I needed to include, such as information about the community colleges, the duties of a trustee, and my work in the LGBTQ+ community. Friends told me that I needed to say more about who I was, so I included my personal background. Through this process, I discovered what most politicians already know: A good speaker is not born; they are made. It was not until well into the second month of the campaign that I got the stump speech memorized so I wouldn't have to panic when I stood in front of a group.

Even though I became physically exhausted near the end of the campaign, I was never emotionally drained. As the candidate, I was the center of attention. People were putting on fundraisers for me, donating money, and singing my praises. These activities would always revive my spirits.

Throughout the campaign, I was continually inspired by the actions of others. I know it took courage for some people to put up a lawn sign for an openly gay candidate. Often these were older men who led closeted lives and whom I only met because friends invited them to fundraising parties at their homes. Sometimes one person in a couple wanted to put up a sign, but the other one did not, fearing what people might say. Eventually, the sign went up because they were willing to do their small part to help me win. I am sure there were other acts of bravery that involved people coming out, most of which I will never know about.

One disappointment I experienced in the campaign was the failure of the progressive community to see the value in electing a qualified gay candidate. Because my main opponent had been involved in union politics, several organizations and individuals endorsed us both. From my perspective, they failed to see the importance of doing a single endorsement of an openly gay man over a liberal heterosexual male. All things being equal, it was time that the queer community had representation, as much as women and other minority groups now do.

Finally, election day came. In the morning, there was nothing more to write, deliver, stamp, or seal, so I went jogging. Later, I heard on the radio that George Bush also went running. I laughed, amused that election-day jogging was the only thing that Bush and I had in common. I then went to vote.

The first results that came in were the absentee voters. I had sent all absentee voters a special mailing that they received prior to getting their absentee ballots. I assumed that none of the other candidates had thought of this, so I was not surprised that I did well with these voters. It was not until after midnight that I learned I had won, racking up 49.9 percent of the vote—a phenomenal percentage given that six people were in the race. Everyone was flabbergasted. One explanation for the landslide was that many people knew me from two decades of community work. Because it was a low-profile race, the opinion of these people carried much weight with their spouses and friends. The lawn signs, the three pieces of mail, and the precinct walking all helped me win by an impressive total.

I was not ready for all the attention I received afterward. As the first openly gay elected person in Santa Clara County, I was interviewed by radio and television stations, although not by the local newspaper, which I originally thought would be the only coverage I would get. I received many calls and letters from friends congratulating me. One friend in the East called to say he heard about my victory on CNN. Flowers arrived. The only time since then that I was happier in a professional setting was a month later when I was sworn in as a trustee. A picture taken of me at the ceremony captured the widest smile physically possible.

My first six months as a trustee of the San Jose/Evergreen Community College District were a whirlwind of activity. I put in many extra hours, just as I had done with all my activities beginning with junior high school. It seemed like there was a meeting to attend practically every other day. I viewed them as opportunities because the more people I got to know, the more information I gained about the district, and the better able I was to bring about meaningful change through understanding the issues and building coalitions with groups and board members.

My top campaign issue was to raise standards so students received the quality education needed to compete for well-paying jobs. As chair of the Committee on Academic Excellence and Comprehensiveness, I worked with department chairs to review and enhance academic standards.

One of my campaign goals was to have the college district work with high schools and San Jose State to create a unified educational system. The district now has joint programs with K-12 districts and the university.

The current library system was inadequate and inefficient. I successfully advocated for the board to allocate funds to install a library automation system similar to the one at SJSU, bringing libraries into the modern age.

I convinced the Board of Trustees to vote to have the district divest nearly $2 million from Bank of America because of its financial support to the Boy Scouts of America, an organization that openly discriminates against gays.

I directed the personnel department to research the cost of offering domestic partnership benefits to employees. After a report showed that the cost would be minimal, the board approved the benefits, making us the second public agency in the county to do so.

At my request, the Santa Clara County Public Health Department started to offer free HIV testing on college campuses.

All told, it was a good first term in office. But was it enough? I wondered what other political opportunities might await me.

CHAPTER 6

"If You Put Your Family First": Gay Baiting in the Assembly Race

Four years after my election to the community college board, I ran for state assembly. Because of term limits, the incumbent could not run, creating a vacancy in the heavily Democratic, multi-ethnic Twenty-third Assembly District. It was an ideal seat for me because my community college district was wholly contained in the assembly district. I knew the area well, and many of the residents had already voted for me. There were three others in the March 1996 Democratic primary: Mike Honda, a Santa Clara County supervisor; David Cortese, son of the incumbent assemblyman; and Patricia Martinez Roach, a school trustee.

I ran on a platform of education reform. This was an important issue for residents of the district because of the high education levels needed for employment in Silicon Valley. Of all the candidates, I was the only one who had a vision and a plan to improve preschools, elementary and secondary schools, community colleges, and four-year universities.

It was a well-executed campaign, built upon the foundation of my first one. I was able to raise the $250,000 needed to run a viable campaign (about $536,000 is today's dollars). This was achieved by holding numerous large fundraisers over a year, having 40 people sponsor house parties, and receiving checks from more than 1,500 individuals.

I was blessed with an army of 400 dedicated and talented volunteers. These friends walked hundreds of precincts, phoned thousands of voters, addressed 30,000 envelopes, stuffed tens of thousands of letters, registered hundreds of voters, hung hundreds of door hangers on the eve of election day, and stood on the street corners election morning with banners blaring "Yeager for Assembly." I could not have asked for a finer group of supporters.

I received most of the endorsements, including that of the *Mercury News*. The officeholders who supported me included two members of Congress, numerous councilmembers, state assembly members, county supervisors, school superintendents, and school trustees. Some of the groups that endorsed me were the Sierra Club, the South Bay AFL-CIO, the California Federation of Teachers, the National Women's Political Caucus, the National Organization of Women, and the San Jose Firefighters.

All along, I knew that Supervisor Honda's name recognition was formidable. For me to win, the other two candidates had to take a sizable block of support away from him, particularly in East San Jose, which was their base of support. If my three opponents could divide up East San Jose, I could win by outdistancing them elsewhere.

Until the last week of the campaign, this scenario was playing itself out. All four of us had the finances to stay competitive. While we each had different strategies, we all were running viable campaigns. Then things turned ugly. Cortese mailed out a classic hit piece against me. It was vicious, misrepresented my record, and arrived in the campaign's final week. Moreover, it explicitly fed into society's view that gay men were anti-women and anti-family.

Most hit pieces are quickly forgotten after the election. Not so in this case. Because the piece was so homophobic, its repercussions were felt by Cortese, Phil Giarrizzo, the consultant who designed it, and David Binder, his pollster.

On one side of the 8.5x11 flyers were three photographs.

Under a photo of a policeman read the sentence, "Cut funding for police." Under an anguished-looking woman read, "Oppose rights for rape victims." Beneath a young boy in a Scout uniform read, "Outlaw the Boy Scouts." On the opposite side, in large bold letters, it read, "These are Ken Yeager's positions. Are they yours?" Then, "If you put your family first, watch out for Ken Yeager. He's an ultraliberal who fights for his agenda, not yours." After a brief discussion of the accusations, the piece ended with, "Put San Jose Families First. No on Ken Yeager."

The facts were distorted, of course. As discussed in Chapter 5, the piece said that I wanted to outlaw the Boy Scouts from San Jose schools. However, the issue was never one of outlawing the Scouts from school facilities. Rather, because the Scouts discriminate based on sexual orientation, I fought against public funding of a Scouts' program in a school district.

Cortese stated that I opposed mandatory AIDS testing for rape suspects. In fact, I took a stand against an emotionally charged 1987 bill to require such testing because it was a political ploy by Republicans to find cracks in California's AIDS confidentiality laws. The bill was not about the health or the medical or emotional needs of women who are victims of rape. Health officials opposed the bill for this same reason.

Lastly, the statement that I voted to cut police protection at the San Jose/Evergreen College District was false. To offset budget cuts at the state level, I supported the chancellor's proposal to eliminate an administrative staff person in the campus police department office. The issue was never one of cutting police officers.

Cortese and his consultant, Phil Giarrizzo, initially said that they did not engage in gay bashing. I disagreed, as did most people who saw the piece. For me, the message of the mailer was obvious: People who fight for the rights of lesbians and gays are a threat to families. Although I was not being personally attacked for being gay, my record had been distorted to confirm people's prejudices that gay people were a menace

94

because they put their own agenda before the concerns of rape victims, children, and ultimately society. My "agenda" over two decades of community work had been education, good neighborhoods, and many other issues beneficial to families.

I agreed with my veteran consultants Carol Beddo and Joy Alexiou that the less media focus on the piece the better. We knew that each time the voters heard the allegations I lost votes. Our main response was to quickly send out a mailer criticizing several votes Cortese had made while on the school board.

To my mind, the *Mercury News* reporter who had been assigned to cover the campaign played right into the hands of Cortese's consultant.[85] It was the front-page story in the local section, complete with a sidebar restating the charges. The local TV station ran a full story. All told, more people heard about the piece from the media than had received it in the mail.

The last week of any campaign is pure hell anyway, but it was made even more so by the hit piece. With 20 years of fighting in the political trenches, I consider myself a veteran campaigner. But as I walked door-to-door, I knew the piece had mischaracterized my position and that some voters were now viewing me, and perhaps other gay people, in a negative light. My years of working to make San Jose a better place to live seemed to have been quickly overshadowed.

On election night, I came in second place. Cortese, with his well-known family name, finished third, barely outdistancing the last-place finisher. Word on the street was that the hit piece turned voters away from Cortese and me and gave them to Honda, who led in the polls going into the final week.

In the months following the campaign, I came to know the personal fallout that Giarrizzo and Cortese experienced because of the piece. Each deeply regretted his involvement in it. It is their story that I want to tell.

Shortly after the campaign, Giarrizzo asked to come before the Harvey Milk Gay and Lesbian Democratic Club in San

----

85   De Tran. "23rd Assembly District Demos Unleash Last-Minute Mail Blitz." *San Jose Mercury News*. March 22, 1996.

Francisco to explain his position on the piece. The president of the Milk Club then called me and asked if I would attend.

Perhaps Giarrizzo had asked to speak because LGBTQ+ Democratic leaders had been circulating a resolution to hold candidates and their consultants who had used homophobic tactics against their opponents accountable. Perhaps he just needed to ask for forgiveness. In any case, the man I saw at the meeting looked as if he was carrying a heavy weight on his shoulders.

Giarrizzo began by saying since the piece was mailed, he had felt "like shit." He admitted that he had committed the major sin of campaign politics by showing poor judgment. He said the piece clearly went over the line, that he accepted full responsibility, and that he wanted to personally apologize to me.

He then proceeded to rationalize his actions. He stated that as a consultant it was his job to win at any cost. He also said that the campaign's gay pollster, David Binder, had reviewed the piece and had not criticized it. Several times he said that although there is a line in campaigns that should not be crossed, he was unsure where that line was.

I then gave my interpretation of the piece, pointing out its misrepresentations and its homophobic message. As an aside, I mentioned that I was uncomfortable with him partially blaming Binder, as if a gay man's involvement somehow justified mailing out the piece.

Several audience members made insightful comments. One person commented that most people learn at an early age where the line between right and wrong is drawn, be it from family, church, or synagogue. What concerned her most about his talk was that he lacked that internal gauge.

Another speaker talked about the high rate of suicide among gay and lesbian youth. In poignant terms, he explained how a troubled teenager might have seen the hit piece on his family's kitchen table, sending him another negative signal that gay people are depraved. It could be one more piece of evidence for the teen that he was inherently immoral and should not keep living.

Giarrizzo seemed shaken by the speaker's words. After revealing that he had a lesbian sister living in San Jose who had not spoken to him since the piece was mailed, he somberly concluded that it would not be easy for him to live with the fact that he might be responsible for someone's suicide.

David Binder, Cortese's pollster, is a well-known San Francisco consultant who has worked for numerous gay and straight candidates. Cortese, too, had tried throwing blame on Binder by saying that a gay man had not objected to the piece. Because Binder is an acquaintance of mine, I felt comfortable calling him to find out if what Cortese had said was true. Binder confirmed that it was.

Binder's complicity seems the hardest to explain. As a gay activist, he should have known better. Over the phone, he told me that he saw his role in the campaign as strictly a consultant. He did not think it was his place to judge whether the piece should be sent, but only if it accurately reflected the data from the polls. Although disturbed by the piece, he had kept silent. Binder has done much soul-searching since the piece went out, and he regrets his actions. Next time, he says, he will not stay quiet.

Five months after the election, I received a second call from Cortese asking if we could get together. I could tell from the tone of his voice that this would be an altogether different conversation from the first when he was still defending the overall intent of the piece.

Over lunch, Cortese again apologized for the piece and confided that he would always carry the burden of his actions with him. He had been taught by the Jesuits at Bellarmine College Preparatory in San Jose that there exists a window of opportunity for a person to make the right moral choice. When he first saw the piece, he knew it was wrong but did not speak out. It was a decision he would always regret.

Although he didn't initially consider the piece as gay bashing, he had come to understand from conversations with several people that it was. It was wrong, Cortese said, to accuse someone of being anti-family solely because he is gay.

Cortese revealed that on the day the piece arrived, he did not want to walk precincts. He was ashamed of himself for sending the piece and expected to be reprimanded as he went door-to-door. In addition, his wife, who was unaware of the piece before it was sent, did not approve of it.

In talks with close friends after the election, Cortese realized that people were beginning to view him differently. In fact, even Cortese's best friend asked for an explanation. A counselor who works with gay and lesbian youth at the East Side Union School District, where Cortese serves as an elected trustee, asked if he was now going to oppose the program. Cortese began to think of the many cousins in his large extended family. He realized the likelihood that some of them could be gay or lesbian. I wondered if they changed their view of him, too.

His eyes welling with tears, Cortese said he wished he could apologize to everyone who had seen the piece and say how sorry he was. He worried that, in some way, the piece could contribute to the anti-gay climate that was fueling the religious right's attempt to overturn a domestic partner registry recently passed by the Board of Supervisors. He asked if there was anything he could do to show his support for the LGBTQ+ community.

I could tell his remorse was genuine. Although I am not a religious person, I do believe in the healing power of personal redemption. I also know that he will now be able to fight homophobia in his circle of influence more effectively than before.

I might add here that over the years Cortese and I have become friends. We served on numerous boards together, and he has always been a staunch supporter of LGBTQ+ causes and projects. As a state senator, he was able to get approval for funding to the BAYMEC Community Foundation for community education, outreach, and activities to preserve and promote Silicon Valley's LGBTQ+ history.

To better understand how I should have responded to the piece, I called Dave Fleischer, coordinator of training for the Gay and Lesbian Victory Fund. I met Fleischer in 1995 when he led a two-day candidate workshop that I attended.

Fleischer explained how hit pieces against queer people fall into three categories. The first is the overt homophobic piece which states that the opponent is unfit to hold office because they are queer. The second is an attack on the candidate's character by pointing to positions they've taken that are against heterosexual norms. Most often, the message is to protect children. It is the hardest piece to respond to because it plays on internalized homophobia. The third is an implicit homophobic attack. These pieces say the heterosexual candidate is more like the voter than the gay candidate. One candidate even sent out mailings titled "Straight Talk" just to be sure that everyone understood his point.

Fleischer said that Cortese's piece fits into the second category because there was little I could say by way of a direct defense. Discussing the particulars would have been useless. The charge was that a candidate was a bad person. Therefore, the only response is to show that the candidate has good character.

Fleischer gave two suggestions for a strategy. The first is to ask the local paper to write an editorial condemning the piece, calling it sleazy and unethical. This could be reprinted and sent to voters identified as undecided. The second is to send a piece with three testimonials: A Boy Scout or Scout leader could vouch for my support of youth programs; a rape victim counselor could detail my work in support of women and social service issues; a police officer could discuss my platform on crime prevention.

Hit pieces will always be a part of a candidate's arsenal.

Despite their dislike from all quarters, they are enormously effective, which is why they continue to be used. However, as Cortese and his consultant and pollster realized, there are lines that should not be crossed when it comes to personal attacks based on race, gender, or sexual orientation.

My assembly race did not preclude me from running for a second term on the community college board. I was unopposed in the November 1996 election. This allowed me to serve for another four years without having to again ask my friends for their money and time. For this, I was eternally thankful, as I'm sure they were, too.

It was unclear what would come next for me politically. I had grown to be more confident as a candidate, but was being gay too big of a target on my back, inviting opponents to always aim at me?

CHAPTER 7

The Loud Whispering Campaign for City Council

I spent the rest of 1996 and most of 1997-98 doing pretty much what I was doing before: teaching full-time at SJSU and organizing LGBTQ+ activities through BAYMEC. I had become rather intrigued by the handful of gays and lesbians across the country who had managed to get themselves elected to office. I had gone to my first meeting of the International Network of Gay and Lesbian Officials in 1992, right after I was elected to the college board. It was here that I met a number of the first generation of gays and lesbians who would go on to have long political careers, like Wisconsin U.S. Senator Tammy Baldwin, Congressman Barney Frank, Minnesota State Senator Allan Spear, Houston Mayor Annise Parker, San Francisco Supervisor Roberta Achtenberg, and Tempe Mayor Neil Giuliano, to name a few.

I was quite fascinated by them, wondering how they were able to be successful. Their numbers were small—only 100 or so had been elected in the whole country by 1992. I was an avid reader of the *New Yorker* and was aware of their long profiles of well-known people, and I wanted to write profiles like those. After people agreed to be interviewed, I traveled to their city and spent three or four days with them and wrote in-depth accounts of their lives.

By 1999 I had completed profiles of 11 individuals and one

of the three gay West Hollywood councilmembers. Published by Haworth Press, *Trailblazers: Profiles of America's Gay and Lesbian Elected Officials,* is the only book that captured the lives of the first generation of those officials. Of course, now LGBTQ+ people are in the halls of power at all levels, but it took a lot of courage and heartache for us to get there.

That my authorship of the book would make its way into the city council campaign would be one source of amazement to me, but that story comes later.

Career-wise, I knew it was never in the cards to get a tenured track position at SJSU because my Ph.D. was in education, and I was teaching in the political science department. One could make the case that I was qualified for an assistant professorship since I was teaching a full load of political science classes, but I knew it wasn't going to happen, a reality I accepted.

So, where was I headed in life?

By 1998, I was 45 years old and a little discouraged that I hadn't made the mark in the world I envisioned myself making. A year earlier, I had met Michael Haberecht, the man who would be my partner for all the years to come, so I was happy with my personal life. But I yearned for more.

It was still a time when no LGBTQ+ candidate had succeeded in winning a major local office in San Jose or any city in Santa Clara County. I was the only one who had broken through the lavender ceiling, and that was with the community college board. There was no evidence that I could overcome prejudices against LGBTQ+ people or survive future hit pieces.

The political scorecard across the country was just as bleak for LGBTQ+ candidates. For my book, in 1997 I mailed a questionnaire to the country's 124 openly gay and lesbian elected officials. Ninety-four responded. Of that group, 40 were serving as councilmembers. Interestingly, there was a number of gay officials who were not out when they first ran and won. It was only after their elections that they acknowledged their sexual orientation, either due to being "outed," the subject of innuendo, or growing tired of hiding.

Thankfully, today things are much improved. According to the *Out For America* website, there were a total of 1,174 LGBTQ+ officials nationwide in March 2023. Of that number, 721 were serving at the local level, 59 of them mayors.[86]

When I bought my house in 1992, I was aware of the council district I lived in. I had thought of buying a home in an adjacent district, which included San Jose State and a large enclave of queer residents, but the homes were too expensive. Instead, I bought a nice three-bedroom, two-bathroom 1945 Craftsman house in the Rose Garden area of San Jose, located several blocks from the actual municipal rose garden itself.

I had been acquainted with San Jose's neighborhood groups for several decades, having started my activism at the local level in 1975 while a student at SJSU. I helped create a coalition of central San Jose neighborhoods, including the Rose Garden, and was on the steering committee of the neighborhood group where I lived at the time.

Since moving to the neighborhood, I became involved in the Rose Garden Neighborhood Preservation Association, or RGNPA. As occurs in many suburban neighborhoods, there's a dearth of people who want to serve on these boards. I was asked by Keoni Murphy, the association president who lived down the street, if I would become a board member, to which I readily agreed. Two years later, I became board president.

Around the same time, Fanny Rinn, a much beloved former SJSU political science professor of mine and Rose Garden resident as well, had taken it upon herself to be the patron saint of the aging Rose Garden Library. Rinn had somewhat of a maternal relationship with me, and I think she was always looking out for my political career. She must have known it would benefit me to be on the board of the Friends of the Rose Garden Library, so when I was invited to join, I happily accepted. Shortly thereafter, I became president of the four-member board.

----

86   https://outforamerica.org/?office-level=Local

San Jose elects its 10 councilmembers by districts. The district that I lived in, District 6, was represented by Councilman Frank Fiscalini, a fatherly, old-school type of politician who was termed out at the end of 2000. By early 1999, speculation was beginning about who would run for his council seat. I had already begun to entertain the idea of running. One major impediment was Terry Poche, former Congressman Edwards' chief of staff and my direct boss, who was also thinking of running. She was a respected and beloved person with deep roots in the community and years of activism in Democratic politics, but she was always more comfortable behind the scenes. This caused me to pause as we'd be fighting for the same base in the Rose Garden area.

Back in 2000, the main source of political news and gossip were mainstream and community-based newspapers. In the political gossip column of the *Mercury News*, they wrote a story about the lunch I had with Poche. After mentioning what we both had for lunch, the article continued, "Poche said, 'So I guess you want to know what I'm going to do.' To Yeager's great relief, Poche agreed to step aside. 'Ken has been at it much longer. The both of us running just didn't make any sense.'" [87]

Shortly thereafter, Kristina (Kris) Cunningham entered the race and thus entered my life. At the time of the election, she was 50, two years older than me. Born and living in Willow Glen, she had spent her entire adult life in District 6. Married to Gary Cunningham for 29 years, she had three sons. Growing up, she attended an all-girls Catholic high school in Willow Glen, as well as San Jose State, where she got her degree in political science. She worked as an instructor at a city Pre-K program; her husband taught at the all-boys Catholic high school, Bellarmine College Preparatory, which was in the district.

She was involved in a number of activities, but the association she highlighted the most was the Willow Glen Neighborhood Association (WGNA), where she had served in numerous

----

87   Political Insider. *San Jose Mercury News*. March 18, 1999.

capacities since 1973, including the president. There was no doubt she was a formidable candidate.

In ways that only happen in politics, friends and foes often line up according to former endorsements—for and against. A few of the elected officials who supported Cunningham were people I had opposed or ran against along the way. She got the expected endorsement of Fiscalini, who had once run against Susan Hammer for mayor, whom I endorsed. Her other supporters included more conservative elected officials that I had opposed, like former Mayor Tom McEnery, in whose congressional race I endorsed Zoe Lofgren.

Many of the people I supported for office over the years supported me, including former mayors Janet Gray Hayes and Susan Hammer, former employers Congressman Don Edwards and Supervisor Wilson, and friends such as state Senator Dan McCorquodale, former Councilwomen Iola Williams and Cindy Chavez. And as I discussed in an earlier chapter about state Senator Al Alquist, even he found a way to endorse me. You have to love politics.

My first awareness of the type of impression Cunningham made on people occurred at the very onset of the campaign, which had major repercussions for her. As told to me by Keoni Murphy, the RGNPA president, she had gone to him and all but demanded that he endorse her for council. He had never met her but was so turned off by her that he decided then and there to endorse me. This led him to have my first campaign coffee at his house, sending a message that my neighborhood association was behind me.

In campaigns, it's always funny how minor events outside of your control can make a greater impact than all the strategizing by consultants ever could. Had Murphy endorsed Cunningham before I even had a chance to approach him, the race would have been much different. She would have been able to claim support from my own neighborhood association, removing the drama of the race being between two neighborhood associations' presidents.

Of the four other candidates in the race, only Jim Spence, a retired San Jose police officer, who also lived in Willow Glen, gained any traction.

California had moved the primary election to an early March 7th date to be more of a player in choosing the presidential nominee. Most cities tie their elections to the states as a way to save money. The result of this date change was to sharply condense the time for campaigning after the New Year to mainly January and February. If a candidate was going to walk all the precincts in the district, which I did, it meant starting in July and going until mid-November, when everything stopped for Thanksgiving and Christmas.

Just like in my community college race, I ran the campaign out of the house and garage. This allowed me to keep track of everything that was happening and to chat with the 10 to 15 volunteers who arrived every day to help. The campaign produced numerous position papers on multiple issues, printed campaign flyers, scheduled coffees, and lined up fundraisers. As with my other campaigns, we hand-addressed thousands of neighbor-to-neighbor letters to be stuffed and mailed months later in February.

Many first-time candidates wonder where they will get the volunteers to fuel their campaigns. Not all friends are eager to spend evenings and weekends helping you run for office, but I had already been in the trenches with many of the people who ended up being stalwart supporters, mainly through BAYMEC and the Proposition 64 campaign. Many, like Leslee Hamilton, Arlene Rusche, and Clara Brock, worked tirelessly in the community college and assembly races. They had learned a variety of skills that they used to train others. For some, my candidacy was a cause they believed in, especially those who thought I had unfairly lost the assembly race. It was still a time when no local LGBTQ+ candidate had succeeded in winning a major local office. We were all trying to make history, and we knew it would take all the energy we had. They were aware of the long hours I was putting in, and they wanted to do the same.

While most of the volunteers were LGBTQ+, many were friends I met through my neighborhood activities or my work in the local Democratic Party and union affiliates. Some of my biggest supporters were Patty and Pete Koopman, who were active in Parents and Friends of Lesbians and Gays (PFLAG), and Linda Dittes and Keith Uriarte, neighbors who lived down the street. Some were former students, gay and straight. Some were members of groups that had endorsed me, like the Sierra Club or NAACP. San Jose Firefighters would sometimes park their grills in my driveway for barbecues to feed volunteers when they returned. The San Jose police and fire retirees would always have a handful of precinct walkers on weekends. One of them, Paul Mulholland, was assigned "combat duty" to walk Cunningham's precinct. We roar with laughter years later whenever he reminded me of the precinct he was given. He handled it as the firefighter he was: Going door-to-door looking for supporters amidst the flames.

One thing I always insisted upon was having Polaroid snapshots taken of all volunteers with their names written below their photos and posted on the Wall of Fame. This served two purposes. First, it showed appreciation for their work; second, it helped me get to know the names of people new to the campaign so I could give them a personal greeting and words of gratitude.

In between teaching and grading papers, I would be walking precincts, raising money, and attending forums and community events. I made it a practice never to go to bed until every "thank you" note had been written. I did this because if I ever let the notes begin to pile up, I'd get discouraged by the sheer volume that needed to get done and perhaps not finish. I knew every note I sent to a supporter was one more vote I could definitely count on. Should a donor talk to their friends about the race, possibly one or two more.

Unlike today, free weekly community papers were a factor

in the campaign. One was the *Resident*, which had a Willow Glen and a Rose Garden edition. The other was the San Jose *Metro*, a paper found in news racks throughout downtown and coffee houses. They were both owned by Dan Pulcrano, a young entrepreneur who generally sided with the downtown business establishment and relished stirring up shit he could find about his detractors.

These papers were at their heyday from around the mid-1990s to 2010s. Largely supported by local advertisers, they had enough writers to cover issues in targeted communities. As social media became more of a source of news, newspapers such as these either went out of business or drastically scaled back. Their numerous stories on all aspects of the campaign brought an increased awareness of issues and personalities that wouldn't have occurred otherwise. I dreaded walking to the sidewalk Thursday evenings to pick up the free paper thrown on everyone's driveway, never sure what negative story would be there about me.

The big dog of the papers remained the *Mercury News*, San Jose's hometown newspaper. In their glory days, they were a force to be reckoned with. They always had writers assigned to city hall and were known for their investigative journalism. Politically, they certainly leaned Republican, a la John McCain, pro-business and anti-union to the core. Despite this, they were very progressive when it came to women, minorities, and LGBTQ+ rights. After all, they were the ones who published my opinion piece in 1984 denouncing an anti-gay assemblyman discussed in an earlier chapter.

Of the newspaper endorsements, the one I received from the *Mercury News* was definitely the most important. After listing my community and political involvement, the editorial concluded, "We believe Yeager's broader experience, including serving in public office and working as a policy analyst, give him a better, big-picture view of city leadership."[88]

----

88   Editorial board. "The Top Council Candidates." *San Jose Mercury News.* February 25, 2000.

Cunningham won the *Resident*, which meant both the Willow Glen and Rose Garden *Resident*, along with the *Metro*.

The slant in both the *Resident* and *Metro* was basically the same: Cunningham was a native San Josean, a mother, and a neighborhood leader. Moreover, "She has an epic-length list of donors dotted with small contributions from neighbors, teachers, and small businesses."

I, on the other hand, although active in neighborhood issues, was a "polished politico," with support from the business community and labor groups. And just in case readers didn't know it, *Metro* felt the need to mention my sexual orientation: "An openly gay candidate like Yeager—who has leaders in the community backing him—would be a welcome addition to strait-laced city hall, and he will hopefully continue his active role in local politics."

Gee, I thought, *thanks for the pep talk when I lose.*

I always laughed when the *Resident* and *Metro* brought up my being gay, trying hard not to be anti-gay but always including it, perhaps betting on the fact that it would be the one thing that readers would remember the most about me. "*Oh, isn't he the gay guy?*" The odds were greater that people would remember that over any of my credentials, such as my being president of my neighborhood association.

As I found out, it was a journalistic bias that would continue to the general election.

There was one additional worry. As luck would have it, Proposition 22, also known as the Knight Initiative for the state senator who led the campaign, was on the ballot. This was the state initiative that banned gay marriages in the state constitution. Polling showed it passing by high numbers. Would anti-gay marriage sentiment carry over to anti-gay sentiment for me? We just didn't know.

The night of the primary, March 7, my team was feeling good. As it turned out, I had done well, coming in first with 38.6 percent of the vote. Cunningham followed with 32.8 percent,

1,100 votes between us, and the other four candidates racked up 29 percent. As stipulated by the San Jose city charter, if no candidate received 50 percent plus one of the votes, the top two vote-getters go on to the general election in November.

As for the ban on gay marriage, a disappointing 61 percent of California voters supported it. Thankfully, in Santa Clara County, it was much closer, with 52 percent of the people voting in favor of the ban.

But the long, hard fight was yet to come. For eight months, from March to November, it was hand-to-hand combat, which just about killed me. I wrote numerous times in my journal, "Buck up, Ken, buck up. Don't let this get you down. You can beat this." At times I wasn't so sure.

The General Election

The campaign began to heat up after the summer. The first skirmishes related to my qualifications. I presented myself on my brochures as "Teacher," "Elected Trustee," and "Neighborhood Leader." The Cunningham campaign couldn't challenge "Elected Trustee," so they turned their attention to the other two.

For people considering running for office, here is an example of the silliness you have to deal with.

First, there was the issue of whether or not I was calling myself a professor.

The SJSU Political Science Department secretary received a call from a woman asking if the *Mercury News* was accurate in calling Ken a "professor." "*Is he not a lecturer?*" she asked. The caller was told that was correct but stressed that I had a Ph.D. The woman went on to tell the secretary that I called myself a professor in my book, and wasn't that wrong, too? *Shouldn't someone write a letter to the Mercury News?* [89]

----

89   Note: In *Trailblazers* "About the Author" it reads: "I teach at SJSU," not that I'm a professor.

That led a *Mercury News* editorial page editor to email the chair of the Political Science Department, Terry Christensen, saying that somebody had pointed out that the *Mercury News* referred to me as a professor, which I wasn't. The *Mercury News* editor wondered if lecturer was the better title.

Christensen repeated that my official title was lecturer. He advised her that as long as the *Mercury News* didn't capitalize professor as a formal title, they were fine.

This was a predicament I was always conscious of. Most people who teach at the university, regardless of degree, are routinely referred to as professors. That is different from capitalizing the word, as in Professor Ken Yeager. Regardless, I avoided the problem by always saying I taught at SJSU or was a teacher.

In the end, the *Mercury News* didn't see an issue with it. Mischievously, in their endorsement, they referred to me as "a political science professor at San Jose State." [90] Love it.

On that skirmish: A Yeager victory.

Then there was the matter of whether or not I was a neighborhood leader.

A good example of this type of tussle was the San Jose International Airport, which technically is in another council district but was close to the border of District 6 and greatly impacted its residents with late night and early morning arrivals and departures. Former Mayor Janet Gray Hayes lived close to the airport and had worked with other neighbors to form Citizens Against Airport Expansion or CAAP. In 1994 she asked me to join the group, and I worked closely with them to monitor issues dealing with noise and airport expansion. A few years later, the city council established a curfew monitoring committee, which had a slot for a community member, to which I was appointed.

Therefore, it came as a surprise to see "Ken Yeager chose

90   Editorial Board. "For San Jose City Council." *San Jose Mercury News.* October 16, 2000.

not to become involved in the issue" plastered on one of Cunningham's flyers, saying that she had been working with neighborhood leaders on the airport.

Hayes followed with a scathing letter. She wrote that Cunningham's assertion that Cunningham had been involved in the issues was misleading and that people in the organization had never met her until she attended a meeting seeking their endorsement. Secondly, Cunningham's statement that I had not been involved went from "misleading to outright falsehoods," and she was asked to withdraw the flyer immediately.

Hayes ended the letter by writing, "Reasonable people can disagree on the issues, but your flyer is not credible, accurate, nor true." She was asked to stop distributing the flyer.

She didn't, of course. But on that skirmish: Another Yeager win.

Another issue in a long list of squabbles was a proposed maintenance yard on the edge of the district to service trains from the popular Caltrain line, which runs from San Francisco to San Jose. During testimony on a cooperative agreement between the City of San Jose and the Caltrain Joint Powers Board, I restated my opposition and said a better location for the project would be further south near Morgan Hill and Gilroy, where the train also ran. I said that until such time that we can convince Caltrain to move the facility elsewhere, we must make sure there is no negative impact on the surrounding neighborhood.

Like the neighbors, I was concerned about the 24-hour operation of the facility. I stressed in my remarks that the best way to protect the neighborhoods was a night-time curfew. I was pleased to report that Mayor Gonzales agreed with my position and had publicly come out in favor of the curfew.

But it was all to no avail. It felt like I literally got hit by a train. A flyer called "Railroaded" had a picture of a railroad crossing warning sign with my face in the middle where the two sticks crossed. Nearby residents accused me of being a traitor. While Cunningham would always oppose the maintenance yard, I only spoke of mitigations. "This experience made us feel 'railroaded' by Ken Yeager," said a campaign piece signed by some neighbors, "and caused us to reconsider our support."

I might add here that the following year a curfew was imposed, and a curfew monitoring committee was established between the residents and Caltrain. Because so few complaints were filed, the committee was eventually disbanded.

Still, Cunningham won that skirmish.

In September, right in the midst of this warfare, Mayor Gonzales was caught having an affair with a member of his staff. Gonzales, who had recently filed for divorce from his wife of 22 years, was 49; the staffer was 25. It was, of course, front page news in the *Mercury News*. The affair was discovered when the two of them were spotted at a cabin in Mendocino. At first, Gonzales denied it, then at a press conference, acknowledged the affair and apologized for it. The romance was between two consenting adults and not against City of San Jose policies, so there were no legal consequences, just political ones.

Gonzales' enemies were all over the issue, many demanding his resignation. I was in a tight spot. Gonzales' endorsement of my campaign was certainly helpful, yet it was hard to be silent. My public statements revolved around being disappointed in his action and advocating that the City adopt the same policy we had at the community college district, which prohibited employees from engaging in sexual relationships with individuals employed by the district over whom they have a direct line of supervision. Whatever bounce I had gotten from Gonzales' endorsement was certainly reduced. Not surprisingly, Cunningham was much more critical of him.

If the race were to be solely decided by Willow Glen voters, I would have lost. I believe Cunningham thought this was the case. Willow Glen was always seen as a more white, middleclass, conservative council district. After the city went to district elections in 1980, the first councilmember, Nancy Ianni, resided there. Even though Fiscalini lived in a neighboring area, everyone thought his home was in Willow Glen. In subsequent elections, the races were all won by the more conservative candidates over union-supported ones. Cunningham could be viewed as fitting into that mode, while I was the interloper.

But there were larger forces at play, some of which were to my advantage. To win, I knew I had to have as many factors going my way as possible.

One advantage I had was being a more seasoned activist who had built relationships with other organizations over the years. Wiggsy and I made sure that BAYMEC supported other groups who, in turn, supported us. On the SJSU campus, Wiggsy was a leader in the California Faculty Association (CFA), becoming its campus president. Thus, from the beginning, BAY-MEC had formed a close alliance with the unions, as well as the closely aligned local Democratic Party. This was a world that Cunningham would not have been familiar with.

I had always been a union supporter and member. I joined CFA when I was hired by SJSU in 1991 and later became the lecturer representative on their statewide board. This allowed me always to claim union membership when I went before their endorsement committees. I also mentioned the elected officials I worked for, like Iola Williams, Susie Wilson, and Don Edwards, all of whom were admired for their support of working families.

In a 2022 email exchange with Amy Dean, the CEO of the Central Labor Council in 2000, she shared how important my race and the race of Dolly Sandoval for county supervisor were for the unions. Both of us were running in districts with lower levels of union membership than other seats they had targeted. The importance of District 6 was the opportunity to pick up a seat that they had never held, so they were excited to go all in for me. Just as significant, the San Jose Municipal Employee Union made my race a top priority and put similar resources into it.

Tied to labor was the local Democratic Central Committee,

chaired by Steve Preminger, a close labor ally. Having Preminger as chair of the party meant labor could earmark their field operations in coordination with the United Democratic Campaign. In races like Sandoval's and mine, they moved more resources into our districts, like precinct walkers, phone bankers, mailers, and Get Out the Vote activities.

As Dean recalled, there was never any discussion about not endorsing me or splitting my endorsement with Cunningham. She wrote that "the years Ken had been associated with Supervisor Susie Wilson cemented his reputation with the trades and the labor movement. Overall, he was extremely well-liked, respected, and seen as competent and credible. His race was an important one for us for a number of reasons."

As a visible sign of that support, the South Bay AFL-CIO Labor Council sent a mailing to union members in District 6 with the headline "An Important Message for Working Families," which highlighted my campaign. Similarly, the Santa Clara County Democratic Party did a mailing supporting my candidacy that included a list of almost all Democratic elected officials. Although I was always able to raise the $89,000 maximum allowed in the race, independent expenditures were helpful.

Other groups supported me as well, including the Sierra Club, League of Conservation Voters, San Jose Police Officers Association, San Jose Firefighters, and San Jose Retired Police and Fire Association. There were dual endorsements from Democratic Activists for Women and the San Jose/Silicon Valley Chamber of Commerce, a conservative business group where I had enough friends to deny Cunningham a sole endorsement. Along with those two groups, she had the Tri-County Apartment Association. That was it.

As could be predicted, I received the *Mercury News* endorsement again. Some of the anti-gay rhetoric must have been known by the editorial board because after mentioning that I was a "co-founder of BAYMEC, the highly effective gay and lesbian political advocacy group, some Cunningham supporters—but not Cunningham herself—try to paint him as a one-issue activist, but it's a bum rap. He has a solid record of broad community service spanning more than a decade, and he would be a fine addition to the city council."[91]

Important as endorsements and support from organizations were, it was the voters who mattered. Although no other neighborhood in the district was as large as Willow Glen, it only comprised a third of the total votes. I knew I would win in the Rose Garden and neighboring Shasta/Hanchett, Cory, and College Park neighborhoods. What Cunningham and her consultants must not have recognized is that the remaining third of the district was in neither of these neighborhoods. Bordered by the 880 Freeway and the busy thoroughfares of Bascom and Winchester Boulevards, they were in more undefined housing subdivisions. We hit them hard with mailings and walkers, all addressing their specific needs. Overlooked by Cunningham, we pretty much had the entire territory to ourselves. It would end up making all the difference.

The Loud Whispering Campaign

For the Assembly race, the anti-gay assault came at the last moment; for the council race, it was a daily drip-drip-drip of innuendo and homophobia.

The battlefield became the precincts, and the soldiers were the precinct walkers. For those unfamiliar with this campaign activity, when someone registers to vote they are informed of which precinct they live in. It's all public information, so it's easy to know who is registered to vote, their address, political party, and other information. Volunteers are given sheets of paper with this information and head out to walk the area, house by house.

We soon heard what Cunningham's volunteers were saying.

One of my volunteers, Linda Dittes, reported back that when

---

91   Ibid.

walking in a particular neighborhood she witnessed several alarming incidents. She talked with one voter who told her that the president of their neighborhood association was telling people I was gay, and for that reason, voters should not support me. One woman handed back the literature and said she would not vote for someone who was gay. Dittes' husband, who was walking across the street, got into an argument with a man who said I would push a gay agenda when I got to the council.

It just kept getting worse. I had one person tell me she was aware of a Cunningham supporter driving in her neighborhood and stopping at houses where she saw a Yeager lawn sign. She would stop, go to their door and ask the person if they knew I was gay. Of the people my friend talked to, she said that several people said yes, they knew and were fine with it; one person, however, said she didn't know I was gay and subsequently had the sign taken away.

Buck up, Ken. Don't let it get to you.

My partner Michael remembers more vividly than I do all the nights I spent lying in bed, wide awake, worried about what was happening and whether I was handling it correctly. I know it took an emotional toll on him, too.

Another volunteer, Bob Sippel, wrote an email to Assemblyman Honda saying that when he was approached by Cunningham and he informed her that he was supporting me, she became "less than polite, to put it nicely." Sippel mentioned to Honda that Cunningham had a supporter who was gay-bashing and making hurtful remarks about me. He went on to say that he had no proof that Cunningham had knowledge of this, but many people were aware of it, and that he could only conclude that she was not stopping this behavior. Based on all the evidence, he hoped Honda would withdraw his support of her.

Dittes asked for the same retraction in a letter she wrote to Honda, Councilwoman Linda LeZotte, and Supervisor Blanca Alvarado, outlining all the things she had seen and heard. "Each of you has the right to endorse and support the candidate of your choice. But may I remind you that as 'public' friends of the gay and lesbian community, you do a disservice to the people who support you and the constituents you serve by continuing to support a candidate like Kris Cunningham."

The two neighborhood associations—WGNA and RGNPA—were much more active in 2000 than they are now. Membership was large; newsletters were left on doorsteps; attendance at board meetings was high. People really cared who their councilmember was, and candidate forums were always packed full of people and tension. This made candidates' nights a battlefield of their own.

At the debates, Cunningham would have five of her supporters sit in the front row and scowl whenever I spoke and cheer at whatever she said. It was a bit unnerving, which was obviously the plan. "Buck up, Ken," would echo through my mind.

Since I was still president of the Rose Garden Neighborhood Association, I had the support of the board members. At our candidate forums, people were asked to write their questions on index cards and turn them in. Board members filtered them before handing them over to the moderator. After the forum was over, I was told about some of the questions that were rejected:

What can be done to stop some of the activity in the men's restroom in the Rose Garden?

Why did Ken oppose the Boy Scouts being able to use school facilities?

Will the growing gay population in D6 change the character of our area?

The same types of questions were submitted at the Willow Glen candidates' forum. Although I didn't have supporters on their board, the moderator had the courtesy not to ask them.

I don't know how I would have responded to those questions in the debate. I hope I'd have the wits about me to say something like I was expecting our residents to be better than to ask derogatory questions meant to embarrass and humiliate a member of our community solely because of his sexual orientation.

Things were not much better with the mainstream and community press. As in the primary, *Metro* endorsed Cunningham in the general election. The editorial repeated most of the reasoning from their prior endorsement, saying that Cunningham—"soccer mom, neighborhood do-gooder"—would better represent the interests of her district.[92]

As for Yeager? The *Metro* said, "If he got elected, he would be the city council's first openly gay member." Clearly no soccer dad here.

Cunningham reproduced the short *Metro* endorsement and had precinct walkers take it door-to-door. Later, when we were discussing the piece at campaign headquarters, a volunteer wondered why she chose it to be the last piece to be distributed before the election. An astute person thought it was her way of telling people I was gay without being the person to say it.

It was interesting how a reporter for the *Mercury News* would talk about Cunningham's "grassroots neighborhood leadership" but would always find a way to mention that I was gay. In an article a month before the election, she topped herself by mentioning three times I was gay in a span of four sentences. After mentioning my election to the community college board, she felt it was important to add that I became the first openly gay person elected in the county. The next line was about how I co-founded BAYMEC. Other reporters left it at that, but she added "a gay and lesbian political advocacy group." Not satisfied to stop there, of all things, she then wrote, "His book, *Trailblazers: Profiles of American's Gay and Lesbian Elected Officials,* was published last year." [93]

Christensen sent an email to the reporter, saying her emphasis on my sexual orientation was excessive. "One or two mentions might have been enough; I doubt three were necessary—especially since none of the three is pertinent to the race."

----

92 Editorial Board. "Metro Endorses Kris Cunningham for City Council, District 6." *San Jose Metro.* October 26, 2000.

93 Janice Rombeck. "Candidates for City Council Split on Only a Few Issues." *San Jose Mercury News.* October 2, 2000.

The reporter responded that she agreed that sexual orientation was not an issue in the race. "But Ken's involvement in gay rights activism is part of his record. I was writing about his accomplishments, not his sexual orientation."

Okay. So, being the first gay elected official, starting a gay political organization, and writing a book about gay and lesbian elected officials were not about my sexual orientation but about my activism. Huh?

I tried not to let all the anti-gay bullshit get to me, but I was nevertheless extremely anxious about it. I was worried I wasn't being effective in countering it. We kept contacting the *Mercury News* when we thought articles were slanted toward Cunningham, but it was hard to know if that helped much. We also asked people who had endorsed Cunningham to withdraw their support. We were only successful with one person: Michelle McGurk, who was Fiscalini's chief of staff.

But worse things were still to come.

Besides the Willow Glen Neighborhood Association, the other influential organization was the Willow Glen Business and Professional Association, which was in the process of printing its new business directory and was seeking advertisers. Denelle Fedor, my campaign manager, had seen the solicitation and asked them if we could put in an ad for the campaign. They said yes, so into the directory our ad went.

Well, you would have thought we had snuck it into the King James Bible. All hell broke loose. Cunningham's supporters were livid that they were not given an opportunity to do a similar advertisement. Moreover, they said it was a clear example of favoritism toward me.

The headline in the *Mercury News* about the story made me once again shake my head in disbelief: "Mailing alleges bias for gay candidate." [94] Yet again, there was no reason to point out that I was gay. This would not happen now in San Jose or

----

94   Janice Rombeck. "Mailing Alleges Bias for Gay Candidate." *San Jose Mercury News*. November 3, 2000.

other urban cities, but it was standard practice when LGBTQ+ candidates were first running for office.

Officers of the business association countered that everyone was welcome to put in an ad: You just had to ask. Moreover, they were struggling to get enough ads to pay for the printing of the directory and weren't out to endorse any candidate. A move by a Cunningham supporter to file a complaint with the IRS fell through when it was determined that the association did not violate its tax-exempt status.

Then things really started to snowball into a strange and homophobic hell.

Soon after the directory was distributed, an anonymous letter was mailed to all Willow Glen merchants. It reiterated the complaint against the association and made derogatory statements about me, accompanied by a gay slur. On the back of the letter was a homophobic cartoon. There was no return address on the envelope, but the letter was signed by Phillip Rossignol, one of Cunningham's supporters. Rossignol denied sending it, and after an investigation by the San Jose Police Department, it was determined to be a copy of his signature.

Here is my attempt to describe the cartoon, which was basically a representation of the famous photo of the six U.S. Marines raising the American flag at Iwo Jima. The Marines are hoisting a flag with the words "Cunningham for City Council" in place of the stars. There were names on the Marines' helmets like "WGNA" and "Kris." A caricature of me on all fours with my pants around my knees has "Ken Yeager" written on my helmet, with the word "gay boy" on my rump. The flagpole is being strategically planted in a part of my anatomy.

It's hard to know what to make of it or who did it and why. Cunningham denied any responsibility, then pathetically said my campaign may have done it, which is beyond absurd.

The anti-gay crap wasn't over quite yet.

Next up was a letter written by Dennis Henderson, senior pastor of Willow Glen's First Baptist Church, sent to all the pastors in District 6. According to an article in the Willow Glen *Resident*, Henderson's letter said he was concerned "not because I have animosity toward homosexuals, whom God loves, but because I am uncomfortable with the homosexual agendas."[95]

The mailing included copies of my endorsement by the Gay and Lesbian Victory Fund and the *Mercury News*, both of which referenced my leadership in BAYMEC. It also included excerpts from my *Trailblazers* book.

"We're not homophobic; we welcome everybody," Henderson said to the reporter about his church. "We think the Bible teaches God loves everybody. But I think the Bible is clear in saying that homosexuality is unnatural and wrong."

Glad he cleared that up.

In a column in the gay paper, The *Point*, Vaughn Beckman, a gay minister, asked why there was not more denouncement of the letter in the straight community. "No public outcry, except in the gay papers, suggests that we still have a long way to go to guarantee dignity for our LGBTQ+ citizens. Our community has failed in its silence."[96]

One straight ally did speak out. Art Mills, a pastor of one of Willow Glen's progressive Presbyterian congregations, Stone Church, was quoted in the *Resident* article saying that he was surprised and shocked by the letter. "I thought that we were way beyond that sort of thing. It's just a veil for a bigoted attack. It prompted me to put up a lawn sign for Ken Yeager."[97]

After the reporter pointed out I was a Unitarian, I was quoted as saying: "I've been around this type of bigotry all my life and fought very hard against it in San Jose. I'm saddened to see it rear its ugly head, especially in the name of God."

----

95   Kate Carter. "Baptist Pastor Sent Anti-Yeager Letter to Other Local Clergy." Willow Glen *Resident*. November 2, 2000.

96   Vaughn Beckman, Reverend. "Beyond Homophobia in Elections." *The Point* Newspaper. December 6, 2000.

97   Kate Carter. Ibid.

When I had the chance, I thanked Pastor Mills for his courage to speak out when so few people were willing to do so. I would later ask him to do the invocation at my swearing-in.

The *Metro* was blessed with an iconoclastic editorial cartoonist named Steven DeCinzo, who just signed his drawings "DeCinzo." Like many newspaper cartoonists, he must have been allowed journalistic license if his opinions were separate from the publisher, who happened to be a Cunningham supporter.

Shortly before the election, the setting of his weekly drawing was the interior of a storefront with a sign that read "D6 Campaign Office." There are several people working inside, with one woman holding a box saying "Anti-Gay Rhetoric." A Greyhound bus has just driven up, and passengers are getting off. They include a neo-Nazi, a Ku Klux Klansman, and some Hells Angels types, all walking into the campaign office.

The caption underneath the drawing said it all: "We got here as soon as we could. How can we help?"

I loved it. It was a brilliant statement as to how homophobia can ignite other hate groups into action, certainly something we are seeing today. DeCinzo was the only journalist who saw this phenomenon.

I knew editorial cartoonists' drawings were sketched out in a larger format than the size that appears in the paper, so I thought it would be wonderful to get a bigger copy of it. I had never met DiCenzo, but I called him and asked if we could have lunch in Willow Glen, adding if, by chance, I could have the original artwork. To my surprise, he said yes to both.

At lunch, he brought the original as promised. I knew at once I would treasure it, which I have all these years. It stood framed in my various offices as a reminder of what I had to deal with to get to where I was.

DiCenzo was very candid with me when I asked about the cartoon and whether he got any pushback from the publisher. In fact, he had. In the first version, he had the entire name of "Cunningham" spelled out on the window. He was asked to change it; thus, "Dist. 6 Campaign Office" was drawn in to cover most of the letters of her last name except "NGHAM." With a smile, he remarked how the publisher didn't catch that the last letters were still there. Also, there was a change of the word in the caption. Originally the sentence read, "We got here as soon as we heard." He was to switch it to "as soon as we could." I don't recall what he said about adding a sheet of paper that read "Homophobic Cartoon," but it must have been a reference to the Iwo Jima drawing.

As the election grew closer, I became more anxious. This just made me grit my teeth and work even harder. I knew how high the stakes were for me, politically and personally. First, I wanted to prove that a qualified gay man could win in a large urban city. Second, once elected, I wanted to show that I could represent the whole community. If I lost, I knew it would be many years before another seat would open up. I knew Cunningham wanted to win, but I knew I wanted it more. With all the strength I had within me, I was willing myself to come in first.

Election Day finally came. I went on my normal three-mile jog. Volunteers were out holding signs for me at the entrance of freeway on-ramps and contacting people who we knew were supporters to make sure they voted. I called up the people who were especially helpful to thank them.

Michael was very sweet. He reminded me that I had done everything within my power to win the race, but it was now out of my hands. People were either willing to support a qualified gay candidate, or they weren't.

This was true for candidates throughout the country who were trying to crack the lavender ceiling in places that had never elected an LGBTQ+ person before. It's always the hardest for the first one.

After the phone calls, there really wasn't much left to do except wait until the polls closed at eight. Just as it was in the primary, my victory party was at a restaurant called Lou's Village, an old Italian, unionized restaurant with autographed photos on the walls of people like Tony Bennett and Rosemary Clooney, who ate there God knows when. Years later, I knew I had arrived when they added my photo to the wall.

By 10:00 p.m., enough of the votes had been counted and posted for the results of the election to be clear. It was then that I went up on stage. The large crowd grew quiet.

"I want everyone to know," I shouted into the microphone, "that I just called my mother." Long pause. "And told her we had won." Everyone roared with delight. I had done it.

The final vote was 53.8 percent (13,166 votes) for me; 46.2 percent (11,297 votes) for Cunningham. Where I had won by approximately 1,000 votes in the primary, I won by about 2,000 votes in the general.

For her congratulatory wishes on November 8, Cunningham sent me the following email: "I wish you luck in your new job representing the great people of District 6. Sincerely, Kris."

My swearing-in ceremony at the Three Flames restaurant on Meridian Avenue was a glorious event. The owner estimated that 500 people filled their huge banquet hall. Everyone was so full of joy, happy for me and happy for San Jose.

The program couldn't have been better. It was with such great pleasure that I had my former boss, Supervisor Wilson, give the welcoming remarks. This was followed by the invocation by Reverend Mills of the Stone Church. Next, there were words by political ally Councilwoman Cindy Chavez, followed by Mayor Gonzales, who couldn't believe the number of people there. The oath of office was administered by Superior Court Judge and civil rights activist LaDoris Cordell.

My speech was very short. It was all I could do not to tear up. I thanked everyone for their help and love and expressed how much I was looking forward to working with them to make San Jose an even greater city.

Six Years Later

I had a weak opponent when I ran for re-election in 2004, easily winning in the primary. In June 2006, I ran for the Santa Clara County Board of Supervisors with two opponents: San Jose City Council Member Linda LeZotte and City of Santa Clara Mayor Patty Mahan. To their shock and everyone else's, I avoided a runoff by winning 52 percent of the vote, a feat seldom accomplished in contested primaries with multiple strong candidates.

That meant leaving the city council with two years left in my second term.

The Willow Glen *Resident* article about my six years in office was very complimentary. In large print, the headline "Kudos for Ken" set the profile's tone. It was a nice turnaround by the paper for all my hard work.[98]

The article highlighted how my efforts and commitment during the last six years had not gone unnoticed by the community. Said Cara Finn, co-owner of a wine shop on Lincoln Avenue in Willow Glen, "He's a leader and a doer. I wouldn't even say he's a politician. He's a city and county activist who was willing to step into a political position."

As the city's first LGBTQ+ councilmember, I was proud to take leadership on a number of issues. First, I proposed that the City of San Jose provide recognition for all valid marriage licenses of city employees and retirees who are in same-gender relationships, resulting in full and equal benefits to all married couples or registered domestic partners, regardless of sexual orientation. This passed on an 8 to 1 vote. I then successfully advocated successfully for a policy to waive fees charged by the City of San Jose on property transfers for same-gender couples, just as it does for opposite-gender couples. I authored an amendment to the city's harassment policy to include protections for gender identity in addition to existing protections

----

98   Mary Gottaschak and Alicia Upano. "Kudos for Ken." Willow Glen *Resident*. December 6, 2006.

for race, color, ethnicity, national origin, disability, age, sex, marital status, sexual orientation, and religion. I also helped secure nearly $2 million in funding to remodel the Billy De-Frank LGBTQ+ Community Center and operate its senior lunch program. The Rainbow Flag was raised for the first time over San Jose City Hall in 2001.

One hurdle that any minority candidate has to overcome is the belief that he or she will only focus on issues related to their constituency and not the whole community. This is especially true when they are the "first," and voters don't have anyone to compare them to. Part of the whispering campaign against me was that I was better suited to run in San Francisco than San Jose, or that I would only focus on gay issues, because that *must* be what gay politicians do.

Which, of course, is total nonsense. Although I am proud of my record on LGBTQ+ issues, they took up relatively little time in the overall scheme of things. Try slowing down traffic in the neighborhoods, expanding the trail network, or getting an airport curfew. Now those take up a lot of time.

I believe that the work my staff and I did was much appreciated by my constituents. Our work targeted a variety of topics, from parks to fire safety. We were able to create six new parks, including Hummingbird, Fuller, River Glen, Buena Vista, Cahill, and O'Connor, open the new Rose Garden Library, and complete the design of the new Willow Glen Library. At my urging, the City hired a trails coordinator, developed a master plan for the trails, and allocated funds to purchase more trail property (including $5 million set aside to purchase the abandoned Willow Glen railroad spur for a future trail). We led the fight for the FAA to approve a new and better airport curfew and to impose fines for violators—a feat no one thought we could achieve.

We worked with residents throughout the district to slow down traffic in neighborhoods by adding stop signs, painting new crosswalks, reducing speed limits, adding signage, installing speed bumps, and building median islands. I served on the

Caltrain board and supported the creation of the Baby Bullet, which allows passengers to go from San Jose to San Francisco in under an hour. Even after Mayor Gonzales proposed cutting staffing and fire apparatus at the Willow Glen Fire Station, I successfully lobbied the council to maintain the status quo.

I proposed landmark policies that provide healthy food and beverage options in all city vending machines; kept the Willow Glen Senior Center as a City-operated facility, winning approval for an audio loop system for seniors with hearing devices. I chaired the City's Ethics Task Force and strengthened ordinances on lobbyists, gifts, and campaign finance. In addition, the task force wrote a new code of ethics, streamlined the process for censure, and instituted ethics training for councilmembers and top City employees.

We vastly improved the district's four commercial streets (Lincoln Avenue, The Alameda, West San Carlos, and Winchester Boulevard) by adding pedestrian safety features, more parking, more trash pickups, and more neighborhood retail. Five new neighborhood associations were created, all of which are active and communicate with each other. Lastly, I chaired the Aging Services Plan Committee and led the effort to identify how the city and county could continue to provide our growing senior population with the best possible services.

In the *Resident* article, I summed up my feelings about the six years I served on the council. "I'm sad to be going," I said. "I don't think there's another person who knows every square inch of District 6 like I do."

CHAPTER 8

Running a
Perfect Campaign

By May 2005, I still had more than two and a half years left in my city council seat. As any politician who is subject to term limits knows—which I was with a two-term limit—the hourglass quickly depletes of sand. I had thoroughly enjoyed being on the council and wasn't sure if I wanted to leave early. Looking around, I knew my only real option was an office few people were aware of but which carries a great deal of authority and responsibility: the County Board of Supervisors. The seat was currently held by Jim Beall, who was termed out and was running for state senate.

Most people know what cities do—land use, parks, police, etc.—and what mayors do—run the meetings, cut ribbons, be quoted in the paper. But far fewer know what the county government does, least of all what a supervisor does. "Who do you supervise?" I was inquisitively asked.

First, a brief synopsis: California is divided into 58 counties, all with five supervisors, except San Francisco, which is a city and a county and has 11. Counties, by design, are agents of the state. Their main functions primarily deal with services that are viewed as state responsibilities, like public health, mental health, drug and alcohol, child support, public safety, criminal justice, foster children, elections, aging adults, and dependent children. Some provide critical medical care by operating their own hospitals and clinics, serving the insured and uninsured alike.

Santa Clara County has the sixth largest county population in the state, after Los Angeles, San Diego, Orange, Riverside, and San Bernardino. It has 1.9 million people, an $11.7 billion budget, and 23,000 employees, making it the largest employer in the county. All this results in county government having a major impact on the lives of its residents.

The election wasn't until the following June of 2006, but I wondered if I was starting too late. Already in the race were San Jose Councilwoman Linda LeZotte, Santa Clara Mayor Patricia Mahan, and state Assemblywoman Rebecca Cohen, who would later drop out and endorse me. I knew it would be a competitive race, and I worried about how well I would do against three women. Of the three cities in Supervisorial District 4, San Jose had 55 percent of the district voters. The other two cities had far fewer, with Santa Clara at 28 percent and Campbell at 11 percent. These numbers boded well for me as I had good name recognition in my Willow Glen/Rose Garden council district, as well as an adjoining district that included many Willow Glen neighborhoods.

I called upon some good friends who had excellent political skills to meet at the home of my SJSU mentor and friend, Terry Christensen, to guide me in my decision. Most had helped me in the city council race, including political consultants Ed McGovern, Don Cecil, and Dustin DeRollo. My loyal friend Leslee Hamilton joined us, along with my City Hall Chief of Staff, John Mills. I asked them if they thought the county was a good fit for me and if I stood a fair chance of winning. They answered in the affirmative to both questions and offered to help in any way they could. That sealed the deal. With my partner Michael's support already, it was all systems go.

As with the City of San Jose, the County required a 50 percent plus one vote to win in the primary. Primaries are generally less aggressive than general run-offs because candidates spend most of their money promoting themselves rather than attacking their opponents. My assembly race was a little different because the race was about which Democrat would face the winner of the Republican primary, so the primary was the real competition.

Because of this, I wasn't too worried about an anti-gay attack in the primary. Moreover, I had been in office for more than five years, primarily working on neighborhood issues, with the occasional LGBTQ+ issue like same-sex marriage coming up only now and then. One upside of electing queer people to office is the public has the opportunity to assess how they are doing. Once they realize we have no "*gay agenda*" and, in fact, have the same goals as everyone else about what is best for the community, the election of the next queer person is much easier.

I will never forget the September campaign kick-off held at the Rosicrucian Egyptian Museum near my home in the Rose Garden neighborhood. Many San Jose residents and visitors know of this museum devoted to Egyptian history because of its Karnak-style entrance and statue of Tawaret. I had gotten to know its director, Julie Scott, fairly well, and when I was looking for a no-cost venue that held a lot of people, I thought of their large indoor courtyard. I had it catered by Antonella's Restaurant, which was just across the street and where Michael and I often had dinner. More than 200 people attended, so the venue was a perfect size. There were so many people standing or sitting around the courtyard that I didn't have time to say hello to everyone before introductions began.

Terry Christensen did the opening welcome. Because it was important to have speakers from all three cities in the district, he was followed by David Keller of the Campbell Kiwanis and Jamie McLeod, a lesbian City of Santa Clara councilwoman.

The highlight was words of support from former Mayor Susan Hammer. She talked about how we had worked side by side for many years, how I built coalitions to make sure everyone in the community was included in decision-making, and that if anyone could help the City and County to work well together, it was me.

In my remarks, I touched on a number of issues but stressed public and physical health the most. "People ask me what my number one priority will be, and I answer: making sure we provide comprehensive health care to our most vulnerable citizens, particularly seniors and children," I said.

I went on to say, "Physical health is a big issue for me, and I worry about the growing rate of obesity in the county. Obesity, poor diet, and lack of exercise can lead to a number of serious illnesses like diabetes, heart disease, and stroke."

I then talked about completing the trail system, providing more AIDS education and treatment, increasing mental health services, providing more housing for the homeless, and improving our public transportation by bringing BART to San Jose.

"Today is the start of the campaign," I concluded. "I thank you from the bottom of my heart for being here. It's a long road, but with your help, we will be victorious on election day."

Raising money is never easy or fun. I can't tell you how many candidates I've listened to bemoan that task. Of most importance is having a good database. Since 1984, I had started collecting people's names, addresses, and phone numbers when I started BAYMEC. Emails would come later. Initially, names were printed on 3x5 index cards, then converted to a database by my friend Paul Morrell. As anyone who has worked for me knows, I was obsessive about making sure any contact I had with someone resulted in getting their information inputted correctly. "We live and die by the database!" I would shout. Thus, from all the BAYMEC years, the Proposition 64/No on LaRouche/AIDS Quarantine Initiative, and my campaigns for community college, state assembly, and city council, my database was humming with about a thousand up-to-date donors just waiting to be asked to make a contribution.

And boy did they. An email went out the third week of May,

and by June 30 I had raised an impressive $45,000, all without spending a penny on fundraising or making many calls. This was achieved even with the County-imposed limit of $500 per person. By November, I had raised $150,000. This allowed me to concentrate principally on walking precincts, which I did with great enthusiasm.

As with all my other races, I accumulated an impressive list of individual endorsements. I do believe that many voters look for names that they know and, barring other factors, vote for that person. As in my city council race, my list of 150 names included elected officials from the U.S. Congress, the state senate and assembly, the City of San Jose, school trustees, business leaders, nonprofit leaders, and neighborhood association officers.

Organizations are important as well. Getting their endorsements takes much more time than one would think. First, if it's an organization whose endorsement you want, there is a multi-page questionnaire to complete. Often, these contain esoteric questions that are specific to the organization, and research is needed to formulate your position. Then there is the interview, which can be very stressful. You walk into a large room filled with their members, and you and the other candidates in your race sit at a table with sweaty palms and hope for the best. If you've been around politics for as long as I have, you already know many of the key people and have talked to them beforehand to get a sense of their support. Some groups will take a membership vote immediately afterward; some wait until their board of directors takes a vote later.

One of the unions that is part of the South Bay AF-CIO Labor Council is the Service Employee International Union, the County's employee union. Because supervisors determined the wages and benefits of County employees, they are the most affected by who was elected. Having been a union member when I was on faculty at SJSU, as well as supportive of union issues as a councilmember, I knew I had a good chance of getting their support, which I received after a lengthy process.

This gave the go-ahead for union members to work on my campaign and to support me at the ballot box.

The other important group was the local Chamber of Commerce's political action committee or COMPAC, a body that is separate from the chamber membership and which has a more conservative board. Getting their endorsement would be much more difficult. I obtained a list of their board and called those that I knew. My campaign team looked over the other names to see which of my supporters could contact them. I thought I did well in the interview but figured that it was unlikely they would endorse me. Under those circumstances, the best I could hope for was that no one got the endorsement.

The following day I received a phone call I will never forget. I was standing in the kitchen preparing breakfast when I got a call from Pat Dando, a former San Jose councilwoman and colleague who was now the president and CEO of the chamber. When she said, "I'm calling to tell you that COMPAC voted to give you a sole endorsement for the County race," I literally dropped to the floor. I knew my getting the chamber's endorsement would be big news and would considerably increase my chances of winning.

So, along with COMPAC and South Bay Labor Council, I was able to list a number of organizations in the mailer, including the San Jose Teachers Association, Democratic Activists for Women Now, Santa Clara County Democratic Party, BAYMEC, Log Cabin Republicans, Deputy Sheriffs Association, and the San Jose Police Officers Association.

The last crucial important endorsement was the *Mercury News*. I thought the interview went well, but you can never really tell. I had taken several votes on the city council that the editors supported, so I held out some hope. One of those votes dealt with a proposal by Mayor Gonzales to bring a Grand Prix-like road race through downtown San Jose, which was nonsensical given our narrow downtown streets, so I voted against it. The other was my vote to censure the mayor for his shady dealings over a contract with a garbage company.

The day that the *Mercury News* first publishes its endorsements begins the nail-biting countdown for candidates as to when theirs will appear. I subscribe to the paper, so from the second day onward I would go out to the sidewalk, pick up the paper, climb back into bed, and then ever-so-slowly open it to the editorial section to take a peek and see if they had written about the supervisorial race. I was always deflated when there was no endorsement, knowing I needed to wait another day or perhaps two maddening weeks.

One morning I stayed in bed a little longer than usual, so Michael went out to get the paper. I remember him bounding into the bedroom, all excited with the newspaper open to the editorial page, yelling, "You got it, Ken. You got the endorsement!"

I couldn't have been more pleased with the text. The May 16, 2006, headline read: "Yeager leads the list of good candidates." The editorial stated, "Yeager has spent the past six years representing District 6 on the council. His engaging personality and his track record of building consensus make him particularly well suited to tackle the city-county rift, which lately has played out in lawsuits and countersuits."

The editorial mentioned that I had the endorsement of the Labor Council and the Chamber of Commerce, "which speaks volumes about his ability to reach out to a wide range of constituents."

The endorsement ended on an upbeat note: "Yeager doesn't relish confrontation, which sometimes makes it difficult for him to say no—an important skill in the county, where needs always exceed funds. But he proved his leadership on the council by tackling tough issues, such as lobbying reform and standing up to Mayor Ron Gonzales on matters of ethics and openness. Chairing the Ethics Task Force, Yeager deftly handled competing interests and brought about serious reform." [99]

----

99   Editorial Board. "Yeager Heads List of Good Candidates." *San Jose Mercury News.* May 16, 2006.

There it was: The Chamber, the Labor Council, the *Mercury News*. A rare trifecta in San Jose and Santa Clara County politics.

Under California law, all local city, county, and school board races are non-partisan, meaning political parties cannot follow a candidate's name on the ballot. This allows people to vote for any candidate, regardless of party. This encourages candidates to reach as broad of a base as possible. Getting COMPAC's endorsement suddenly—and surprisingly—opened the door to consider a targeted mailing to Republican voters, something which I had never done before. Today, with our hyper-partisan divide, it is hard to imagine a progressive candidate in a non-partisan race getting support from pro-business Republicans, but back then, most Republicans in the county were fairly moderate in their politics.

So, the decision was made to mail to Republican voters. The outside cover read: "An important message for Republican Voters about the June 6th election." Then inside, the headline read, "Republicans, Business, Education, and Public Safety Leaders Support Ken Yeager." Dando gave me a very supportive quote to include: "Ken Yeager's ability to unify and bring consensus to even the most troubling and complex issues makes him a perfect candidate. Ken will help our local economy continue to rebound and help Silicon Valley stay on top in the 21st Century global economy."

Also important was the endorsement from County Supervisor Don Gage, the only Republican on the five-member board—and a mild Republican, at that. If I were to win, it would bode well that we could work together. His quote stressed my ability "to work with people from all parties to get results. I urge you to join other Republican leaders and me in supporting Ken Yeager for County Board of Supervisors."

The issues I listed as my top priorities were not inconsistent with a moderate Republican agenda. They were to fully hire and train the sheriff and County fire departments, ensure the County trauma centers were fully staffed, make sure the County had strict ethics rules, work with local businesses to cut red tape, and attract and retain quality teachers by investing in teacher training and housing.

A targeted flyer also was mailed to Democrats. Along with stressing healthcare, education, and public safety, there was a quote from the chair of the county Democratic Central Committee that read: "Ken is a life-long Democrat who fights to protect civil liberties, a woman's right to choose, and anti-discrimination policies."

By election night, we had hand-addressed 38,000 envelopes with 15 versions of neighbor-to-neighbor letters, recruited 140 precinct walkers, called 20,000 voters, distributed 800 lawn signs, compiled 900 endorsements, held 25 coffees at people's homes, six fundraisers, and raised $270,000, far more than my two opponents.

Going into election night, my campaign team was optimistic about my winning, even predicting that I would get over the magic mark of 50 percent to avoid a runoff. To me, that seemed like an impossibly high bar. Maybe because the assembly and the council race were so awful, the universe decided that I had suffered enough and finally paved a smoother election path for me. I say that jokingly because it was really all my years of hard work in the community and, along the way, making friends, not enemies, that actually helped me to surpass the 50 percent plus one total. After all the votes were counted, I received 51.96 percent. To say people were stunned is an understatement. It was a blessing not to have to run another campaign in November. For those six months, I was able to finish up my projects on the council and get prepared to provide new energy and visionary leadership in my new position. Santa Clara County, here I come.

CHAPTER 9

LGBTQ+ Health Assessment and Creation of the Office of LGBTQ+ Affairs

People run for office for any number of reasons. Perhaps some grievance has arisen that they want to address, or they disapprove of the votes taken by their representative, or maybe they just want to serve their community in a broader way. Although they may know what problems they want to tackle, they are probably unsure how to solve them. Often, when their tenure is at its end, they may be left wondering what overall difference they made.

As mentioned, from the onset, I wanted to focus on health. As I often said in speeches, the greatest gift you can give to someone is the gift of health. I say that because if you have good health, you can focus on reaching your full potential. You can be more active and involved in the outside world. Poor health limits you.

Every year supervisors choose among themselves who will be the chair for the coming year. In Santa Clara County, we call them presidents. Normally this position rotates to the supervisor who has gone the longest without serving in that position.

One duty of the incoming Board president is to give a State of the County address. The occasion is often a big deal, with lots of dignitaries attending and much pomp and circumstance.

Because these speeches outline the new initiatives that the president wants to introduce during their term, County staff and community organizations pay much attention to what is said.

When I was president of the Board in 2013, one of the most important policy announcements I made in my State of the County address dealt with conducting health assessments for the LGBTQ+ and African/African Ancestry communities, the latter which I will discuss in a moment.

There were numerous reasons for the LGBTQ+ assessment. LGBTQ+ adults represent an estimated three to four percent of the adult population in Santa Clara County, or more than 50,000 people. Despite the size of the population and its unique needs, information was scarce on the health status and related social experiences of LGBTQ+ residents, making it difficult for leaders to shape policy or allocate funding to improve LGBTQ+ health and well-being. The purpose of the assessment was to fill in these knowledge gaps. I knew from my years of graduate school at Stanford the importance of research supporting a thesis. Anecdotal stories are useful in getting a sense of people's lives and struggles, but a more rigorous examination carries more weight.

In March 2013, following my address, the Board voted to allocate $245,000 for the assessment. I asked two well-respected gay leaders in the community to join me in being co-chairs of the report: recently retired County Health Officer Dr. Marty Fenstersheib and Health Trust CEO Fred Ferrer.

The Public Health Department hired a public relations firm to help with outreach to the LGBTQ+ community. Data collection included an online survey to obtain feedback from a wide spectrum of individuals representing youth, seniors, and a range of social and economic backgrounds, as well as representatives from diverse sectors, including business, education, and advocacy groups. In addition, the firm worked to recruit and facilitate focus groups and conduct key informant interviews.

By the end of November, data from 1,175 people, 17 focus groups, and two key informant interviews were gathered. Because the queer community in a suburban area like San Jose has no gay enclave like the Castro or Greenwich Village, locating queer people to take surveys can be difficult. But I felt good about the numbers and confident it would give us the important information we needed.

In December, the Public Health Department released the first comprehensive health report for our diverse LGBTQ+ communities. Entitled *Status of LGBTQ+ Health: Santa Clara County 2013*, the groundbreaking report uncovered the health disparities and inequities faced by queer people, while also identifying key priority health issues.

Acknowledging that the Bay Area had a well-deserved reputation for tolerance and diversity, the report showed that the LGBTQ+ community still had very real, unique, and unmet needs.

It is an extensive list, but here are some of the key findings:

- LGBTQ+ individuals comprised nearly one-third of homeless youth and young adults under the age of 25 and 10 percent of homeless adults ages 25 and older.

- One in 10 middle and high school students was harassed or bullied on school property in the past 12 months because they were gay or lesbian or someone thought they were.

- One in 10 LGBTQ+ respondents was physically attacked or injured, and one-third had been verbally harassed in the past 12 months due to sexual orientation and/or gender identity.

- More than one in 10 respondents reported some type of discriminatory treatment by healthcare professionals in the past 12 months.

- Many community conversation participants report that they are not aware of available healthcare services or that the services they are aware of are perceived as not LGBTQ+-competent.

- Nearly half of the respondents felt they might have needed to see a professional in the past 12 months because of concerns about mental health or substance use.

- Nearly one-quarter of all respondents and nearly half of the transgender respondents seriously considered suicide or hurting themselves during the prior 12 months.

- Approximately one in 12 LGBTQ+ respondents have used injection drugs, and most of the respondents remain users.

- A high percentage of respondents (between 38 percent and 65 percent) from each LGBTQ+ subgroup have never been tested for STIs.

- Discriminatory experiences were more commonly reported by transgender respondents.

- Nearly four in 10 Black respondents agree or strongly agree that sometimes they dislike themselves for being attracted to people of the same sex.

- More than one in five respondents have been physically abused by an intimate partner, and 13 percent have been forced into non-consensual sex. Rates of both physical and sexual violence were highest among bisexual women.

- Moreover, three in four LGBTQ+ survey respondents who experienced intimate partner violence did not report the incident(s) to law enforcement.

In order to guide the next steps, the report detailed the strengths and resources available in the County and proposed strategies based on participants' input. They recommended an improved awareness of available health and social services, including those that are low- or no-cost, among LGBTQ+ residents through education, outreach, and development of directories and inventories.

They wished to address the shortage of health and social services providers who are LGBTQ+-friendly and LGBTQ+-knowledgeable through competency training, aiming to provide additional funding, training, and technical support for existing LGBTQ+ services.

Clearly, we had work to do. Which begged the question, who was going to do it?

Creating the Office of LGBTQ+ Affairs

It was fortunate that during this period of time, from 2012 to 2014, the County's Juvenile Probation Department was working to achieve greater dignity and fairness for LGBTQ+ youth in our juvenile justice system. Known as the Equity Project, it was funded by a national consortium of nonprofits, including Legal Services for Children, the National Center for Lesbian Rights, and the National Juvenile Defender Center. The grant brought together local probation staff and leaders from community-based organizations, such as the Bill Wilson Center and the LGBTQ+ Youth Space. Alex Shoor from my office, an ally who had a background in LGBTQ+ media training, was an active participant who helped signal that I was in full support of their work.

It is somewhat remarkable that the Probation Department would even undertake such a progressive project. When it was first introduced, there was pushback from staff. Fortunately, it had the full support of the chief of the Probation Department, Laura Garnett, an out lesbian. She was well respected in the profession and had the full backing of County Chief Executive Dr. Jeff Smith, who had appointed her, bypassing a more tenured and traditional deputy probation chief.

The group created a new Probation Department policy for how LGBTQ+ youth are processed, housed, and treated in County facilities. They also designed training to instruct County staff and community-based organizations on issues that LGBTQ+ youth face. By 2014, the training had been presented to Santa Clara County Superior Court judges, as well as 850 community stakeholders and County employees from 10 different departments connected to the juvenile justice system.

Although the partnership with the Equity Project came to an end, the work it fostered continued. The steering committee and its workgroups renamed their efforts Collective PRIDE: Promoting Respect, Inclusion, Dignity, and Equality.

Everyone involved in the training did not want to lose momentum in educating the County workforce on LGBTQ+ issues. Moreover, the results of the health assessment demonstrated such a significant need. In conversations I had with Garnett, we agreed that some agency needed to have it as its mission or it would fall by the wayside. The County's Human Relations Commission was one option, but it had no staff, so I knew that wouldn't work. I then suggested we create a new office to assist Collective PRIDE in its next steps and institutionalize support for its efforts. She enthusiastically agreed. Thus, the nation's first county Office of LGBTQ+ Affairs was born.

Although I was excited about the idea, I wanted to make sure others felt the same way. I held two meetings with representatives of numerous County departments and community organizations, particularly those in the areas of public safety and health and human services, to solicit their feedback on the Office. The agencies and organizations that participated in the meeting included: the Sheriff's Office, Department of Corrections, Probation Department, Public Defender's Office, County

Executive's Office, Behavioral Health Department, Public Health Department, Social Affairs Agency, Department of Aging and Adult Affairs, Equal Opportunity Department in the Employee Affairs Agency, The Health Trust, and the Asian Americans for Community Involvement.

Once I knew these departments would utilize the services of the Office, I was all in. Several months later, in March 2015, I spoke at a Board meeting and asked my fellow supervisors to vote on a referral to establish it.

I began my remarks by saying I was pleased to put forward my proposal. "While the LGBTQ+ community has tradition-ally been underrepresented in government and underserved by institutions, this county has a long tradition of working to eliminate disparities among its residents."

I then thanked the County staff I worked with to reduce those disparities, acknowledging Dr. Smith in particular. "From my heart, I really appreciate all that everyone has done.

"An Office of LGBTQ+ Affairs could provide staff training, external relations to the LGBTQ+ community, resource devel-opment, and evaluation. Its goal would be to provide leader-ship, accountability, and effective outcomes."

I made a brief reference to the LGBTQ+ Health Assessment that the County undertook, touching on a few statistics, wor-ried that a long list of issues could be difficult to fully assimilate in that setting. "Despite these statistics," I stated, "this county has been quite innovative recently in trying to address these disparities. However, up until now, these efforts have been ad hoc. An Office of LGBTQ+ Affairs would keep these programs on track while ensuring adequate resources and collaboration across departments.

"Over the last month, I held meetings with the leaders of numerous county departments and community organizations to solicit their feedback on this idea. Overwhelmingly, they were all very encouraging and pointed out tangible ways that the Office would be of use to them. Once I knew they were supportive, I made the final decision to take my proposal to the full Board," I explained.

"Therefore, I am asking the County Executive's Office to report back to the Board of Supervisors preliminary considerations for an Office of LGBTQ+ Affairs."

My motion was seconded and passed unanimously.

My staff helped me write my comments for the referral, which I had rehearsed beforehand, so mentally I was ready to speak. What surprised me was that emotionally I wasn't.

The first time that I welled up and my voice cracked was when I thanked Dr. Smith and the County staff "from my heart." I seemed to have jumped from the professional to the emotional in an instant. I really did appreciate all the help they had given me in implementing programs for the LGBTQ+ community, and I saw this as my opportunity to recognize and thank them for their help. It's the tears I hadn't planned on.

Somewhat embarrassed, I said, "Now I'm going to get choked up." I carried on, talking about the need for the Office, which was as far as I got. Then I began sniffling and stopped talking altogether. I sniffled some more.

As I tried to compose myself with several deep breaths while wiping both eyes with my hands, I heard my friend in the audience, Gabrielle Antolovich, who was the board president of the Billy DeFrank LGBTQ+ Community Center, shout out, "We love you," and the rest of the audience followed suit with sounds of support.

After a long pause, I was able to say, "I wasn't quite expecting this." In an attempt to give some explanation of my emotions, I said, "I was getting choked up, Gabrielle, when you were talking earlier because I remember the Billy DeFrank Center 30 years ago in a small storefront on Keyes, and since then, we've all come so far."

After presenting more reasons for the Office, I was ready

to make the pitch. I felt I had made my case and, more importantly, composed myself. After another breath, I began again, but out of nowhere, after one sentence—bam! I went straight into sobs. Talking while crying is not easy, but I didn't have any other choice. For a brief moment, I thought of handing over my remaining remarks to Supervisor Chavez, who was sitting next to me. But I soldiered on, taking three deep breaths, hoping that would help, picking up where I left off mid-sentence. Thankfully, I was finally able to collect myself and finish my remarks. Everyone cheered and laughed when I said, "My motion, finally...."

For those interested, the speech can be viewed on a website I created on the history of the LGBTQ+ movement in Silicon Valley: queersiliconvalley.org/yeager-proposes-office. Every time I watch it, I still wonder why I lost my composure, never having anything like that happen before.

Perhaps it was because when you are a person caught up in a protracted civil rights struggle like I was for almost 40 years, you aren't aware of how far you've come until you've climbed all the way up the hill and looked back on the battlefield below. For many LGBTQ+ Americans who fought for marriage equality, that feeling happened when the U.S. Supreme Court validated same-gender marriages in California in 2013 and then in the entire country in 2015. Progress was suddenly measurable.

To a lesser degree, I had that same sense of progress with the proposal to create the Office of LGBTQ+ Affairs. It was the culmination of my work at the local level, where I had decided I could make a bigger difference.

That is why when my friend from the DeFrank Center shouted, "We love you," it wasn't just the Center that had come a long way from its original storefront on Keyes; we all had. That realization overwhelmed me. As the weight of all those years slowly lifted, I found myself shedding the best tears to shed: tears of joy.

Creation of the Office

An article in the *Mercury News* was very positive.[100] Rebecca
Famer, a spokeswoman for the American Civil Liberty Union,
was quoted as saying her group had not seen that model before.
"A lot of city governments have a liaison, but this is something
unique and new." She further stated that the "state has legal
protections for the LGBTQ+ community, but a County office
could help make sure some of those great laws are a reality for
a group that continues to face discrimination."

All my colleagues made supportive remarks in the story.
Dave Cortese, as Board president, said, "It was comforting to
have a civil rights advocate on the Board. He'll keep moving us
on to the next issue. Instead of declaring victory, he sees the next
area that needs to be addressed and acts on it." I was heartened to read an editorial in the *Mercury News* two weeks later
entitled "LGBTQ+ Office in the County still is necessary." [101]
It pointed out some of the anti-gay laws being considered or
passed elsewhere in the country and added, "So yes, Supervisor
Ken Yeager's proposal, unfortunately, is timely." The editorial
cited some of the health statistics I mentioned in my referral
and even provided a link to it.

The editorial concluded with these words: "A Santa Clara
County Office of LGBTQ+ Affairs need not be a budget buster.
It can coordinate other agencies' works, educate healthcare
and other professionals and reach out to LGBTQ+ populations
so they're aware of available resources. And, by its very existence, show that this county cares about the needs of minority
communities." Amen.

After an extensive recruitment process, in January 2016,
the County hired Maribel Martinez, a lesbian Latina from East
San Jose, as the Office's first executive director. She had spent

----

100   Eric Kurhi. "Planned for LGBTQ+ Office Praised." *San Jose Mercury
News.* March 15, 2015.

101   Editorial Board. "LGBTQ+ Office in the County Still is Timely." *San
Jose Mercury News.* March 30, 2015.

the previous 20 years working with various nonprofits, dealing with issues ranging from education reform to community safety measures to health care and social services. For nine years, she served as the founding director of the Associated Students Cesar Chavez Community Action Center at San Jose State University. While there, she developed and facilitated cross-cultural educational programs and trained as many as 30 on- and off-campus units in the areas of social justice, community issues, and advocacy.

Martínez, after serving in the Emergency Operation Center and helping start the Language Access Team during the COVID-19 response, was later promoted to program director of the Division of Equity and Social Justice, overseeing the LGBTQ+ Office, Gender Based Violence Prevention, Disability Affairs, Hate Crimes/Incidence Prevention, and division-wide communications. Sera Fernando, a transgender woman of color, was promoted from senior management analyst to manager of the LGBTQ+ Office in June 2022. As an equity and inclusion practitioner, she also serves as the chief diversity officer for Silicon Valley Pride. Prior to this position, she was a retail manager at Microsoft.

If something like the Office had existed when I was a new SJSU graduate, I would have been ecstatic to either work or intern there. It would have been a dream come true that would have made me love San Jose even more. Maybe one of the biggest gifts our older selves can give to the next generation is to create jobs we would have wanted for our younger selves.

The Primary Functions of the LGBTQ+ Office[102]

The work of the Office is centered around seven different areas. These include:

102　Note: For more information about the Office of LGBTQ+ Affairs go to lgbtq@lgbtq.org

- **Training:** Train County staff and community stakeholders on best practices while raising awareness of LGBTQ+ issues that are relevant to our interaction with clients, constituents, residents, and employees.

- **Individualized, case-specific assistance:** Offer guidance to County departments and community members seeking support and referrals to local and national resources.

- **Cross-departmental best practices:** Work collaboratively with all County departments and local agencies to ensure that our programs and policies are pushing to expand options to LGBTQ+ clients, residents, and employees.

- **External relations:** Represent the County and build partnerships with local, state, and national government agencies, school districts, and nonprofit organizations on LGBTQ+ issues.

- **Communications:** Develop the Office's communication strategies and develop resources to address them.

- **Resource development:** Identify gaps in services to LGBTQ+ residents and develop resources to address them.

- **Community engagement and mobilization:** Play a role in promoting and collaborating on LGBTQ+ community events, building support and platforms to strengthen and amplify community voice.

In terms of written research reports, the first to be completed was a comprehensive assessment of older LGBTQ+ adults, their quality of life, gaps in their care, and the services that are available to the community.

A second study identified existing resources for transgender, gender expansive, and non-binary people, outlined needed resources, and reported on their educational and professional experiences.

A third was an employment study of the county's transgender, gender expansive, and non-binary members to learn what barriers and problems they face in their jobs and career paths.

A fourth was the Support OUT Initiative, which is a multiyear collaboration with Shannon Wilber of the National Center of Lesbian Rights, Ceres Policy Research, Rhodes Perry Consulting, the Office of LGBTQ+ Affairs, and the County Probation Department. It was designed to promote the health and well-being of LGBTQ+ youth living in the county, especially LGBTQ+ youth of color.

I knew it was important to propose policies that would bring about institutional change and remain in existence after I was gone. Along with other policies to be discussed next, I am confident this is the case with the creation of the nation's first county Office of LGBTQ+ Affairs, as well as the other policies I initiated.

CHAPTER 10

Passage of Eight Pieces of Legislation and Celebration of Marriage Equality

Few big initiatives in government get accomplished alone. That is especially true in county government, where you must work not only with your fellow supervisors but with a powerful and sometimes entrenched staff. Great staff can help you achieve your goals; recalcitrant staff can undermine you at every turn. I was fortunate to have two top administrators, the County CEO and the chief health officer, to work with, not against me, as I tried to make progress on my legislative priorities.

In most small to moderate-sized cities, the top administrator is not the mayor, whose position may rotate among the councilmembers, but the city manager, who is appointed by the city council. They are the ones who have the authority in the charter to hire and fire department heads, prepare a budget, and ensure council directives are implemented. In counties, the corresponding position is the chief executive officer. Like city managers, the CEOs are hired and fired by elected officials. Most city managers and county executives are sufficiently adept at keeping at least a majority of their board happy, thus remaining in their jobs for a long time.

When I arrived at the County on December 12, 2006, I was eager to shake things up. Early on, I had a sense that County Executive Pete Kutras and I were not in sync, even though we had a friendly relationship. It was evident that Kutras had the backing of the supervisors who had appointed him in 2003. He was a career County employee, having worked his way up the ladder for more than 35 years, serving as director of labor relations, of personnel, of employee services, and then deputy county executive. Over the years, he had acquired much loyalty from people he had mentored and promoted. To the surprise of many, in June 2008, he announced his October 31 retirement.

Early in 2009, the Board began its search for a new County executive. It soon came down to two people. One was the Deputy County Executive under Kutras, Gary Graves, who was his heir apparent; the other was Dr. Jeff Smith, a county health administrator from nearby Contra Costa who had a most impressive resume. Not only was he a medical doctor and lawyer, but he had served one term as a county supervisor, having chosen to run (unsuccessfully) for a state legislative office when his first term ended.

While I liked Graves, I was in full support of Smith, mainly because he knew how to run a hospital system. Our County hospital took in all patients regardless of ability to pay, so we were hemorrhaging money as this required more general fund dollars. This resulted in fewer dollars for other County services. Even though Dr. Smith was an unconventional choice, I pushed hard for him and was able to secure the votes needed for his appointment.

I cannot express how significant this was. Over time, he improved the County Health and Hospital System, convincing a number of health administrators to retire and be replaced by experts in their fields. It also allowed the County to fully implement the Affordable Care Act, which gave more people health insurance, thus helping to reimburse County costs. In March 2019, about a year before the COVID pandemic hit, he was able to negotiate the $235 million purchase of the 358-bed O'Connor Hospital, the 93-bed Saint Louise Regional Hospital, and the DePaul Health Center, which were owned by Verity Health at the time of their bankruptcy. This gave the County more capacity to deal with the dramatic increase of COVID patients, along with saving millions of dollars if new hospitals needed to be built. In keeping with the County's mission to care for everyone regardless of ability to pay, the new facilities' financial assistance program ensured that the most underserved in the community would have greater access to high-quality care.

With the retirement of another supervisor in 2010 and the election of a new one, I had sufficient seniority to be appointed to the committee on which I most wanted to serve: the Board's Health and Hospital Committee. In 2012, I became the committee's chair, serving in that post until termed out at the end of 2018. It was this position that allowed me to push through most of my health agenda.

Dr. Smith became an essential ally in all the work I did, not only on health issues but on LGBTQ+ matters as well. As discussed in the prior chapter, he was in full support of the creation of the Office of LGBTQ+ Affairs. After the U.S. Supreme Court decision on gay marriage, he was the one who proposed to me that the Rainbow flag fly over the County Government Center every workday, not just one day in June for Gay Pride Month. He also hired a significant number of "out" LGBTQ+ department heads, signaling that a person's sexual orientation was not an issue in the County's promotional and hiring practices.

These and other actions led BAYMEC to award him "Ally of the Year" in 2018. As importantly, he helped make sure that the Getting to Zero initiative of having zero HIV infections, zero deaths, and zero stigma had the resources and staff it needed. Never once did he say to me, "slow down." The response to all my requests was always to proceed forward.

The second key person was Dr. Sara Cody, who later became well-known nationally during the COVID crisis. I got to know her when she worked as the deputy public health officer under Dr. Marty Fenstersheib, a gay physician who worked with HIV/AIDS patients since the early days of the pandemic.

The California State Constitution requires each county to have a health officer and gives them enormous powers separate from county governments when dealing with such health issues as infectious diseases. When Fenstersheib retired in 2013, the County needed to hire a new health officer, and Dr. Smith and I discussed who it should be.

There was some question as to whether the Board or the County Executive had the authority to appoint the health officer. While the Board selects a handful of department heads, such as the Clerk of the Board, the County Counsel, and the Public Defender, the County Executive appoints everyone else. I thought Cody would be an excellent choice. She was bright, articulate, and someone who worked well with others. I was president of the Board at the time, so I had a little more leverage with Dr. Smith on matters like this. I suggested that he announce the hiring of Dr. Cody, and he agreed. This way, I knew we'd get the best person possible.

Dr. Cody had gotten to know my Chief of Staff, John Mills, and I remember Mills telling me how surprised and self-effacing Dr. Cody was when Dr. Smith and I told her the news. Her first reactions were, "Who, me?" and "What are they thinking?" I think Dr. Smith and I saw the potential in her that she had not seen in herself.

A couple of years later, in 2015, our director of the Public Health Department resigned. This is a position separate from the health officer and is the person in charge of running the entire 450-member Public Health Department. With my full support, Dr. Smith appointed Dr. Cody to that position in tandem with being the health officer.

Being both the health department director and health officer allowed her to run both offices without interference or turf wars. She became a trusted friend and collaborator who hired excellent staff, many of whom I worked closely with on my health agenda.

As luck would have it, one of the first diagnosed cases of COVID-19 and the first death from COVID-19 in the U.S. occurred in Santa Clara County. Soon, the entire country learned of Dr. Cody when she became the first mainland U.S. official to implement a stay-at-home order to combat the COVID outbreak in March 2020. Her bold actions throughout the pandemic kept infection rates much lower in the county than the national average, leading to fewer hospitalizations and deaths than there otherwise would have been. She has been recognized nationally for her work and is one of the true heroes of the battle against COVID.

Next is a discussion of eight programs I worked on at the County, six of which are related to health. Given their broad scope and impact on County services, they would not have been successful if Dr. Smith or Dr. Cody had tried to stall them, as can happen unbeknownst to elected officials. I always viewed the three of us working as a team. The last section deals with marriage equality in San Jose and Santa Clara County.

African/African Ancestry Health Assessment and the Creation of the Roots Clinic

The path for an assessment of the African American community was a little different from the one for the LGBTQ+ health assessment. I had become friends with leaders of the local Black community, mainly through serving as a member of the Valley Transportation Authority Board, the agency that operates the county's bus and light rail lines. Two of the leaders of the Black Leadership Kitchen Cabinet of Silicon Valley, Walter Wilson and Reverend Reginald Swilley, were critical of the lack of contracts being awarded to Black-owned businesses. I promised to help however I could. It was that process that led to the development of a close working relationship with them. However, it took the hiring of Nuria Fernandez, a Black woman, as the new general manager in 2014 to finally achieve the goals set for minority-owned business contracts.

As I was preparing for my second State of the County speech in early 2013, Wilson and Swilley met with me and told me of their interest in focusing attention on issues concerning educational challenges facing the African American community. While obviously important, county government deals with many issues but not education per se. I suggested redirecting their efforts toward the field of health, which was more in line with the mission of county government and the board's authority. Knowing the health disparities of their community, I thought it would be more beneficial. They readily agreed. This is how the idea came about of including the African/African Ancestry health assessment in the speech.

Several months later, when it came time to submit proposals for the following year's budget, I requested and won approval for $250,000 for both the LGBTQ+ and African/African Ancestry health assessments.

A disagreement soon arose over who should conduct the African/African Ancestry health assessment. Justifiably, the Public Health Department felt it should take the lead, just as it had done with the other health assessments. They believed they had the expertise and would take an unbiased, scientific approach to the research, resulting in findings they could support.

Wilson and the Black Leadership Kitchen Cabinet were having nothing of it. They believed they knew their community best and wanted to be in charge of the process, including hiring professors who were highly regarded in their fields.

The two groups came to an impasse, with the health department having a slightly stronger hand because they had all the money.

Since I had a good relationship with Wilson and then-Public Health Director Dan Peddycord, I was asked to bring everyone into my office and act as a referee of sorts. This had happened numerous times over the years when there was an issue between a County department and a community group. I prided myself in my ability to guide the at-odds parties involved to finding a satisfactory solution. In this situation, Alma Burrell, who was in charge of the County Black Infant Care program, assisted in helping to resolve the impasse. She knew people on both sides and, following my lead, established a consensus.

Two years later, a well-regarded report was released. I think the health department learned they didn't need to be so rigid in their procedures, and Black leaders realized the County's expertise was beneficial. When all was done, everyone had great respect for each other and had become friends. I couldn't have been more pleased.

The final draft of the *Status of African/African Ancestry Heath: Santa Clara County* was released in 2015. Many of the findings were not surprising but alarming, nevertheless.

Key informant interviews and community conversations conducted for the assessment revealed a mistrust of the healthcare system due to a lack of cultural knowledge about the African/African Ancestry community. This resulted in a lack of participation in the healthcare system and contributed to health disparities. These findings led to perhaps the most important recommendations from the health assessment: Establish an Afro-centric health clinic that provides both physical and mental health services with an Afro-centric perspective to address client needs in a holistic way.

It was Wilson's belief that what his community needed was their own health clinic because current public health facilities were not meeting their needs, to put it mildly. "You have people who would see doctors who didn't want to touch them," he said.

With these findings in mind, the East Oakland-based Roots Community Health Center was approached about providing primary care and services in Santa Clara County. Founded in 2008, Roots was a community health center serving area residents who needed it most. It had expanded significantly and also was operating a standalone pediatrics clinic and a second clinic in Union City.

Everyone was interested in learning more.

I'll never forget our field trip to Oakland. We brought all the major players along: Drs. Smith and Cody, Wilson, Swilley, Burrell, members of the hospital executive team, and myself. Led by Roots' Chief Executive Officer Dr. Noha Aboelata and Chief Operating Officer Aquil Naji, we learned of its mission and programs. We were blown away by what we saw.

By the end of the day, we knew that the founders of Roots had created a prototype that would work for our African American community. Everyone was very excited. In politics, where it can take forever to get something done, we were jubilant in knowing this would be a reality.

At an August 2016 board meeting, Dr. Smith asked for approval of $350,000 to cover initial clinic construction, planning, and infrastructure costs for Roots Community Health Center, Santa Clara County. It was unanimously approved.

In November 2016, other expenditures were approved for start-up costs, as well as for personnel and operations. At the time of the opening, the clinic had five full-time employees, including a physician and several additional health workers. It was expected to provide primary care for more than 1,300 African American county residents who had significant health issues and were high utilizers of medical services.

The Ribbon Cutting was on May 4, 2017. What a grand day it was. Wilson, Swilley, Aboelata, Naji, Board President Cortese, and I were there, along with the newly named Roots South Bay Manager Burrell.

In my remarks, I stated how the Roots Community Health Clinic was exactly what our county needed and how, when we work together, we move so effectively and efficiently. "The opening of this clinic is a perfect example of the great things that can happen when community-driven organizations work together with public agencies to address a common challenge."

Soon thereafter, there was an article in *San Jose Inside* about the Roots Clinic's opening. In it, Burrell called the clinic a labor of love, adding, "Black patients want to go to a place where they feel at home, where they feel welcome, and people understand them and their culture. They're not getting that in San Jose or in the county overall. When you come to Roots, I want you to feel like you've just come home," she said.[103]

Like all health clinics should be.

Since opening in Santa Clara County, Roots Community Health Clinic has served more than 5,000 residents with medical and or navigation services. When the pandemic hit, Roots was positioned to provide testing and vaccinations for all residents but particularly to the African/African Ancestry community who face historical mistrust of healthcare delivery systems. In fact, the Roots Clinic was the first community clinic to provide free COVID testing to the community by partnering with Sean Penn's Community Organized Relief Effort, or CORE, and the County of Santa Clara. Roots eventually provided vaccines and boosters to thousands of county residents and continue to do so.

Because healthcare is an issue mostly addressed at the county level, I continue to encourage LGBTQ+ people to consider running for this post in their counties. You can literally help save lives.

Opening of the Gender Health Clinic

When the survey for the 2013 LGBTQ+ health assessment was being designed, I wanted to be sure that the transgender, non-binary, and gender-expansive community was included. Anecdotal evidence existed that medical services were inadequate, but I knew more quantitative data was needed to justify asking the Board for funds for a specialized clinic.

----

103   Tori Truscheit. "County Study Identifies Health Disparities, Leads to Funding for African American-Focused Clinic." *San Jose Inside*. May 3, 2017.

The findings on the *Status of LGBTQ+ Health* were alarming. Transgender respondents reported higher levels of discrimination than non-transgender respondents. Nearly one in five (18 percent) reported that they were refused needed care in the past five years, and nearly one in 10 (nine percent) reported that healthcare professionals were physically rough or abusive, compared to non-transgender respondents.

According to the responses, 38 percent of transgender individuals reported a need for medical care but were not able to access it; 82 percent agreed with the statement, "Not enough health professionals are adequately trained to care for people who are LGBTQ+."

Many transgender residents reported having to drive to San Francisco, Santa Cruz, or Fremont in order to access medical providers. They also noted fear of harassment from local medical providers and a desire for medical providers who are knowledgeable about transgender health needs.

Furthermore, County healthcare providers reported a lack of knowledge (41 percent) and experience (58 percent) in addressing the health concerns of transgender and gender nonconforming patients.

Although several constituents shared their personal stories with me over the years, these findings illustrated the daunting problems this community was facing. Clearly, there was a significant and rapidly growing need for transgender and gender-expansive healthcare services. Exactly how to achieve this was outside my expertise. I was happy to foster communication between the Office of LGBTQ+ Affairs and the staff from the Santa Clara County Medical Center to devise a plan.

They brought the proposal for a creation of a transgender/ gender-expansive family clinic to the Board in March 2018. It would be the first transgender primary care facility of its kind in the county. The staff would comprise of a physician, psychiatrist, psychologist, nurse practitioner, medical social worker, health education specialist, clinical nurse, and licensed vocational nurse. Anticipated expenditures would be offset by an increase in revenues.

In my remarks, I stated how proud I was of the action we were taking. I mentioned that I was aware of the lack of health resources for transgender people in the county, forcing people to travel elsewhere. This was people's number one complaint and biggest frustration. I said opening a Gender Health Clinic shows that the County continues to take a leadership role when it comes to health issues, especially for marginalized segments of our population, like the transgender/gender-expansive community.

My motion to approve the clinic was passed unanimously.

The need for the clinic has been well substantiated. In fiscal year 2021/22, the number of patients remained around 600, and the total number of visits was steady at about 1800.

Dr. Chyten-Brennan, a transgender man, was hired as the founding medical director in 2019. We have continued to keep in touch as various issues have arisen that I was able to provide guidance on.

Given the physical and verbal harassment that transgender people are experiencing throughout the country, along with laws penalizing parents whose children receive transition care, I am even more proud of Santa Clara County for recognizing the unique medical needs of its transgender, non-binary, and gender-expansive community residents. I would urge policy-makers who have responsibilities over medical care to explore opening up such clinics. They are badly needed everywhere.

"Who Made You the Toy Police?" Fighting the Fast-Food Industry Over Kids' Happy Meals

My most far-reaching policy dealing with children's health was the 2010 passage of the so-called toy ban or restricting restaurants from offering toys or other incentive items in conjunction with food marketed to children that fail to meet specific nutritional criteria. For my efforts, the California Restaurant Association labeled me "the toy police."

I began working on childhood obesity issues shortly after being sworn into office at the end of 2006. Partially from my work trying to get sodas and junk food out of city vending machines, I was aware of the increasing rates of childhood obesity and the severe health issues children could face, perhaps for their entire lives. I couldn't stand by and do nothing.

I started my crusade during my first year at the County. In partnership with FIRST 5 Santa Clara County, I invited local elected officials to join me for an October 2007 meeting to brainstorm ways to prevent obesity in children and adults. We discussed some promising strategies to prevent obesity in children from birth to five years of age. These included increased breastfeeding, improved feeding and eating practices for young children, reduced television watching, and the elimination of the marketing of unhealthy foods to children.

A month later, I wrote an editorial in the *Mercury News* about the need for aggressive action to reduce childhood obesity, acknowledging the difficulties parents face when cartoon characters wave at children from cereal boxes filled with sugar and fat, convenience stores offer few or no healthy eating options, and low-income areas are crowded with fast-food restaurants.

"One thing is clear," I wrote. "Solving a problem as massive in scope as childhood obesity can't be accomplished in small, timid steps. Government, the private sector, and schools must do more if a substantial change is to occur.

I concluded by putting out a call to arms to elected leaders at all levels to add healthy eating and exercise to their agendas in order to "save a whole generation from a fate of ill health." [104]

I was able to help get some early wins, particularly with vending machines and assisting Supervisor Liz Kniss with a

----

104   Ken Yeager. "Aggressive Action Needed to Reduce Childhood Obesity." *San Jose Mercury News*. November 21, 2007.

menu calorie-labeling ordinance. But the big culprit in the battle was the so-called Happy Meals.

It was well known that the fast-food restaurant industry was shameless in its marketing to children, having spent $520 million in 2006, including $360 million on kids' meal toys and having sold 1.2 billion meals with toys to children. Studies showed that 10 out of 12 meals that came with toys exceeded the recommended caloric limits for children. Further research showed that parents frequently made purchases based on requests made by their children.

It was the public interest group Public Health Law & Policy (PHLP) that came up with the idea of restricting the giveaway of toys in kids' meals that did not meet certain nutritional standards. With their knowledge of the legal issues connected to such a policy, they approached our County Counsel's Office to see if it was something our legal department would support. It was a no-brainer for them. They were all in.

As can be the case, "think tank" researchers may come up with ground breaking policies that are backed by compelling research and a call for action, but often one important element is missing: an elected person who will not only champion it but can get his or her governing board to adopt it.

I still remember when people from PHLP and the County Counsel's Office came into my office with binders of evidence proving the fast-food industry was intentionally marketing to kids. Of course, the industry denied it (just as tobacco companies deny marketing e-cigarettes to teenagers), but our lawyers felt we had a good case if we were sued.

After about an hour of listening to all the facts, I was asked if, as a county supervisor, I was willing to be the face of a campaign to ban the toys. They knew of my established record on health issues and mentioned my January 2010 State of the County address in which I had called for bold ideas to deal with childhood obesity. I readily agreed.

From there, we brought in other partners, namely the Public

Health Department. They were very useful in supplying data about the health of the county's children and the consequences of obesity. Also included were community-based organizations like FIRST 5. They proved invaluable when it came to recruiting experts to attend public hearings.

The ordinance imposed specific restrictions. Restaurants could not use toys as rewards for buying foods that have excessive calories, excessive sodium, excessive fat, or excessive sugar.

Right on the heels of the introduction of the ordinance in April 2010, the California Restaurant Association commissioned a poll of Santa Clara County residents concerning their perceptions related to local government involvement in regulating the availability of toys that were included in restaurant meal promotions. In a letter addressed to me, they reported the following:

Eighty percent of residents said the issue was not important enough for lawmakers to be involved in; 87 percent did not believe that local lawmakers were better informed than ordinary citizens about what kind of food sold in restaurants is healthy and nutritious; 73 percent believed they should have the option of buying a meal at a restaurant that includes a toy that is part of a meal promotion, and lawmakers should not be allowed to take that option away.

The poll results were included in a full-page ad in the *Mercury News* on April 25, the Sunday before the Board vote. There were three games to play, each made to look like a kid's word game. One was matching percentages to poll questions, a second was a word search with the answer being "Listen to Constituents," and the third was a word scramble looking for "Are they serious?

The bold, enlarged headline above the three games was "HEY MOM AND DAD, GUESS WHAT?" Then: "The Santa Clara County Board of Supervisors wants to make it illegal to offer toys in kids' meals. Supervisor Ken Yeager introduced a

proposal to ban toys in restaurants. But the v
Santa Clara County residents think the propo:
time and is not the proper role of governme:
instructed people to "tell their supervisors
games with our tax dollars" and listed the nam...
bers of the five supervisors. I'm not sure the "game playing
gimmick worked. A reader turning the pages of the *Mercury
News* probably didn't even pause to figure out what the ad was
for. In any event, we received a fair amount of calls the next
day, but I think many were from people connected with the
restaurant industry.

The California Restaurant Association wasn't done yet. In another *Mercury News* ad the morning of the vote, there was
a photo of a young girl in a pink sweater and skirt, with her
hands behind her back, holding a small toy dog. If you looked
hard enough, you could spot a handcuff on her left wrist. The
text next to her in red read: "TOUGH ON CRIME?" Then, below
in black ink was: "The Santa Clara County Board of Supervisors wants to make it illegal to offer toys in kids' meals." Then
in bold type: WHO MADE POLITICIANS THE TOY POLICE? It
then listed our names and numbers. There was a packed crowd
of about 300 people at the Board meeting. A fair number of
supporters representing public health agencies and children
advocates were in attendance, but the majority of people were
opponents, including lobbyists from the restaurant industries,
several fast-food franchise owners, and many fast-food workers. Their arguments were several: toys don't cause obesity;
healthy options were already being offered; politicians should
focus instead on education; school lunches are just as bad; the
government had better things to do.

In my remarks, I repeated what other proponents and I
had said before: that restaurants encourage children to choose
specific menu items by linking them with free toys, and research shows that parents frequently make purchases based
on requests made by children. "This ordinance levels the playing field," I said. "It helps parents make the choices they want

₋heir children without toys and other freebies luring them ₋ward food that fails to meet basic nutritional standards."

The ordinance barely passed by a 3-2 vote. Supervisor Don Gage, the only Republican on the Board, but a centrist at that, said he would rather see County funding go toward teaching parents how to buy and prepare more healthy food. Supervisor George Shirakawa, who represented the most ethnically diverse parts of San Jose, felt the ban would hurt low-income kids the most by taking away the toys. Supervisor Dave Cortese was a reluctant "yes," trying to see if a compromise could be reached. He amended the motion to add a 90-day grace period for the restaurant industry to come up with alternatives that would meet the Board's standards, which they never did. The other "yes" vote came from Supervisor Kniss, who had been working on children's health issues alongside me.

Reaction

There was widespread media coverage of our vote. Articles appeared in the *Washington Post, Chicago Tribune, Los Angeles Times,* and even the *Economist* and *Financial Times*, to name a few. Stories aired on all the Bay Area channels, as well as Fox News, NPR, Nightline, and The View.

As an aside, *The New York Times* ran several stories about the ban, always including quotes from me. I often joke that everyone's name will someday, somehow, for unknown reasons, end up in *The New York Times*. The first instance for me was in a story related to a censure vote for San Jose Mayor Ron Gonzales, but they spelled my name wrong, so I don't think that counted. The two stories on the toy ban got the spelling right.

It was the first—and last time—I appeared on CNN, along with a spokesperson from the California Restaurant Association. The interview increased the number of negative emails and calls the office received. A YouTube posting also solicited a number of responses. One said, "I want to know when the pitchforks and torches and rope are going to come out. We need to run these Frankenstein political monsters the hell out of town."

Yikes! *Pitchforks!*

My office tried to keep track of policies enacted by other jurisdictions. San Francisco passed a similar ordinance shortly thereafter, as did several other cities. Brazil fined McDonald's $1.6 million for targeting children with advertising and Happy Meal toys. Chili's eliminated the practice of including free toys in their packages. KFC stopped offering toys with their meals.

The County's Environmental Health Department was needed as a partner. They were the ones responsible for the enforcement of the ordinance. As it turned out, rather than contesting the ordinance or trying to abide by nutritional standards, all the restaurants involved stopped handing out the merchandise just to be safe.

It is hard to know how much of a difference our first-in-the-nation ordinance changed the whole fast-food industry, but we were the snowball that created the avalanche.

It is heartening that there has been an industry shift away from associating toys with children's meals. While some fast-food chains still sell toys, they are no longer part of their advertising campaigns. Also noteworthy is that kids' meals now conform to the County standard in handing out toys: For example, McDonald's Happy Meals hit the scales with 10 calories to spare, weighing in at 475 calories.

At the end of the day, I hope our work gives parents and kids a fighting chance against those who seek profit over the health of our children.

The Fight Against Big Tobacco

Although the gift of health was something I wanted others to have, I was slow in bestowing it upon myself.

A healthier lifestyle came to me a bit later in my life, around my mid-30s. I was never athletic in junior or senior high school. I was lousy at baseball, basketball, football, swimming, tennis, you name it. For popularity's sake, I went the student government and journalism route instead.

I was probably around 16 when I started smoking, lured, I'm sure, by ads of the Marlboro Man looking rugged and masculine. As it is with a lot of smokers, it began with a cigarette now and then, then slowly increased as the years went by. I really amped it up when I was in graduate school. By the time I was 36, I was a walking smokestack, smoking several packs of True cigarettes a day.

My only physical activity was playing racquetball. My father and I had taken it up some years earlier when I'd come home for vacation, and I continued to play it while at Stanford with a friend. Even though I felt I was more skilled than him, I was finding myself more winded. To compensate, rather than quitting smoking, I decided to see if I liked running. I'll never forget running the quarter-mile track on campus and nearly collapsing from being out of breath. It was then that I decided to stop smoking.

I began to wean myself off cigarettes as I depleted my last couple of packs. I loaded up with Nicorette gum, Nicorette patches, and sugar-free gum as I counted down my last smokes. Five, four, three, two, one, zero. I haven't had so much as a puff since 1989.

To say quitting smoking changed—if not saved—my life might be a bit of an exaggeration, but it comes close. Determined to get my lungs healthier, I made a commitment to start running in earnest. The next time I went to the track, I ran around it twice. Then three times, then four, a mile. Then two miles, then three—during my first 5K race I thought I'd never make it to the finish line. Then my first 10K, then my first half marathon, followed by my first marathon at the age of 39 in San Francisco in 1992, where the last six miles almost killed me. I swore I never would do another, but six months later I ran the

Los Angeles marathon. I ended up running a total of 33.

Because I never had an image of myself as being athletic, I was always in awe that I was even participating in races, never caring that I finished them in the middle of the pack. Qualifying for Boston eluded me by 10 minutes. Then I started doing triathlons and half-Ironmans. After those came the Spartan and Tough Mudder races with my friend Forrest Linebarger—crawling through mud, climbing ropes, scaling walls, carrying buckets of sand, jumping over a fire—all pure joy. In 2018, wanting to get better at cycling, I signed up for the 545-mile, seven-day AIDS Lifecycle bike ride from San Francisco to Los Angeles. Once unthinkable for me to complete, I crossed the finish line with energy to spare, having raised $20,000 for AIDS research and services along the way.

I say all this because being healthy and active has improved my life in ways I can't even measure. I feel better, sleep better, and who knows, maybe I'll even live longer. If, as a public official, I gave this gift of health to others—young and old—in whatever way it is manifested, then I would feel I had accomplished what I set out to do.

Given my personal experience with smoking, perhaps it wasn't surprising that one of the first health issues I worked on dealt with tobacco. As has been well documented, smoking is the single largest preventable cause of death. Smoking kills more people than alcohol, AIDS, car crashes, illegal drugs, murders, and suicides combined.

The best way to prevent a lifetime of smoking and the chronic conditions that come along with it is to never start in the first place. Unfortunately, the vast majority of smokers pick up the habit when they are teens and young adults. This is alarming since there is mounting research that adolescent brains are uniquely susceptible to the effects of nicotine and nicotine addiction. Since brain development continues into a person's early 20s, teens and young adults are particularly vulnerable to harm.

Because it is so hard to quit as you get older, it is best to try to prevent teenagers and young adults from smoking at all. This, along with limiting unwanted second-hand smoke, became my main policy focus.

Collaborating with some great people in the Public Health Department and the County Counsel's office in 2010, I was able to get the unanimous approval of a package of new tobacco laws that are among the most comprehensive in the nation.

Knowing that a state survey showed that 17 percent of county retailers still illegally sold tobacco to youths under 18, County staff and I decided that the first ordinance needed to focus on reducing youth access to tobacco.

A new tool that some jurisdictions had begun to use was requiring stores that sold tobacco to obtain a tobacco retail license. This is separate from a retail permit, which carries no enforcement or penalty with it. A tobacco retail license gave the County leverage over stores that sold to anyone underage by having the ability to revoke it. The strategy behind this is that stores would do better at self-monitoring, given that tobacco sales made up a large part of their profits, which they would risk losing.

There were several other measures relating to the selling of tobacco, such as barring underage employees from selling tobacco, limiting window advertisements to 15 percent of window space so that authorities can properly monitor tobacco transactions, and banning tobacco sales in pharmacies within 1,000 feet of a school, or within 500 feet of another tobacco retailer.

Two other ordinances dealt with secondhand smoke. For these ordinances, Dr. Suzaynn Schick, an expert on secondhand smoke from the University of California, San Francisco, was asked to come to a Board meeting to speak in support. According to her research, even short exposures to low levels of secondhand smoke have cardiovascular effects that can increase the risk of heart attacks. Moreover, smoke can easily seep through walls and air ducts of multi-unit residences, and it does not necessarily dissipate quickly in outdoor areas. Smoke-free policies are the best way to protect a resident's health from someone else's smoke.

The ordinance also banned smoking in all county parks and at the county fairgrounds, as well as smoking in outdoor service areas, including ticket lines and outside seating areas of restaurants or bars, and made hotels and motels entirely smoke-free.

Perhaps the most controversial part of the ordinance was prohibiting smoking in all living units and common areas of apartments, condominiums, and townhouses. One thing I always tried to do with any ordinance I introduced was to have meetings with people or organizations affected by them to hear their concerns.

My first meeting was with the Tri-County Apartment Owners Association. I remember walking into a large conference room packed mainly with middle-aged white men. My initial reaction was that this was not going to go well. After talking about the effects of second-hand smoke and how it seeps through ventilators and windows, I was asked if the apartment managers were the ones needing to enforce the ordinance.

I responded by saying that the way it would work is that the County would pay for signs saying that smoking was not allowed in the apartment units or common areas, only in designated smoking areas. This alone would have a major impact. I mentioned how in parks with "no smoking" signs and even with no police around, the vast majority of people abide by the law. If someone *does* smoke in their unit or common area, someone could report them to the County Public health office or the apartment manager.

The next day I got a call from the CEO of the association. He said the group had voted to support the ordinance once they understood more about enforcement. He also explained how banning smoking would make it much easier to clean apartments without the residue on the walls, as well as reduce fires from unattended cigarettes. I was floored. Those arguments had never crossed my mind. As the expression goes, "Where you stand depends on where you sit."

The only other group I heard from were residents in a condominium complex near Stanford University. It was on unincorporated land and thereby affected by the ordinance. Several people called me and were vehemently opposed. This concerned me, so I told them I'd be happy to meet with them. They said that first they needed to bring up the matter at the next homeowners' meeting.

It was at that meeting that the membership voted overwhelmingly in favor of the ordinance. Non-smokers were, by far, in the majority and didn't like second-hand smoke. I was told I no longer needed to attend.

As mentioned earlier, these cutting-edge ordinances only covered the unincorporated areas of the county. However, our Public Health Department received a Communities Putting Prevention to Work grant under the American Recovery and Reinvestment Act. That grant allowed the County to do more education and advocate for similar, comprehensive tobacco control policies with 11 of the 15 cities in the county. Collectively, the policies enacted across the cities had the potential to impact 1,530,000 residents.

All of this work made Santa Clara County a national leader when it came to anti-tobacco and anti-smoking policies. In 2011, the County was recognized for its efforts by the American Lung Association in California, which raised the County's tobacco control report card grade from an F to an A. I could not have been more proud.

The County continued to work on anti-tobacco policies throughout my tenure on the Board. In 2013 we added e-cigarettes to existing tobacco and secondhand smoke ordinances. And in 2015, we raised the purchasing age to 21 for tobacco and electronic smoking products.

I would like to believe that all this work is the main reason why residents of San Jose have the second-lowest smoking rates in the nation. According to the Centers for Disease Control and Prevention, only the residents of Seattle smoke less.

I was honored to receive the Cities Champion Award in 2018 by the Santa Clara County Cities Association for my leadership and work on the Healthy Cities Program and "for being an outstanding partner to cities through the Cities Association." I was the first County supervisor in their long history ever to be given that award. Mazel tov.

Getting to Zero[105]

It was at the 2011 United Nations World AIDS Day that the international Getting to Zero (GTZ) program was launched with the goal of achieving zero HIV-related deaths, zero new HIV infections, and zero stigma.

In 2015, I worked with the Public Health Director, Dr. Cody, and community stakeholders to explore how to start such a program in Santa Clara County. Once we knew how to create a GTZ program that suited our needs, I asked the Board of Supervisors in 2016 for funding and received approval for a $6 million budget spread over four years to 2020.[106]

PrEP, or pre-exposure prophylaxis, is an HIV prevention tool based on taking a daily medication designed to prevent HIV RNA from replicating itself in the body. PEP, or post-exposure prophylaxis, is a month-long course of antiretroviral medication that can prevent a patient from becoming infected with HIV if it is taken soon after exposure.

I was aware that there was great skepticism in the medical

----

105   Note. Some portions were included in "Battle Against AIDS. A Look Back at the First Decades of the Santa Clara County Experience." Ken Yeager. Booklet is Appendix D.

106   Ken Yeager. "New HIV-AIDS Strategy is Needed for the County." _San Jose Mercury News_. December 17, 2015.

field about PrEP. There was also a lack of information and misunderstanding about insurance coverage. Moreover, according to a health assessment conducted by the Public Health Department for the LGBTQ+ community, many gay people do not talk openly about their sexuality with their primary doctors. These are all significant barriers that have had to be overcome since then.

This is why I was glad when the Santa Clara County STD/HIV program administrators began sending expert health education specialists to clinical sites to teach medical personnel about prescription barriers to PrEP and PEP and to offer personalized resources. As a result of these efforts, in 2018, 11 new provider sites posted their availability to offer PrEP/PEP on the website www.pleaseprepme.org. I am thankful for how much ground has been covered.

In 2017, the CDC announced that individuals with undetectable viral loads have essentially no risk of sexually transmitting HIV. This is a significant breakthrough that helps to reduce transmission, a pillar of Getting to Zero. This only applies to people who take antiretroviral therapy daily as prescribed and achieve and maintain an undetectable viral load.

A good opportunity to test for HIV is when a person gets an STD test. If tested positive for an STD, it might be a sign of risky sexual behavior and, thus, possible HIV infection. That is why in 2016, I advocated for the creation of a full-time STD/HIV controller to elevate the County's STD/HIV prevention work through a dedicated, physician-level position. Dr. Sarah Lewis Rudman filled this position. In 2017, I worked with the Public Health Department to double the hours at the STD clinic and implement the first-ever mobile STD testing site during Silicon Valley Pride.

Also, in 2017, the Board allocated County general fund dollars for an additional Communicable Disease Investigator who works to improve the speed and thoroughness of HIV and STD investigations due to the increase in STD cases. A new nurse manager was also hired to oversee the STD/HIV Client Services Team.

In Getting to Zero's first year, training was provided to health care providers and youth peer educators oriented around reducing HIV/AIDS stigma to zero. Providers and educators are trained on how to have stigma-free examinations and encounters with patients and the public. GTZ funds also support a health education specialist responsible for broadening the knowledge about public health in county schools with an emphasis on reducing HIV/AIDS stigma.

Of the three goals of Getting to Zero, reducing stigma is the hardest to quantify and requires the most sustained effort and funding. Through collaboration with the County's Office of LGBTQ+ Affairs, the GTZ initiative supported nine mini-grantees to conduct unique projects that reduced HIV-related stigma. The Office works on a wide variety of issues related to the LGBTQ+ community, with GTZ being just one of its initiatives.

Finally, at my urging, the County sponsored two extensive marketing campaigns geared to inform young Hispanic/Latino men who have sex with men about the option of PrEP. According to a Public Health Department October 2018 memo, the first campaign—"Get Liberated"—resulted in more than 2.4 million media impressions; the second—"PrEP is for..."—received more than 13 million. A third PrEP Awareness campaign was specific to African-American residents.

By the end of 2018, the County was seeing increases of more than 50 percent in PrEP prescriptions compared to the baseline before the County began Getting to Zero. The initiative set a new precedent for increased STD clinic hours and staff, a greater number of healthcare workers trained on PrEP/PEP, and other public health advancements.

Looking back 30 years, I am proud to have proposed the creation of the Santa Clara County AIDS Task Force in 1986 and to serve as its first chair. This was very early in the epidemic, with less than 100 people having died from AIDS in the county. At the time, when a person was tested for the virus, it took weeks to get results. We had no thoughts then of getting to zero deaths, zero new infections, or zero stigma. We were just trying to get care for the sick and dying, obtain funding for research, and gain recognition from an often indifferent, if not genuinely hostile, society that this was a significant public health crisis. From 1984 when the first AIDS deaths were reported in the county, to the end of 2021, there have been a total of 2,732 deaths from AIDS. What a tragic loss.

We have come so far since those early dark days. But much work still needs to be done. I am confident that the goals of Getting to Zero are within our grasp, and I remain committed to doing everything I can to ensure that we reach them. I've been fortunate to have had a public career spanning 40 years to work on an epidemic that has taken the lives of so many people in my community. My heart is full of both sadness and hope.[107]

Six Million Meals a Year That Meet Nutritional Standards

I have always been fortunate to have excellent staff. The four staff members I had as a councilmember came with me to the County. To learn more about the County operations, they met with the various department heads and took tours of facilities. One such exploration was to the County's Juvenile Hall.

While they were taking a tour and being told by officers how the kids are taught about nutrition, the lunch cart came by. It was loaded with nachos, chips, brownies, and soft drinks. My staffers, John Mills, Megan Doyle, Tony Filice, and Laura Jones, were somewhat horrified. They came back to the office and told me how kids were taught to eat healthily but only had unhealthy foods to eat.

---

107   Ken Yeager. "Supervisor Reflects on the Long Fight Against AIDS." *San Jose Mercury News*. November 30, 2018.

That was when the idea of establishing nutritional standards started. I knew I wouldn't be able to lower the high obesity rates of adults and children in the county overnight, but I knew change happens one meal at a time.

Establishing nutritional standards turned out to be an enormous undertaking. At the time, the County government, with more than 30 departments and agencies, was the second largest employer in the county with a workforce of 15,000 (it is now first, with over 24,000 employees). The County serves tens of thousands of meals a week to custodial populations, as well as to thousands of community residents that participate in its programs, meetings, and events each year. In addition, meals and snacks are served to both employees and the public on County owned and/or leased properties at 12 cafeterias and cafes, 200 vending machines, and nine County-leased properties.

As I was preparing my referral to the Board to create nutritional standards, the U.S. Department of Health and Human Services (HHS) awarded $31 million to 10 communities and one state. Santa Clara County was one of the recipients. The $3.6 million grant allowed the County to expand efforts to reduce obesity, increase physical activity, and improve nutrition.

Early on, we got an estimate of how many meals the various departments served or contracted out. All totaled annually, the Department of Corrections served four million meals, the Department of Probation 500,000 meals, the Social Services Agency's Senior Nutrition Program 1.2 million meals, and the Santa Clara Valley Medical Center 300,000 patient meals, in addition to 450,000 meals to patrons in their cafeteria and cafés. The figure was eye-popping: over six million meals a year. I'm sure it is even higher today.

What guided me throughout this endeavor was the knowledge that offering healthy options with maximum nutritional value was one of the most direct ways the County could promote the prevention of chronic diseases for employees, visitors, and the custodial populations. It was also my hope that people would see that food lower in salt, sugar, and fats was still delicious, and maybe even begin to eat better at home.

After I got approval from the Board to study the issue, a Nutrition Standards Committee was formed. Because any department that would be affected had to be involved, the committee consisted of the Office of County Executive, County Counsel, Public Health Department, Facilities and Fleet Department, Department of Corrections, Probation Department, Procurement, Health and Hospital System, and Social Services Agency.

Trying to reach an agreement on the standards was an arduous task. It was important for stakeholders to know that there was no preconceived notion of what the nutritional standards would be or even if there was a one-size-fits-all model that could be applied to all departments. The hope was for staff to study the issue and come back with recommendations. I was fortunate that my staff person who had a master's in public health, Laura Jones, represented me at the meetings and was an excellent facilitator.

Some departments, such as the jails, had their own kitchens and could more easily make changes. Departments like Social Services contracted out for food and beverages, so those contracts had to be amended. Vending machine companies were sometimes limited in the options they had or were concerned they wouldn't generate enough income to keep the machines profitable.

Although there was some resistance to making the changes, after 10 months of meetings, the consensus was reached, and my proposal went to the Board in February 2012.

Implementation dates varied, but some departments had to be ready by July 1. Perhaps sensing some pushback, Dr. Smith issued a memo in June to all agency and department heads stating that the "County is committed to supporting healthy living by ensuring that food and drink offered, purchased, or served at County facilities and provided by County departments are of maximum nutritional value." At the end of the memo, he left no doubt of the role of department heads, which was "ensuring the new standards are implemented correctly within your department."

One of the most important regulations dealt with sodas, which was very straightforward: No sugar-sweetened beverages would be served or purchased by the County. In place of soda, tap water, seltzer water, coffee, and/or unsweetened tea should be served. If there was no tap water available, then bottled water could be used.

Food standards were a bit more nuanced for obvious reasons. The guidelines required healthier food options be provided that incorporated more fruits, vegetables, whole grains, and low-fat and low-calorie foods. Processed foods were to be minimally used, without added sugar and less sodium; foods were to be prepared using healthy cooking techniques; foods were to be provided that contained no trans fats; smaller portion sizes were to be offered; vegetarian options were to be available.

I was glad that the guidelines also applied to all County contracts where a contractor's scope of work involved the purchase of food or beverages with County funds.

I wanted these nutritional standards to be adopted by as many governmental, educational, and social services agencies as possible. My involvement with FIRST 5 proved to be another reminder of the value of networking with other people and groups: Your reach is far greater when others get involved.

FIRST 5 California was created in 1998 by a voter-approved initiative spearheaded mainly by television actor and director Rob Reiner to tax tobacco products to pay for early childhood development programs. Each county established its own FIRST 5 commission and hired its own executive director. Jolene Smith was the CEO for Santa Clara County when I was elected to the Board of Supervisors. She was known for leading one of the most successful and innovative FIRST 5 agencies in the state.

The commission was comprised of nine members, one of whom was a member of the Board of Supervisors. This was a coveted spot. Because the incoming Board president made the yearly appointments to various commissions, they would normally appoint themselves to FIRST 5. This is exactly what I did in 2010. The problem was that I enjoyed serving on it so much that I didn't want to leave after a year. I had a good working relationship with my four Board colleagues, so I asked each succeeding Board president if I could remain the Board's appointee. To my delight, they all said yes. This is how I was able to stay on for an unprecedented nine years and to work with Jolene Smith and staff on a wide range of programs for children zero to five, from family resources centers to screening for developmental delays to showcasing First 5's popular mascot Potter the Otter, who is reported to love water.

As a commissioner, I knew that FIRST 5 provided funding to 300 in-home childcare programs, 135 after-school sites, schools with which they partnered, and 27 family resource centers. I spoke to Smith about having them all adhere to the nutritional guidelines when purchasing food or beverages with FIRST 5 dollars, and she readily agreed. I knew it would help to educate childcare providers about nutrition that they otherwise would not have.

Later on, Smith relayed to me that parent and teacher surveys showed there was a 90 percent reduction in the consumption of sugary drinks at many of these sites. She believes that it would be hard to find a sugary juice box in a child's lunch box or served in a cafeteria.

San Jose is fortunate to have a well-loved Children's Discovery Museum, which thousands of kids and families visit each year. One year they were holding an event sponsored by the County called Rethink Your Drink, a catchy phrase meaning to rethink drinking sodas and sugary beverages and choose water instead. Afterward, the museum's dynamic executive director, Marilee Jennings, invited me to see their food court.

She was very proud that the design of the long lunch tables incorporated fruits and vegetables. What caught my eye, however, was the food for sale on the counter. There was a big heated container with two huge pizzas and a large display of chips. This was followed by soft drinks. Yes, there were some healthy options, but they were barely visible.

When I pointed this out, Jennings was horrified. As we talked, she admitted that she just hadn't taken notice of the food choices available. She immediately began to change the items for sale. The museum revamped its food court to only serve healthy food to the thousands of kids and families who visit. She worked with FIRST 5 to create a centerpiece exhibit around Otter the Potter's healthy drinking and healthy eating, which traveled throughout the state to all other children's museums.

It was gratifying that our efforts dovetailed with First Lady Michelle Obama's challenge to elected officials across the country to join her Let's Move! campaign to solve the problem of childhood obesity within a generation. The main pillar of her campaign encouraged jurisdictions to make healthy foods more accessible. One of the suggested strategies for expanding healthy food in communities is passing food policies that require food and beverages purchased with government funds to meet certain nutritional standards. We're on it, Michelle!

The First Lady must have heard our cheer because she honored the County and FIRST 5 by recognizing our efforts. We were invited to the White House for an awards ceremony, and I, along with several partners, had our photo taken with Mrs. Obama. I displayed it proudly and prominently in my office.

I also received a nice letter from Mrs. Obama, congratulating us for being designated a 5 Gold Medal Achiever as part of Let's Move! Cities, Towns, and Counties. She wanted me to know how proud she was of all my work to make my community a healthier place.

She ended by thanking me for all I've done and will continue to do to make health a priority. She wished me all the best and had high hopes for my continued success.

The photo of us and her letter is something I will always cherish.

I was pleased when, in 2017, the Robert Wood Johnson Foundation and the University of Wisconsin named Santa Clara County the third healthiest county in California, only behind Marin and San Mateo. Our success has been based both on the County's ability to work closely with other government bodies and agencies and our willingness to serve as a trailblazer and model for new policies and regulations.[108]

I'll Take My Water To Go

As much as I tried to limit the number of sugary sodas available to kids, I couldn't expect them to drink water if it wasn't available. Having bottled water for sale everywhere wasn't going to happen. Plus, I wouldn't have wanted that anyway, given how bad disposable plastic bottles are for the environment. Water fountains were sometimes an option, particularly at schools or parks, but they were often too dingy for anyone to actually use them.

So, what to do? I remember when I saw my first water hydration station at the San Francisco International Airport. I realized their potential right away, especially at airports where you can't bring fluids past security. As I was filling up my water bottle, I was already visioning these hydration stations installed all over town.

One of the reasons I was excited about being a commissioner on FIRST 5 in 2010 was the possibility of creating greater synergy with the County Public Health Department. Combining dollars and resources on shared objectives could double the results. Both organizations had an emphasis on reducing childhood obesity, so attractive filling stations that provided

----

108   Ken Yeager. "Collaboration Makes Santa Clara County one of the Healthiest." *San Jose Mercury News.* January 10, 2017.

easy access to water would help reinforce efforts to encourage children to make water their beverage of choice over sugar ones.

Installing more stations would also assist schools to be in compliance with the Healthy, Hunger-Free Kids Acts (SB1413), which required access to drinking water during school meal-times in food service areas.

I was glad to learn about concurrent efforts underway by FIRST 5 and the Santa Clara Valley Water District to install hydration stations. I encouraged Public Health staff to find a way to partner with them, which they were happy to do.

"Water to Go" was created from that partnership. The County Public Health Department allocated $125,000 to install 25 stations in community locations such as parks and libraries, FIRST 5 put in $125,000 to install five stations in schools and childcare centers, and the Water District was in for $254,000 for 50 stations in partnership with FIRST 5 and school districts. We had a big press conference with all three partners announcing the program.

By the end of three years, we had 100 stations blanketing the county at schools, parks, community centers, and other public spaces where families gathered. I felt a sense of accomplishment when I was able to get several installed at the San Jose/Mineta International Airport.

Not satisfied with that goal, I introduced a County ordinance requiring an equal ratio of water filling stations to drinking fountains in new and renovated buildings. I also requested the County explore the feasibility of installing water filling stations in all current and future construction of County facilities. It was heartening when the day came that water stations were installed at the County Government Center where the other supervisors and I worked.

Because these efforts made progress toward the goal of enhanced public health and sustainability, I'd encourage other elected officials to investigate doing something similar. The advantages of the program are numerous: Water stations increase access to and utilization of safe, fresh, tap water; promote water conservation and minimize disposable plastic bottles from entering the waste stream; educate people, children in particular, about the health benefits of drinking tap water in comparison to other beverage choices and reduce the consumption of sugar-sweetened beverages; and shift the perception among residents about the safety, health, and taste of tap water. Just as important, it complies with a state mandate that requires access to drinking water during school mealtimes in food service areas.

Here's to a healthier generation of kids and adults.

Playing the Long Game to Construct the 880/280 Freeway Interchange

One issue that most elected officials in urban areas have to deal with is traffic congestion, whether it occurs on neighborhood streets or state and federal highways. The bigger and more expensive the problem, the longer and more players it takes to solve, if it's solved at all. One such case existed in an area that was in both my council and supervisorial districts. If I hadn't served on numerous boards that financed transportation projects over a 10-year period, I doubt my top project would have been funded, given the competition over scarce dollars.

People who lived in the valley prior to 2015 know the interchange I'm talking about: I-280/I-880/Stevens Creek Boulevard. Constructed in 1959, the interchange was not built to accommodate the number of cars and trucks that commute through the area every day. With the opening of the upscale shopping center Santana Row in 2002 and the large shopping mall Valley Fair across the street, it soon became known as "The Nightmare Before Christmas" during the holidays. I knew the problems well, living about two miles from the intersection and often taking the off-ramp home.

This stretch of road had one of the highest crash rates in the Bay Area. Gary Richards, the *Mercury News* traffic reporter, called it a "white-knuckle ride no matter what direction motorists were headed." The recurring congestion resulted in traffic slowdowns, unsafe merges and, most hazardously, a standing queue with free-flow traffic on either side of I-280 when drivers were waiting to merge onto northbound I-880 during rush hour and weekends.

As Richards wrote, "During holiday weeks, Caltrans would set up warning signs pleading with drivers to slow down, and the California Highway Patrol put cars on the shoulder with lights flashing. Nearby residents had to tolerate motorists cutting through their neighborhoods in droves." [109]

Piecing the funding together for construction was not easy, but first I needed to have money allocated to begin an engineering study. This is a strategy veteran politicians know: Once you start spending money on a project, it can take on a life of its own. This is because administrators are reluctant to stop a project once funds are being spent. Soon after the opening of Santana Row, I lobbied to have the council identify improving the corridor as a high priority for future regional funding. Subsequently, the Valley Transportation Authority (VTA), which served as the county's congestion management agency, did as well. In 2006, the city council allocated $1.5 million toward project planning, environmental clearance, and preliminary engineering that was done by VTA, on whose board I was appointed in 2001 and served until I was termed out in 2018. The estimated cost of the project was $63 million.

The next big break was when San Jose U.S. Representative Mike Honda got $20 million in a federal earmark for the project.

Then there was some good luck followed by some bad luck. In

109   Gary Richards. "280-880 Interchange Project Near Valley Fair Shopping Center is Almost Done." *San Jose Mercury News.* June 16, 2015.

November 2006, state voters approved a $20 billion infrastruc-
ture bond measure, with $1.8 billion designated for northern Cal-
ifornia. Naturally, I thought some of these funds would go to
the interchange project. But it was not to be. To my disappointment and despite VTA's request, the Metropolitan Transportation Commission (MTC), which is the regional transportation
board, voted not to include the project in their submission to
the state.

But all was not lost. Beginning in 2007, as a new supervisor, I became Santa Clara County's representative on MTC,
having taken the seat held by then-supervisor but now state
Senator Jim Beall. This opportunity fell in my lap when none
of the other four supervisors wanted it.

Most of the public is unaware of the number of regional
governing bodies that exist and the authority they have. As a
good example, MTC is responsible for long-term transit and
transportation planning for the nine-county Bay Area region,
distributing state and federal transportation dollars to cities
and counties within its boundaries.

While much of the money MTC allocates is based on pre-
set formulas, a significant portion is decided by those serving
on the Commission. Based on population, Santa Clara County
has one-quarter of the Bay Area's total. However, it doesn't
receive that much from the pool of discretionary funding. According to estimates by VTA, the county was losing up to $15
million in regional funds each year.

A big part of the problem had to do with the makeup of the
commission. When MTC was created by the state legislature
in 1970, each of the nine counties received one voting member
on the 19-member board. San Francisco, as the largest city
in the Bay Area at the time, had an additional seat for the
mayor or their designee. That allocation had not changed in
40 years, a length of time when Santa Clara County grew by
leaps and bounds ahead of other Bay Area counties in terms
of jobs, economic growth, and population. Moreover, San Jose

out-populated San Francisco decades ago and is now the third largest city in California, behind Los Angeles and San Diego. While this also meant that the region was eligible to receive more federal money, it didn't mean the money went to Santa Clara County.

Another issue had to do with term limits. While many cities limit the number of terms a person can serve, few counties do. Santa Clara County is the exception, with three terms for supervisors. Because of how important MTC is, most commissioners choose to serve on MTC for many years, thus giving them institutional knowledge and prestige that newcomers don't have.

The other disadvantage Santa Clara County had was its location: Of the nine counties, it is the southernmost. Given the long driving distances from northern and eastern counties to Santa Clara County, most commissioners were unaware of our congestion and traffic jams.

Given these larger problems, I set about doing two things: Getting an extra seat on the commission for San Jose's mayor and educating other commissioners about Santa Clara County.

One thing I learned early in politics is that relationships are key. That is why I invited commissioners to tour the county, making sure to include the I-880/280/Stevens Creek Interchange. In return, I consistently accepted invitations to travel and learn about their counties.

The strategy proved successful. Working with Supervisor Cortese, San Jose Mayor Chuck Reed, San Jose Council Member Sam Liccardo, and Silicon Valley Leadership Group CEO and California Transportation Commissioner Carl Guardino, we got the Commission to agree to increase equity by adding seats for the mayors of San Jose and Oakland.

With all hands on deck, in 2009, we were able to get MTC to acknowledge that Santa Clara County had not received its fair share of funding and awarded $32 million for the interchange. At this point, we had $53 million of the money needed but were still $10 million short of the $63 million price tag.

The other big player in this financing puzzle was the California Transportation Commission (CTC), which also allocates state highway funds. Fortunately, one of the commissioners was Carl Guardino, a good friend and county resident. Attention shifted to them for the additional dollars.

While it was unfortunate that the Great Recession was happening at this time, there was one plus side: Because construction companies were desperate for work, their bids were coming in under engineer estimates, thus creating a budget surplus. Zeroing in on these dollars with the help of Guardino, I was able to get the approval for the additional $10 million from the CTC. With that, we had all the funding we needed.

Shovels were in the ground by 2012, and the construction was completed by 2015. I served as master of ceremonies for the ribbon cutting. Although I didn't mention it in my remarks, I did reflect that here I was, the son of a family that built freeways across Southern California and who had a sign designating the Highway 60/I-15 Interchange in Ontario as the E.L. Yeager Company Interchange. I chuckled to myself as I cut the ribbon that this was as close as I would get to my father's occupation and legacy.

Marriage Equality

The hurdle for people to marry someone of the same gender always seemed too high to ever become a reality. Throughout the 1990s, when there began to be more public discussion of the idea, polls in California and throughout the country showed levels of opposition so high to make same-sex marriages seem unobtainable.

One by one, states were passing constitutional amendments forbidding same-gender marriages. Congress passed, and President Clinton signed the Defense of Marriage Act on September 21, 1996, prohibiting any federal recognition of marriages. In

November 2000, with 61 percent of the vote, California passed Proposition 22, which declared that only marriages between a man and a woman would be recognized.

Perhaps the biggest shift in public opinion toward LGBTQ+ people in general, and gay marriage in particular, occurred on February 14, 2004, when Mayor Gavin Newson allowed the County of San Francisco to begin issuing marriage licenses. Thus began a chain of events that ended 11 years later with the U.S. Supreme Court allowing same-gender marriages to proceed nationwide.

I was serving on the San Jose City Council at the time. Seeing the long lines of gays and lesbians stretched around the block at San Francisco City Hall, I wanted so much to be part of that historic moment. However, there was one major impediment in my way: Counties, not cities, issue marriage licenses.

It was not an option for me to sit on the sidelines and watch history unfold before me while doing nothing. Undeterred, I sought a way for San Jose to be part of this momentous occasion. I found it when it came to my attention that one of our City employees was married in San Francisco and attempted to enroll her spouse in our employee benefits program. She was told, however, that she would have to wait for the open enrollment period later that year because current policy treated her same-sex marriage as a domestic partnership. This was not the case with straight City employees who could enroll their spouses immediately upon their marriage.

I believed it was right and just that benefits provided to spouses of City employees should be applied equally in accordance with San Jose's strong and progressive commitment to ending bias and discrimination in the workplace. With Mayor Ron Gonzales joining me as an enthusiastic co-signer, we issued a memorandum for the council's consideration on March 9.

Immediately, all the council offices were flooded with calls denouncing the proposal. There was certainly a number that was full-throttle homophobic, but the main thrust was either that gay marriages were against God's will, they were against the law, voters opposed gay marriages, or spousal benefits would cost too much. We heard the same arguments hour after hour at the council meeting.

Speakers in favor were outnumbered by those who opposed, but they gave heartfelt testimony about the years they had been with their partners and how the council's actions to recognize gay marriage would move us toward equality.

In my remarks, I responded to several of the arguments that opponents voiced, first about the legality of our actions. I referenced an opinion by our City attorney, Rick Doyle, that there was nothing illegal about changing our retirement policies to grant spousal benefits to a City employee with a same-sex partner. On the second issue dealing with costs, the employee benefits department concluded that there would be minimal impact on the budget.

In my way of personalizing the issue, I mentioned how it was 20 years to the day that I had read an opinion piece in the *Mercury News* by a local assemblyman saying that gays and lesbians were undeserving of any legal, moral, or social standing. This angered me because, at the age of 18, I had moved to San Jose from a town where I knew I couldn't be who I was.

That was when I came out publicly, deciding to stay in San Jose because it was a city that I knew would accept me for who I was.I mentioned that most people who didn't believe in what we were doing changed their minds when someone they knew and loved came out to them as gay. "That is when it becomes a personal issue for you. It's how you'll gain an understanding of the type of love they have and how important it is for society to recognize that love."

I concluded by saying that I believed we were on the right path. "San Jose has a long history of non-discrimination and inclusion. I urge my colleagues to join me in supporting this resolution."

After the mayor and several councilmembers spoke, the

item came up for a vote. It passed 8-1, making San Jose the first city in California to recognize marriages that take place elsewhere. Councilman Chuck Reed voted no, and Councilmembers Pat Dando and Forrest Williams were absent. All three of them had issued a prior memo directing staff to follow California law in recognizing marriages of City employees, adding that "San Jose should not take actions or make decisions on same-sex marriage licenses until the Supreme Court rules on the Attorney General's request or the law is changed by the legislature or voters."

The backlash from social conservatives was fierce. One pastor publicly said, "People make jokes about San Francisco. We don't want them making jokes about San Jose." Because San Jose had the largest concentration of evangelical megachurches in Northern California, the threats of a recall of Mayor Ron Gonzalez and myself were real.

That didn't materialize, which finally indicated the waning power of the religious right in San Jose politics. Gone were the days when, in 1980, they forced a referendum to overturn City and County laws prohibiting discrimination against gays and lesbians in housing and employment and won with 67 percent of the vote.[110]

Jump ahead to May 15, 2008, when the California Supreme Court struck down Proposition 22. This meant marriage licenses could begin being issued on Sunday, June 16 which, in practice, meant Monday, June 17. As a County supervisor, I wanted to make sure our County Clerk-Recorders' Office was ready to go. Clerks were trained to use the right pronouns; "husband" and "wife" were changed to "Spouse 1" and "Spouse 2." The idea of my officiating over the first marriages in the county came when David and Richard Speakman contacted me, asking if they could be the first couple to tie the knot. Richard had taken David's last name after they married in San

---

110   Ken Yeager. "We've Come a Long Way, Baby." *San Jose Mercury News.* July 5, 2015.

Francisco on February 15, 2004. I thought this was a great idea. As a County supervisor, I was designated as a Commissioner of Civil Marriages, which allowed me to perform marriages. I then asked Ronni and Hannah Pahl if they wanted to be part of the same ceremony, to which they agreed.

Shortly after 9:00 a.m., when the County opened for business, I conducted the wedding ceremony in the supervisors' conference room, packed with well-wishers and media. What a grand moment it was for all involved. I was so proud to be an openly gay supervisor who had the honor to conduct the first same-gender marriages in Santa Clara County. How fortunate was that?

Unfortunately, however, the marriage window was short-lived. Opponents of gay marriage collected enough signatures to place Proposition 8 on the ballot, which, if passed, would enshrine the one-man, one-woman marriage doctrine in the California constitution.

Panic began to set in as the November 4 election day approached. Many people felt it would be their last chance to actually get married. My chief of staff, John Mills, and his partner were in that category. I married them in my office on Monday, November 3.

It was a much different situation almost five years later. I think most LGBTQ+ people will remember that fateful day in late June 2013 when political insiders predicted the U.S. Supreme Court would make rulings on the Defense of Marriage Act and the Hollingworth v Perry case that would overturn Proposition 8. On June 26, I turned on my radio shortly before 7:00 a.m. PST. It was sheer jubilation when I heard the good news. Gay marriages could proceed.

I knew it would be a busy day full of exhilaration and media coverage, so I jumped out of bed, showered, and drove down to the County building, giddy about entering into a world that had suddenly changed for the better.

The six days to July 1, when the first marriages could again be performed, were full of excitement. We worked closely with Clerk-Recorder Gina Alcomendras to make sure everything worked smoothly. To speed things up, she created a new Express Marriage Ceremony Service Window. With that, walk-in couples could purchase a license and have the deputized clerk perform the marriages at the same time. That way, clerks could not only fill out the paperwork but perform the quick "I do's" as well. Later, I was able to present Alcomendras with a commendation from the Board for all her outstanding work.

I remember going over all the preparations with County Executive Dr. Smith that morning. I brought up the issue of flying the Rainbow flag in front of the County building.

Traditionally, it was flown only one day for Gay Pride Day, but later I thought it should fly the entire month of June. But now it was July. After I mentioned the idea of raising the flag on that historic day to Dr. Smith, he said, "Why not fly it every day?" To which I responded, "Exactly! Yes, why not?" From then on, it has flown every day. Being a bit lonely up there on the flagpole, it was joined several years later by the Transgender Awareness flag. Now in their place flies the Progress Pride flag.

The following is the op-ed I wrote describing the joy everyone felt on that momentous day.[111]

"More people in Santa Clara County applied for marriage licenses on July 5, 2013, than on any other day ever. Explanations abound: Same-sex couples could finally marry; July 4 fell on a Sunday, so many people had the following Monday off; due to all the attention, marriage was back in fashion.

"All totaled, I performed 27 same-sex unions in my office. Being among so many loving couples and their families was awe-inspiring. I opened each ceremony with a reflection about how their visibility with friends and family helped let love prevail.

----

111   Ken Yeager. "Joy in Same-Sex Marriage Blitz." *San Jose Mercury News.* July 14, 2013.

"The 54 individuals who took their vows were as wonderful and unique as human beings in general. They were of all races, ages, heights, and weights. Some giggled; some had tears streaming down their faces. Having waited so long for this day to arrive, some couples seemed like their hearts would burst if they didn't wed that very second.

"One aspect of the Supreme Court's gay wedding ruling that has received little attention is its importance to the couple's friends and families. They, too, had a genuine stake in the decision. Attendees ranged from a three-month-old baby to a 96-year-old grandmother. Couples were accompanied by their children, parents, co-workers, and friends. All expressed love for the newlyweds; they wouldn't have missed the occasion for anything. That the couple was of the same gender was 100 percent inconsequential to them.

"Throughout the day, I felt I was witnessing how public opinion changed about gay marriages. Over the years, as more gays and lesbians came out of the closet, straight friends and relatives have become accustomed to gay colleagues and family members. For them, the anti-gay rhetoric of political and religious conservatives no longer rings true. All that matters is the person they know and love, not their sexual orientation.

"By 4:30 that afternoon, the last of the couples had sealed their marriage with a long kiss, and my office was empty again.

So, what's next? I wondered.

"While anti-gay political and legal barriers are collapsing with rapid speed, social and psychological stigmas will be harder to overcome.

"The ultimate goal must be for any girl, boy, or binary person who is questioning their sexual orientation to have family and friends accept them, regardless of whether they are gay, straight, bi, trans, or binary. Conversations in the dining room and classroom need to encourage acceptance of everyone's sexual identity. Clearly, the LGBTQ+ people who got married in front of their friends and family that day in 2013 represent an important step in this process of change.

"Full acceptance of us by society may not happen in my lifetime. But you never know. I never thought I'd see the day that same-sex couples could marry, not to mention seeing myself preside over 27 of those weddings in a single day."

> <

At a festive June 26 Day of Decision evening rally in front of San Jose City Hall organized by BAYMEC, a fellow celebrant told me that "a slice of today's victory belongs to you, Ken." While grateful for the recognition of my efforts, it made me think about how credit truly goes to the thousands of people in San Jose and Santa Clara County who, time and again, stood up to the voices of hatred and intolerance until love won.[112]

---

112   To see a short video of the rally, go to youtube.com/watch?v=WPtjL wjaWik

CHAPTER 11

Run, Baby, Run: Planning and Executing a Winning Campaign

When I reflect upon the profiles of LGBTQ+ elected officials in my 1999 *Trailblazers* book and my own experience as the first "out" candidate to win election in Santa Clara County, I can't help but pause to appreciate how much has changed in the past few decades for LGBTQ+ candidates and elected officials.

When I conducted my survey of current LGBTQ+ office-holders in 1997, there were only 124 of us. Now, according to the Victory Fund, 436 candidates won their elections in 2022, the most ever.[113] This included the nation's first lesbian governors, Tina Kotek of Oregon and Maura Healey of Massachusetts. They join Jared Polis of Colorado, who was our country's first LGBTQ+ governor. Granted, these are blue states, but if voters elect a queer governor, they will certainly be open to supporting queer candidates at all levels.

Of course, this is not true everywhere. Even today, in some communities, tactics related to homophobia, gender identity discrimination, and "gay-baiting" are alive and well. But just recently, in 2022, voters in Missoula elected Zooey Zephyr, a transwoman, to the Montana House of Representatives, so you know anything is possible, even though they have met with tremendous opposition in the Republican-controlled legislature.

----

113   https://outforamerica.org/

LGBTQ+ people need to be represented at all levels of government—federal, state, city, and school—but the fact is most will not be running for high-profile seats such as governor or congress. Rather, they will run in low-profile races in cities that have never elected an openly gay person before. With approximately 89,000 cities in the U.S., there are many opportunities to be "the first." In my county, only five cities out of 15 have elected someone LGBTQ+. Nationwide, the prevalence of LGBTQ+ school board members is probably even less, though such positions are especially important now that MAGA Republicans are competing for those seats. They also provide a critical first win for those who want to run for higher office.

It is usually the case that fewer outside resources are available for candidates running for offices lower on the ballot than statewide or congressional offices. This often results in limited funds available to hire a campaign consulting firm or a full-time manager. This means candidates must either have campaign experience or know where to get the information directly. If they expect people to suddenly appear out of the blue and provide assistance, their campaigns will never leave the starting gate.

As Shay Franco Clausen, who ran for San Jose City Council in 2018, said to me, "A candidate's ability to raise money, get volunteers, and get important endorsements will be based on their name identity and commitment to service."

The following is an assessment for candidates to think about when considering a run for office. It is not meant to discourage anyone from running. Rather, its purpose is to help candidates avoid jumping into a campaign without forethought, only to raise false hopes for themselves and the LGBTQ+ community.[114]

----

114   Note: Sections of this chapter appeared in my essay "Running with Limited Resources" in *Out For Office: Campaigning in the Gay Nineties*. Kathleen DeBold, editor. Gay and Lesbian Victory Fund.1994.

Timing

When to run for office is influenced by the availability of an open seat, an incumbent being up for re-election, or circumstances like an unexpected vacancy. Even if there is an office to run for, it is critical that any candidate evaluates the circumstances of their personal and professional lives. Many offices have term limits, so there will always be a chance to run in the future if now is not the right time. As queer California Assemblyman Alex Lee (D-Milpitas) told me, "Know that the office you're running for is the right job for your goals."

Professionally, there are never enough hours in a day to do the work required of a candidate in a political campaign while holding a traditional job, although the pandemic radically changed where and when people are working. That is why it is critical that candidates have a flexible schedule. If the boss requires the candidate to be available during business hours, either at home or the office, then it will be difficult to run errands, attend meetings, and make countless phone calls. Remember, in many local campaigns, there is little to no staff, so the person doing most of the work is the candidate. If the candidate doesn't have time for campaigning, there won't be much of a campaign.

You must determine if your home and family life can accommodate a campaign. The time to focus on your personal life is not when you have already added the stress of running for office. As California State Senator John Laird (D-Santa Cruz) advised, "Make sure you have your eyes open about the time commitment and stress the campaign will have on your family. Everyone needs to be on board with it before you launch a race."

However, there is also no "perfect" time to take on the challenge of running for office. If most aspects of your life are stable and flexible, then it might be the right time to gauge support, line up endorsements, and announce your candidacy.

Getting Prepared

In most winning campaigns, a tremendous amount of pre-campaign work is needed to increase your viability and chances of being elected. One strategy that Michael Vargas used when he ran and won a seat on the Elk Grove (CA) School Board in 2022 was to meet with community and political leaders starting two years before the election. This way, he could introduce himself to people, learn the issues, and most importantly, hear the scuttlebutt on who liked whom and who may or may not run for election or re-election. This was all valuable information in his decision about which seat to run for and, as importantly, which seat not to run for this time around.

As I wrote in Chapter 4 about Paul Wysocki's campaign for San Jose City Council, nothing is more frustrating than being everyone's second choice. In a competitive campaign, you need to be the first choice of a handful of prominent leaders and elected officials, as well as some influential community and political groups. Ask yourself, is there another candidate more qualified and who is supported by the people I need to win the election? If yes, see if other "like-minded" candidates can be convinced not to run, thus increasing your chances of winning.

Understanding the Ups and Downs

If you do decide to run for office, you will be undertaking an emotional journey, unlike almost anything else one might choose to do willingly. Every day will be managed chaos. There will be 20 critically important tasks to accomplish and only time for 10. People will tell you how to prioritize the 20 tasks differently, and you have to manage their expectations.

You will be disappointed by people whom you expect to support you and don't. If yours is a particularly tough race with much at stake, the campaign will consume you, exhaust you, and force you to work every spare moment during every day. It will stretch the limits of your capacities to smile, talk to strangers, attend events, sustain small talk, and absorb details and facts needed to engage with many different groups. You must also prepare for a level of negativity most people only read about.

But you will also meet the most incredible people and be uplifted by those who are there for you that you never expected or may have never known before the campaign. You will meet people who believe in you after meeting you. You will leave encounters more energized and wanting to win so you can make a difference in their lives.

And all of these ups and downs are likely to happen over the course of each day of the campaign.

You're Running—Now You Need to Win

The following is a checklist of campaign readiness, resources, and activities that candidates running for local school board, city, and county offices need a basic understanding of if they expect to run a viable campaign. Candidates need not excel in all areas, but the list does provide a reality check that will help in deciding if this is the year they should run.

Fundraising and Non-Monetary Contributions

Fundraising is often one of the most difficult and uncomfortable tasks for any candidate. Asking people for money is awkward and can seem self-serving. One has to work through these challenges if they exist and ask a broad scope of people to support their campaign. The number one rule of fundraising is that a candidate does not get a large contribution unless they specifically ask for a large amount. So, if you think someone can contribute $500, then you have to ask for $500.

Because name identification is essential for winning public

office, and the only way to increase that is through expensive direct voter contact like mail or advertising, it often takes a lot of money to get elected.

One way to get a handle on fundraising goals is to determine a budget and then figure out how many donors are needed. Let's say the budget is $10,000. Estimate that 100 people must give $25, 50 people must give $50, and 50 people must give $100. Put names of people after these dollar amounts and begin making phone calls. If the candidate cannot determine who will give the money, chances are fundraising will not go well.

Almost as good as money, which is saying quite a lot, are non-monetary contributions. Often individuals and businesses who are reluctant to write checks are willing to donate goods and services at a reduced rate or for free. When this is done, it is called an "in-kind" contribution because the campaign benefits from not having to pay for a service or product. There is a wide range of in-kind contributions that candidates should pursue. These include free office space, reduced rates for printing, and discounts on stationery items. Do not overlook having food and beverages donated, especially from queer restaurants and bars.

In-kind contributions must be reported just like monetary contributions. Be sure to get a receipt from the business for the market value of the product or service and include that amount in the report.

Compliance, Filing, and Reporting

Depending on the office you are seeking, the requirements for qualifying as a candidate, filing of regular reports on fundraising and expenditures, and other factors like contributions limits and expenditure limits may be managed by the County Registrar of Voters or other officials like a city clerk.

It is critical that every candidate fully understands all of the rules, requirements, filing deadlines, and unique limitations associated with the office and jurisdiction they seek. Violating the rules may result in otherwise avoidable consequences like disqualification, fines, and opportunities for supporters, opponents, or the media to question one's capability and viability.

If the candidate does not know how to complete the reports, then they need to find someone who can.

Endorsements

Endorsements by elected officials and community leaders are crucial in any race, but even more so in local elections where voters have never heard of the candidates. If there is no political party designation on the ballot, which is true in most local races, then the main way for a voter to determine a candidate's political party is to see who endorsed them. Early endorsements are especially critical because they help establish a candidate's credibility.

Candidates should assess how many big-name endorsements they can get and whether they can personally contact community leaders or if they must go through an intermediary or, worse, send a letter. If candidates do not know the person well enough to call, then the odds decrease that an endorsement will be given because politicians are unlikely to endorse people they do not know.

Volunteers

If a candidate thinks their friends have nothing else to do but work on their campaign, think again. If the campaign strategy calls for the use of volunteers, candidates need to assess if they can get four or five people a night, six times a week, for three or four months. It is best to make a list of the people who might volunteer, then call them. It is not a good sign if the candidate hears a lot of hemming and hawing.

Messaging

Voters want assurances that the candidates they support are credible and have knowledge about mainstream issues. They look carefully at a candidate's experience and qualifications, especially academic degrees, business titles, and community work. A list of five or more solid qualifications in a candidate's brochure looks impressive. If the list is too short, perhaps it would be wise to hold off running and get appointed to several city or county commissions.

Issues

Candidates are not expected to be knowledgeable of all the issues at the beginning of the campaign, but it is essential that they know where to turn for assistance. Candidates need to know people from various ethnic, racial, political, business, and social groups who will assist them in responding to questionnaires and preparing them for candidate forums. This help will increase the odds of winning endorsements and forming coalitions with other minority groups, which LGBTQ+ candidates must do.

For most local elected offices like the school board, city council, and board of supervisors, voters care about core issues related to public safety, growth and development, neighborhood services and programs, potholes, public schools, and overall quality of life. Raising the Pride flag over City Hall may be important in the month of June, but otherwise, how you improve the lives of the average voter is what matters to most people.

A Non-LGBTQ+ Label

In my first campaign, my consultants knew that I should own the title of the "educator candidate." Because I was running for community college board, we emphasized my Ph.D. in education and my faculty job at San Jose State University. Even though I had been involved in LGBTQ+ politics for years, it was my educator's image that was reinforced in my literature. As a result, when I was walking precincts, people did not say, "You're the gay candidate," but, "You're the professor at San Jose State."

Thankfully, things are much different in more liberal-leaning cities and counties. I know that in the Bay Area a candidate's sexual orientation doesn't come up at all in news articles or newspaper endorsements. That is so refreshing. However, in more conservative areas where there are few or no LGBTQ+ elected officials, it is often the tactic of opponents to marginalize queer candidates by saying they only care about a single issue.

Direct Voter Contact

Direct voter contact encompasses the various tools used by a campaign to contact, engage, inform, and persuade voters to support a candidate. The more of the following elements that a campaign can implement, the better the chances of winning.

Direct Mail:

- Production of direct mail should not be left to the amateurs; if it is, it will look amateurish, and voters don't want to be represented by amateurs. A standard format is for a mail piece to have one overall message or purpose, with three subareas to help make the message clear. The most common design errors are trying to make too many points with way too many words.

- Many components go into a quality mail piece: photographs that capture the essence of the candidate, effective writing, a creative design, and a good layout.

- Good, crisp graphics will convey that a candidate is competent and experienced. That is why it is important for the campaign to have a professional look. If possible, ask several graphic artists to come up with a potential logo. Look them over and discuss the pros and cons of each design. Make sure that this process is started early because once a logo is chosen it should not be changed mid-campaign.

- Seasoned candidates know that as goes the printing, so goes the campaign. A candidate can have the best-looking, best-written literature in the world, but if it cannot be printed in time, no one will see it. Printing schedules fill up fast during campaign season, so it is important to establish a good relationship with several printers by taking business-related work to them prior to the campaign.

Data and Targeting:

- It makes little economic sense to mail to every voter in the district since only about 60 percent or fewer go to the polls in a general election. The percentage is much smaller for cities with off-year elections. A vendor who works with voter files can determine which voters should receive the candidate's mail by using various criteria: voter history, political party, gender, etc. These are strategic decisions, and candidates must work with someone they trust. Good targeting is even more important in low-budget campaigns because money cannot be wasted on people who do not vote.

- Micro-targeting is also a highly effective strategy used by winning campaigns to segment the universe of all likely voters into sub-categories of voters broken down by gender, ethnicity, geography, age, etc., and provide them with highly targeted messages intended to speak to their interests and concerns or use third-party supporters from the same sub-categories who provide validation for your candidacy.

Field Campaign Activities:

- There is still no substitute for the proven effectiveness of engaging with voters on their doorstep or the phone. It's not easy to get voters to answer the door or pick up the phone, but when they do, and the candidate or credible supporters can engage in a meaningful conversation about issues and ideas, a voter often appreciates the effort and the outreach.

- Walking precincts and making phone calls is still an effective method of contacting voters utilizing the tools of data and targeting, but texting voters is also an increasingly useful method of contact as more and more voters register with cell phone numbers and eliminate landlines. After ringing the doorbell or knocking, I always find it best to step several feet away from the door to appear as least threatening as possible. This is also a good practice if there are still concerns about COVID.

Social Media:

- There is no doubt that social media can be an effective way for candidates to interact with people, ranging from friends and supporters to a broader group of likely voters, through paid advertising. It's a fast and cheap way to inform supporters about fundraisers, precinct walks, endorsements, the latest campaign news, etc., or to deliver highly visual and multi-media content as advertising campaigns. However, it is not a substitute for traditional ways to communicate with the general voting public. So, while you may be getting a lot of positive feedback and tons of "likes" on your page, it isn't an indication of how the campaign is doing overall unless you're complimenting it with paid social media advertising. Remember, too, that it is mainly older people who vote, and they are less likely to use social media platforms like Instagram or TikTok.

Get Out the Vote (GOTV)

- All of the efforts and activities implemented by any campaign should always be focused on identifying supporters.

- Once identified, tactics must be initiated to make sure voters return their ballots to increase the likelihood a candidate will win.

- The pandemic accelerated the transition to vote-by-mail in many counties and states, with many counties implementing "all mail" ballot voting elections where every registered voter is automatically mailed a ballot to their home.

- In California, for example, all registered voters are mailed a ballot approximately 30 days before the official election date. The result is that campaigns have to plan for a full month of voting and tracking returned ballots to ensure identified supporters actually cast a vote.

- Many local election results are very close, and it is not uncommon for a winning candidate to win by less than 100 votes—so every vote counts!

Paid Staff and Consultant

Depending on the size of the district or jurisdiction in which a candidate is running, it may be necessary to budget for paid staff positions and even a professional campaign consultant or consulting firm. While this can be expensive and considered a luxury resource, sometimes a campaign has to spend money to help implement many of the functions outlined above. Common positions and resources may include:

- **Campaign coordinator or manager:** A candidate should be meeting voters, not spending time with volunteers. Even if there is no money to pay a staff person, the candidate needs to have a friend who can coordinate activities and be responsible for volunteer efforts. This person must be very good with people because nothing will sidetrack a campaign faster than unhappy, sniping volunteers.

- **Professional campaign consultant:** Highly specialized individuals and consulting firms exist in most jurisdictions that provide professional services to candidates and campaigns. These professionals provide a range of services that help a candidate implement all or some of the functions outlined throughout this chapter and can help a candidate stay focused, implement more effectively, and help manage critical elements like direct mail, social media, data, etc. These services come at a cost and are more beneficial in contested and higher-profile campaigns.

- **Campaign headquarters:** Renting a campaign headquarters can be very expensive. Candidates on a low budget need to find an alternative. One option is to find a business owner who will donate the space. A second is to share space with some organization at no charge. A third is to run the campaign out of someone's garage.

Any of the three is better than watching the money go down the drain in the form of rent checks.

> <

If candidates with limited resources don't know enough about campaigns, there are two options. The first and best option is to volunteer for someone's campaign to learn how it is done. The second option, and one I do not often recommend, is to enter the race in order to gain experience, knowing the groundwork is being done for the future. Nothing is wrong with this as long as the candidate does not lose sight of the objective or make too many enemies when running against a well-liked incumbent.

Whether you're ready to run or not, another great option is to take the candidate training offered by the Victory Fund Institute. The four-day training is held throughout the country to provide skills, tools, and realistic campaign scenarios for current and future LGBTQ+ candidates, campaign staff, and community leaders. For more information, contact victoryinstitute.org/training.

Lastly, it is important that LGBTQ+ people not be afraid of running or underestimate themselves or their chances. As California Assemblyman Evan Low (D-Campbell) told me, "Be authentic. Voters may disagree with your policy positions, but most will value a representative who is open, honest, and transparent." I think that describes LGBTQ+ candidates pretty well.

After candidates realistically assess their chances and they think there is a good probability they can win, I enthusiastically encourage them to *Run, Baby, Run!* and make history.

CHAPTER 12

A Love Letter
to My Community

After 26 years of being an elected official, serving in three different offices, and running six contested campaigns, at the end of 2018, I was termed out of my county supervisorial role. I was asked by the chair of the SJSU political science department if I wanted to resume teaching several classes, to which I gave a grateful yes. Shortly thereafter, an opportunity presented itself to become executive director of the nonprofit arm of BAYMEC, the BAYMEC Community Foundation.

The Foundation was created in 2013 by BAYMEC's president James Gonzales in order to receive money either from people who wanted their contributions to be tax-deductible or governmental agencies that are legally forbidden to donate to political committees. Other LGBTQ+ groups like Equality California and the Victory Fund created similar nonprofit arms, whose names are embedded in their newly created organization, making them instantly recognizable and reputable. Although the BAYMEC Foundation had sponsored guest speakers, did candidate training, and supported activities in the community, it needed someone who could devote more time to it. Gonzales thought I'd be well suited for the post. I give him credit for setting in motion the position that availed itself to me six years later in 2019.

Little did I know when I accepted that I was on my way

to carving a new path for myself, separate from my identity as an elected official. Through my volunteer work with the Foundation, I was on the cusp of progressing from activist to elected official to queer historian.

The impetus for this was a trip I took in 2019 to see an exhibit titled "LGBTQ+ San Diego: Stories of Struggles and Triumphs." Located in majestic Balboa Park, the exhibition profoundly affected me. I had never seen anything remotely like it. The history was all there: the meaning of the Rainbow flag, San Diego's early gay bar scene, the impact of the military bases, campaigns against anti-gay propositions, Harvey Milk, the "coming out" movement of the 1980s, the plague years, community heroes, the early trans community, LGBTQ+ politicians, a timeline of significant events in each of the past five decades, etc. There were photographs, newspaper articles, recordings, paintings, outfits, various documents, and assorted memorabilia. It was a feast to behold.

I stood in the middle of the gallery in awe of what I was experiencing. I asked myself, whose idea was this? Who made the decisions on what to include? Where did they get the money? In essence, how the hell did this happen?

Before leaving, I took numerous photos and wrote down all the information I could. That is how I learned that the San Diego History Center and Lambda Archives were key organizations. On a subsequent trip to San Diego, I met with as many people as possible. Bill Lawrence, the San Diego History Center executive director, was particularly helpful.

In the back of my mind was the constant question: Did I have the skills and expertise to do a similar exhibit in San Jose/Silicon Valley?

As fate would have it, a year earlier, in 2018, while I was still on the Board of Supervisors, my colleague Cindy Chavez proposed the County fund history projects in each of the five supervisorial districts. I was pleased to vote for it, and her motion passed unanimously. I had almost forgotten about it until the procedural guide to the historic grant program was issued a year later, in July 2019.

According to the guide, the grant program's purpose was to "celebrate history in Santa Clara County with a preference for projects that acknowledge and celebrate untold stories and/or underrepresented/disadvantaged communities. This can include, but is not limited to, the history of women, Asian Americans, African Americans, Hispanics, Italian Americans, Native Americans, LGBTQ+, individual communities, technology, and politics and government."

Bingo. Suddenly, the opportunity existed to create a museum exhibit to celebrate the untold stories of the LGBT+ community. The next three years of my life would go to making that dream a reality.

Before I could submit a proposal, however, I needed a gallery to showcase the exhibit. This proved problematic since San Jose has few art galleries. It has a beautiful, modern San Jose Museum of Art, but it mainly carries large traveling exhibits of contemporary art. There were several smaller galleries in the old downtown section, but they were typically used for local artists.

I was aware of another option. The City of San Jose operates a "museum of museums" called History San Jose. According to its website, the park is a "14-acre town-like assemblage of 32 original and reconstructed homes, businesses, and landmarks highlighting the culture and history of San José and Santa Clara Valley."

One building was the Old Pacific Hotel, which contained the park's administrative staff and an art gallery named for San Jose's most well-known historian, Clyde Arbuckle. I didn't know the park's Chief Executive Officer Alida Bray well, but I was comfortable emailing her. Her response was very encouraging, noting that she had always wanted to do an LGBTQ+ exhibit but never did. Bray was happy to meet but alerted me that she was soon retiring. Her successor, Bill Schroh, proved to be supportive as well.

My friend and former chief of staff Jim Weston agreed to help me with this endeavor. Over the next few weeks, we met with Bray and other park staff. By the end of July, everything came together. With the understanding that the exhibit's design and installation was the Foundation's responsibility, they agreed to host it. History San Jose did not charge rent, so there was no cost for the gallery space. No exhibits were scheduled after the current one ended, which meant the space was ours as soon as January 2020 to prepare for a June opening. Lastly, we could keep it up for a whole year. This was far and beyond what we had hoped for. For the first time, I felt we could submit a realistic proposal for the museum exhibit.

As we were writing our proposal, we wanted to add two other components to the grant. One was to create a webpage that contained as much information about local LGBTQ+ history as we could find. Unlike the museum exhibit, which had certain space constraints, the webpage could accommodate an unlimited number of stories, photos, and interviews. I particularly looked forward to highlighting specific individuals and giving them a platform to share their histories.

The other addition was to produce a documentary. The concept of the film changed from its original idea of using old footage from a half-hour cable television show called *Outlook Video* to one with interviews of people associated with the local LGBTQ+ movement.

What I lacked in formal training as a historian was offset by my decades of not only making history but possessing archival documents. Over the years, I methodically kept important articles and documents related to local gay history. This was in addition to my papers from when I was a community college trustee, city councilmember, and county supervisor.

While all this material was stored in my garage, it was not organized in any particular manner. A 2021 San Jose *Metro* article about the history project describes the stacks of clutter in my garage this way: "Filed away amongst a trove of yellowed newspaper clippings, fading photographs, and nearly obsolete newsreels, four oversized office cabinets inside former Santa Clara County Supervisor Ken Yeager's garage gradually became an unofficial archive of the last 50 years of gay, lesbian, bisexual, transgender, and queer life in the South Bay.

"You keep these things just so you have them in case you need them, even if you're not sure why," Yeager says jokingly, reminiscing over how he's become one of the area's de-facto gay historians. "By the time it was all over, I had huge cabinets full of material I could use for a history project." [115]

I'm unsure how to explain my impulse to keep historical documents. Maybe it harks back to my junior high journalism classes, where our teacher would bind a year's worth of the school's *Gage Gator* newspapers and give it to us at the end of the school year. The same ritual occurred in my high school journalism classes with the *Poly Spotlight*. This is how I managed to save in my basement all the news stories and editorials I wrote in grades 8 to 12. Maybe my career as a collector started back then.

With all this in mind, along with help from Jim Weston and Leslee Hamilton, the Foundation applied for a $60,000 grant from the County's historical grant program to install a museum exhibition, design a webpage, and produce a documentary film. It took almost a year, but in June 2020, we learned that our proposal earned high marks and would be funded. But because of the COVID lockdown that began in March, the museum needed to be put on hold, so our attention turned to what was doable under the circumstances: the webpage.

The Webpage

One of the first things we needed to decide was a name for the project. I wasn't sure if I wanted to use the words "San Jose"

---

115   Katie Lauer. "Points of Pride: How Ken Yeager Chronicled 50 Years of LGBTQ+ History in Silicon Valley." *San Jose Metro.* June 23-29, 2021.

or "Silicon Valley" in the title because, much to my bruised civic pride, I still came across people who did not know where San Jose was. "Is that near San Antonio?" I'd hear people ask when traveling. For marketing purposes, "Silicon Valley" had more cache.

Then there was the decision of whether the name should be *LGBTQ+ Silicon Valley* or *Queer Silicon Valley*. I knew that the word "queer" was seen by many people, especially older gay men, as derogatory. But it had become more accepted over time, even to the point where younger people proudly identified as queer. Wanting to be as inclusive and politically correct as possible in the ever-evolving nomenclature, I thought *Queer Silicon Valley* worked best.[116]

An immediate need was to hire people to help with researching, writing, and cataloging material for the webpage. The first person I hired was a former student, Steven Peck. Peck had enrolled in two of my classes and was one of my brightest students. I mentioned my project to him, and he was interested in helping.

The SJSU job bulletin board helped me find two Masters in Library and Informational Sciences students, Jordan Evans-Boyajian and Emily Cannon, to assist with cataloging material. I hired Katie Lauer, a freelance journalist, to help with writing. Longtime lesbian activist Rebecca Obryan helped conduct interviews with bar owners and bartenders.

In addition to my collection, gay newspapers were an excellent resource for information, particularly in the 1980s and 1990s. *Lambda News, Our Paper/Your Paper, Entre Nous, South Bay Times,* and *Out Now* were some of the best-known papers. Although some papers have been digitized, most were not. A high priority became collecting as many editions as possible. I contacted two local gay publishers I knew, Whayne Herriford and Mark Gillard, and asked if they had kept copies. Both had and were happy to give them to me. Also, we bought papers

---

116   The webpage is QueerSiliconValley.org

from Bolerium Books, a San Francisco bookstore specializing in American and International social movements, including gay and lesbian studies.

With Evans-Boyajian and Cannon working remotely, Peck in my garage, and me in the house, thus began our socially-distanced scavenger hunt over the summer of 2020 to find and record anything and everything we could find of historical importance.

COVID lockdown or not, we were having the times of our lives. Whenever one of us came across a particularly interesting or provocative story, we'd fire off a message to the group exclaiming, "We have to include this!"

As we collected more information, we decided the best way to catalog everything was on 14 individual pages. These were LGBTQ+ in Tech, Marriage Equality, Sisterspirit, Latinx, the Trans Community, Pride Flags and Proclamations, Bars and Clubs, Elected Officials, San Jose Pride, LGBTQ+ Organizations, the Gay Press, the Billy DeFrank Community Center, the Office of LGBTQ+ Affairs, and Crime. To make access to the files easier, we also created three broad searchable categories: HIV/AIDS, Culture and Community, and Politics and Activism.

Here are some of the stories we included:

- In 1985, Carla Blair opened "Carla's Saloon" in San Jose, an establishment that was a combination of a tearoom, a beauty salon, a boutique, and a social center where transgender men could store their clothes, get their hair done, and socialize. It was purchased in 2010 by Aejaie Franciscus, a transwoman who talks about how she continues to operate the business in East San Jose to this day.[117]

- Years before marriage equality was won, Amy Brinkman and Kathleen Viall tried to get their "commitment" ceremony listed in the *Mercury News*, but the paper's

---

117   https://www.queersiliconvalley.org/carlas

policy forbade it. Activists protested in front of the *Mercury News* on Valentine's Day to bring attention to the paper's discriminatory policy. Finally, the paper changed its policy, and on September 12, 1992, their announcement was the first to appear in the Lifestyle section's wedding page. For more on this, take a look at Robert Greeley's account of the strategy used by the South Bay Gay and Lesbian Alliance Against Defamation (GLAAD) to accomplish this feat.[118]

- Being out and proud isn't always an easy task at any university, let alone on a Catholic Jesuit campus. Santa Clara University has slowly progressed to make that experience easier, from rejecting a gay alumni group in 1995 to founding a Rainbow Resource Center in 2010. The interview with Dr. Joanna Thompson, a queer, biracial woman who revamped student support services to make the university more inclusive for queer students, is available to listen to.[119]

- The first meeting of the largest and most influential gay Latino group, ProLatino, was held in 1992. Thirteen people attended. The group formed out of the need for a safe environment for gay Latinos to meet and discuss their community, health, and HIV/AIDS. A lengthy interview with the founder, Alejandro (Alex) Campos Vidrio, touches on his struggles creating and leading the organization.[120]

- In 1977, Gail Chandler-Croll, a straight woman, bought Mac's Club in downtown San Jose. She ran it for over 20 years. After it was forced to close, she bought another bar on Post Street to keep Mac's going. In an in-depth interview, she talks about the constant harassment

----

118   https://www.queersiliconvalley.org/commitment-story

119   https://www.queersiliconvalley.org/santa-clara-university-lgbtq

120   https://www.queersiliconvalley.org/alejandro-campos

from the police, the ongoing raids, intimidations, and arrests—all without a legitimate reason. She recounts the good times and bad: the tragic years of AIDS when so many of her friends were dying and the drag queens and drag shows that were always a highlight for her regular patrons.[121]

- San Jose has a long history of drag performers and drag balls. As part of the International Imperial Court System, Casa de San Jose was formed in Santa Clara County in the early 1970s and reincorporated as the Imperial Royal Lion Monarchy of San Jose in 1990. An interview with Kevin Roche, His Imperial Majesty 24, is available to listen to; photos of the coronation balls are on display; and the names of lifetime titleholders of the Imperial Family of San Jose/Santa Clara County are also listed.[122]

- Santa Clara County is fortunate to have six "out" judges. Because judges often live their lives outside the public eye to avoid any potential impacts on the perception of their impartiality, most LGBTQ+ people are unaware of them. To highlight these important community members, interviews were held with four of the judges. A story about the County's first openly gay judge, now deceased, is also included.[123]

- The celebration of Pride in Silicon Valley can be characterized as a series of struggles and triumphs. Over the decades, Pride in Silicon Valley has persevered and evolved into a wonderful event that the LGBTQ+ community eagerly awaits every year. We mapped out the 10 San

121   https://www.queersiliconvalley.org/gail-macs/

122   https://www.queersiliconvalley.org/casa-de-san-jose/

123   https://www.queersiliconvalley.org/politics-activism/judges/

Jose Pride locations from 1975 to 2022 in addition to the three different parade routes.[124]

- Santa Clara County has only a handful of openly out elected officials, but one K-8 school district has three of five trustees who define themselves as queer. In an interview with all three of the trustees, they share their vision for the future of the school district and the multilingual, multicultural, and multiracial students.[125]

- Because the federal government did not recognize same-sex marriages due to the Defense of Marriage Act (DOMA), gaining U.S. citizenship for a bi-national married spouse was impossible, as was getting an extension of time to stay in the other spouse's country. Read about San Jose native Judy Rickard's battle to highlight this injustice in her book *Torn Apart, United in Love, Divided by Law.*[126]

- In 1984, three students from San Jose State University met with Amy Caffrey to discuss the need for a women's bookstore and coffeehouse where women could socialize and enjoy live music performed by women. After several meetings, the group named their project Sisterspirit.[127]

I regretted not getting a couple of stories. I wasn't able to speak to San Jose figure skater Rudy Galindo to see if he would agree to have one of his skating outfits displayed in the exhibit. Galindo rose to fame in 1996 when, at age 26, he won the men's U.S. singles national champion title in front of a hometown crowd. He was the first openly gay figure skater champion, having come out before the competition began. Galindo still lives in

----

124 https://www.queersiliconvalley.org/pride/

125 https://www.queersiliconvalley.org/oak-grove-trio/

126 https://www.queersiliconvalley.org/marriage-citizenship/

127 https://www.queersiliconvalley.org/sisterspirit-story/

San Jose and continues to coach skaters. Numerous attempts to contact him failed. His story is on the webpage and was included in the exhibit.

Tim Cook is unquestionably the best-known openly gay business executive in the country, if not the world. He isn't active in the local government scene, so I have never met him. I wanted to have Apple sponsor the exhibit, but working through my government affairs contacts at Apple proved fruitless. Getting an interview with him one day would be a high point of the history project.

Once the webpage was up, we started putting brief descriptions of significant events on a timeline, along with short articles when available. When we were finished, we had over 200 entries on the timeline, almost 100 full-length stories, 16 interviews, and numerous television and YouTube recordings.[128]

In honor of Gay History Month, on October 1, 2020, the webpage was launched. For each day in October, we did a social media post highlighting a story or event of historical significance. I couldn't have been more thrilled. The feedback we received was encouraging. Clearly, there was a hunger for this type of information.

Fundraising

I soon realized that our ambitions exceeded our $60,000 budget, and I would need to raise additional funds. The first group of contributors I went after was local elected officials, many of whom I had served or worked with. Over the years, all had voiced support for the LGBTQ+ community, so I knew they would be inclined to donate.

Letters were sent explaining the three components of the *Queer Silicon Valley* project: the museum exhibit, the webpage, and the documentary. Four different sponsorship levels were

----

128   Note: See Appendix A for a timeline of five decades of important LGBTQ+ historical dates and events in Silicon Valley.

available: Historians ($10,000 +), Archivists ($5,000+), Supporters ($2,500 +), and Friends ($1,000+). To entice them to contribute, I mentioned that donors' names would appear on the acknowledgment section of the exhibit, the webpage's home page, and be listed in the credits of the documentary. Who could refuse such an offer?

The response was overwhelmingly positive. As the day approached when the acknowledgment panel would be printed, I didn't want any hard feelings from those few officials who had not responded. I certainly knew that not all mail is read by busy politicians. That is why I either emailed or texted them about the due date, casually mentioning that they were the only ones of their colleagues who hadn't contributed.

That always did the trick.

In the end, I was proud that we received donations from San Jose Mayor Sam Liccardo, all 10 San Jose councilmembers, the five County supervisors, our eight state senators and assemblymembers, our three members of Congress, and numerous politicians from other cities. All the elected officials gave at least $1,000. Some, like Congressmembers Zoe Lofgren and Anna Eshoo, gave far more. This in and of itself showed how far we had come from 1984 when few politicians wanted BAY-MEC's endorsements, with one even sending us the money back. Now we had achieved 100 percent participation. Except for being short for the documentary, I had the funding I needed.

The Museum Exhibition

Even though one of the grant's deliverables was to create a museum exhibit, I honestly had no idea how that was going to be accomplished. To my relief, History San Jose's Bill Schroh recommended we hire Exhibit Envoy, which we did. Amy Cohen was our visionary project director.

The exhibit came together nicely. Much credit goes to the advisory committee and their sound advice. Rebecca Obryan,

Ray Muller, Bettie Owens, Eileen Hamper, Jeff Levine, and Craig Westly Shannon were particularly helpful.

By June 2021, the pandemic's peak had passed and life was slowly inching back to normal. This meant that we could have a grand opening. We wanted it to happen during Gay Pride month, so we rushed to have it finished by the last weekend of the month.

A week before the June 25, 2021, opening, I submitted an op-ed to the *Mercury News* about the exhibit. I took the approach of what a visitor would see as they walked through. They gave the piece the headline, "History museum tells the story of queer Silicon Valley."

This is what I wrote:[129]

"Historians often turn to cultural centers like the Castro and Greenwich Village to tell the story of the LGBTQ+ civil rights movement. That may explain why the progression of the queer community in Silicon Valley from political outcasts to integral members of society has never been widely chronicled.

"This will change with the opening of 'Coming Out: 50 Years of Queer Resistance to Resilience in Silicon Valley' at History San Jose.

"For people of a particular generation, the exhibit will bring back memories long forgotten. You will see such names as Whiskey Gulch, Sisterspirit, ARIS, Measures A and B, ProLatino, Ms. Atlas Press, and High Tech Gays, among others. All except three bars are gone, as are the newspapers, the bookstores, the baths, and the leather stores.

"Memories of friends long dead from AIDS are fading, too. Where can people, especially suburban gay men, go to reflect on the loss we all feel? Or to feel outraged over the deaths of Gwen Araujo, a murdered transgender woman, or Melvin Truss, a young gay Black man shot by a San Jose police officer while in his patrol car?

----

129   Ken Yeager. "History Museum Tells the Story of Queer Silicon Valley." *San Jose Mercury News*. June 27, 2021.

"All the heartache is displayed in the museum along with the pageantry that only queer people can create. Walk into the exhibit, and the first thing you will see are the outfits of a colorful folclorico dancer, a gown worn at an Imperial Court ball, and a leather outfit for a Mr. San Jose Leather contest.

"A panel describes useful terms to help allies better understand the ever-growing definitions that queer people use to describe themselves, such as transgender, gender nonconforming, nonbinary, intersex, bisexual, questioning, etc.

"Learn how the low point of the LGBTQ+ movement in Santa Clara County occurred in 1980 when 70 percent of voters rejected ordinances that prohibited discrimination based on sexual orientation, scaring off politicians to support LGBTQ+ rights for years to come. In the aftermath of that brutal anti-gay campaign, groups like Sisterspirit and Billy DeFrank Center were formed to counter the negative images that gays and lesbians were feeling about themselves.

"Likewise, the AIDS crisis had just as profound an impact here as anywhere. Approximately 2500 lives have been lost in Santa Clara County since AIDS was detected 40 years ago. A magnificent quilt honors the names of local people who died. The section ends with a poster promoting Getting to Zero—zero infections, zero deaths, zero stigma—and the hope that AIDS will be finally eradicated.

"Next in the exhibit is how activists in local tech companies pushed for domestic partner benefits and anti-discrimination ordinances long before they became industry standards. Their brilliant strategy was to change corporate America first, believing the government would follow, a reverse tactic from the usual approach that was successful.

"Turn the corner, and you will see brighter days after much despair. Political organizations like the Bay Area Municipal Elections Committee (BAYMEC) began to form and fight anti-discrimination measures. LGBTQ+ people started being elected for the first time, beginning with my election to the San Jose/ Evergreen Valley Community College Board in 1992.

"You can see the framed Rainbow flag that was the first to fly over San Jose City Hall—or any city hall in the county—when Mayor Ron Gonzales and I, a newly elected gay councilman, hoisted it up the flagpole in 2001.

"The exhibit tells the history that younger LGBTQ+ people know little about and have limited access to. The hope is that it allows them to see themselves in the continuum of an older queer generation that forged a path for them to walk.

"It's been a remarkable 50 years." [130]

The Grand Opening

Approximately 200 people attended the opening. No one had seen each other in over a year, so everyone was in a festive mood. Given COVID precautions, all socializing occurred outside in the large picnic area in front of the museum. The Silicon Valley Gay Men's Chorus and the Rainbow Women's Chorus both performed. Queer San Jose poet Shane Cota read his poem "Rainbow in the Valley," which included these ending lines:[131]

Pride
Was formed from those
Who fought for our rights
To simply exist
To hold space
In this world

So let's take up space!

----

130   Note: A video of the exhibit can be seen at www.queersiliconvalley. org/exhibit

131   To read Shane Cota's poem, go to www.queersiliconvalley.org/pride-flags-proclamations

And be true to yourself
And
Live your truth

And Know
that you ARE good,
You ARE beautiful,
You ARE all amazing,
together

We are Silicon Valley's LGBTQ+ community,
today
and forevermore
We must be PROUD of who we are.

WE ARE THE RAINBOW IN THE VALLEY

As the first groups of visitors exited, I was as nervous as a director of a Broadway show anxiously awaiting the reviews. I was happy and relieved that the response was so positive. Many people went out of their way to tell me how much they loved and appreciated the exhibit.

In my short comments during the program, I said that the impetus for the exhibit was to tell the history of the LGBTQ+ movement in Silicon Valley and to honor the work of queer folks who created a place where people could be their authentic selves, often with very little support from straight society.

"We have all been through so much together. Walking through the exhibit, I felt like I was reliving 50 years of history. No wonder I was exhausted when I exited," I joked.

I ended with this: "The exhibit is my thank you and love letter to the community that allowed me and so many others to pursue their interests and dreams and be the people they are today."

A friend of mine, Walt Hammon, had arranged for the San

Jose Chamber Orchestra to play throughout the evening. The music gave the event a nice touch of class. As the evening was winding down, I heard the distant sound of "Somewhere Over the Rainbow." I immediately walked over and stood in front of the musicians, absorbing all the notes while quietly singing to the words. It was the perfect ending to the day.

The Documentary

For the documentary, I hired SJSU professor Bob Gliner as the director and Luis Castillo as the film editor; Gliner and I were the producers. Steven Peck and Katie Lauer worked on the documentary as well.[132]

Gliner and I agreed to use *Queer Silicon Valley* as the title for the film, as it accurately summed up what the film was about. It was also short enough to have all the words listed on the station guides. We started filming in the fall of 2021.

We had initially budgeted $10,000 for the film, but newer estimates were closer to $23,000. In a conversation with the deputy superintendent of the Santa Clara County Office of Education, Gary Waddell, he mentioned how the documentary would be an educational tool for classroom instruction and asked if I needed any help. I said there was a gap of $13,000. He spoke to County Superintendent Dr. Mary Ann Dewan, who was immediately supportive and recommended the funding to her board.

The film follows the events in loosely chronological order, beginning with patrons and bar owners discussing how the bar scene helped create a sense of community, along with how they dealt with occasional police raids.

Next, activists in the early 1980s talk about how voter rejection of local anti-discrimination measures ended the gay

----

132   Bob Gliner and Ken Yeager, Producers. *Queer Silicon Valley*. 2022. https://www.youtube.com/results?search_query=queer+silicon+valley+documentary

political movement that was just beginning to form. It would take years before the community could recover.

The LGBTQ+ residents in Silicon Valley are as diverse as its overall population. That is why it was essential to have representatives from the African-American, Latinx, and Asian-American/Pacific Islander communities at the forefront to share their experiences and to discuss the formation of their organizations.

The HIV/AIDS epidemic hit the local gay male community hard, just like it did in other large cities across the country. The documentary includes reflections by doctors, nurses, and community members who lived through those dark years and remembered the pain they felt watching so many people fade before them.

Employees in high-tech companies like Apple and Hewlett-Packard discuss their efforts to have non-discrimination policies adopted. As these and other pro-gay policies began to be approved, more queer employees were drawn to these companies, slowly changing the workplace culture.

The film includes transgender men and women who share their unique experiences in trying to find their authentic selves.

The joy that same-sex partners felt when they were allowed to marry is captured through footage of the first marriages of two men and two women in the county, along with a sample of the Silicon Valley Gay Men's Chorus' rendition of "Chapel of Love."

The struggle for political representation and a seat at the table is covered by people who led the local political movement over the last 40 decades. They discuss the issues they had to deal with and the tactics they used to succeed.

We held the movie premiere at the Hammer Theater in downtown San Jose on February 25, 2022. My friend Fil Maresca organized the party. He suggested we print baseball cards of all 22 people featured in the film, including headshots and some information about each person as a way for audience members to learn and connect with them even before the movie started. To our delight, the documentary received great applause when the ending credits began to roll.

In late spring of 2022, the documentary was sent to PBS stations across the country to be played during June's Gay Pride Month. The response was gratifying. The film aired in 60 percent of the U.S. television market with 246 total airings, including prime time in Los Angeles, Chicago, Washington, DC, San Francisco, Denver, and other midsize markets such as Austin. It also played in the late afternoon in New York City and Philadelphia. In addition, the program was broadcast in the three largest Florida markets, despite the state's anti-LGBTQ+ political climate: Miami, Tampa, and Orlando. The film is available to watch on YouTube: *Queer Silicon Valley* documentary.[133]

The Traveling Exhibition

Amy Cohen from Exhibit Envoy had experience transferring the images in a physical exhibit onto 33.5" x 80" retractable posters. Although I was skeptical at first, to my surprise, it translated remarkably well. All 18 posters were large enough to include almost all of the exhibition's stories and photographs. Each was designed with vibrant colors, making them attractive to see and enjoyable to read. And since they were retractable, they were easy to put up and take down.

Each time the exhibition premieres at a new location, I feel fortunate to have had Exhibit Envoy create it. I would have felt a bit deflated if the exhibit had just gone into a storage locker after all the work that went into creating it. Now, it can travel to any city that wants it. Should the Foundation find a permanent location, the exhibition could remain on display.

The *2021 Metro* article about the creation of the museum exhibit ended with this quote from me: "Most people, especially

----

133   Names of people in the documentary are listed in Appendix C.

younger generations, don't think any gay things were happening in San Jose and Santa Clara County. And why would they? There wasn't anybody to tell them."

Until now.

> <

It's been a tremendous honor to serve my community as an activist, elected official, and now, as a historian. And while all of these pursuits are worthwhile, what matters most—especially during these perilous times—is simply for queer folks to take action. There are so many ways that LGBTQ+ people can get involved in their community. Find one, whether big or small, and get going. Staying silent and doing nothing only erodes our collective strength and hands power back to those who want to do us great harm. If you want to get involved but don't know where to start, here are a few clear-cut ways.

First, register to vote—and then be sure to follow through and actually *vote*. Second, volunteer for a candidate who is running to replace an anti-gay, anti-trans incumbent. Third, consider making annual financial contributions to local, state, or national LGBTQ+ political groups. They need as much funding and support as they can get to continue doing their crucial work. Fourth, if no queer political action committee exists in your area, create one yourself! Fifth, if you have political aspirations, follow along with Chapter 11's "candidate checklist" and take a shot at running for office. You never know where that journey may lead you. And finally, I strongly encourage all queer people to preserve and document their own history so it is never overlooked, misinterpreted, or forgotten. You never know where it will lead. Maybe to a website, museum exhibit, or documentary.

Good luck. You've got this, and I will be rooting for you every step of the way.

APPENDIX A

A Historical LGBTQ+ Timeline for San Jose/Silicon Valley

» August 1966: The Compton Cafeteria Riot marks the beginning of transgender activism in San Franciso

» June 28, 1969: The Stonewall Riots begin in New York City

» 1970: San Jose State gives organizational status to Gay Liberation Front

» December 15, 1973: The American Psychiatric Association's Board of Trustees votes to remove homosexuality from list of psychiatric disorders

» July 1975: Ms. Atlas Press is founded by Johnie Staggs and Rosalie "Nikki" Nichols

» October 3, 1975: First Pride event is held at SJSU

» 1976: Casa de San Jose, the first Imperial Court in the South Bay, is founded by Ray Aguilar

» 1976: The Lambda Association forms; the first edition of *Lambda News* is published

» 1976: Dignity/San Jose chapter forms

» June 26, 1976: San Jose's first Gay Freedom Day rally

» January 8, 1978: Harvey Milk takes office

» February 1978: San Jose City Council passes, then rescinds,

Gay Pride Week resolution

» April 19, 1978: Johnie Staggs and Sal Accardi begin unsuccessful write-in campaign for mayor and city council

» January 1979: Susan B. Anthony Democratic Club forms

» August 6, 1979: Santa Clara County approves LGBTQ+ anti-discrimination ordinance

» August 28, 1979: Following the County, San Jose City Council votes for LGBTQ+ anti-discrimination ordinance

» November 8, 1979: Proposition 6, a.k.a. the Briggs Initiative, fails

» June 3, 1980: City and County non-discrimination Measures A and B go down in overwhelming defeat

» January 1981: Johnie Staggs becomes first "out" lesbian elected to the state executive committee of the California Democratic Party

» March 1, 1981: First Billy DeFrank Gay Community Center opens at 86 Keyes Street

» November 1981: John Laird is elected to the Santa Cruz City Council, one of the first openly gay elected officials in the country

» April 1982: Governor Jerry Brown appoints LaDoris Cordell to Santa Clara County Municipal Court, making her the first African American woman judge in all of Northern California

» 1983: County AIDS/KS Foundation forms

» March 15, 1983: High Tech Gays (HTG) is founded by Rick Rudy, Denny Carroll, and Eric Lipanovich

» April 1983: Santa Clara County Public Health Department reports first confirmed AIDS cases

» June 1983: Imperial AIDS Foundation is founded in San Jose

» June 1983: Silicon Valley Gay Men's Chorus forms

» February 1984: The Gay Liberation Monument at Stanford University is vandalized

» May 25, 1984: Sisterspirit Bookstore is founded by Amy Caffrey, Mary Jeffrey, Marilyn Cook, and Karen Hester

» August 13, 1984: BAYMEC is founded by Ken Yeager and Wiggsy Sivertsen

» August 29, 1984: HTG files federal lawsuit: High Tech Gays vs. Defense Industrial Security Clearance Office (DISCO)

» November 1984: Tom Nolan is elected to the San Mateo County Board of Supervisors

» 1985: San Jose/Peninsula chapter of Parents, Families, and Friends of Lesbians and Gays (PFLAG) is established in Palo Alto

» 1985: The ARIS Project is founded in the living room of Bob Clayton

» 1985: Necessities and More, an HIV/AIDS support group, is founded

» May 4, 1985: San Jose police officer kills Black teen Melvin Truss

» October 2, 1985: Actor Rock Hudson dies of AIDS

» January 1986: Supervisors create Santa Clara County AIDS Task Force and appoint Ken Yeager as chair

» January 17, 1986: Wiggsy Sivertsen conducts sensitivity training for San Jose Police Department

» February 4, 1986: County allots $60,000 to ARIS after BAYMEC lobbies Board of Supervisors for AIDS funding

» March 1986: "Pastoral Guidelines for Ministry to Homosexuals in the Diocese of San Jose" is issued to help the clergy assist gay and lesbian Catholics

» June 21, 1986: Billy DeFrank Center moves to 1040 Park Avenue

» November 4, 1986: Lyndon LaRouche's Proposition 64 fails at the ballot box

» November 21, 1986: BAYMEC celebrates the successful Anti-Proposition 64 campaign with spaghetti feed at Mitty High School

» 1987: Dr. Marty Fenstersheib starts HIV Early Intervention Clinical Program

» March 1987: Larry Kramer founds ACT UP: AIDS Coalition to Unleash Power

» March 17, 1987: County AIDS Task Force issues its first report

» March 19, 1987: FDA approves AZT, the first drug to treat AIDS

» May 31, 1987: President Ronald Reagan mentions AIDS for the first time

» June 1987: After months of lobbying by BAYMEC, San Jose Mayor Tom McEnery issues a proclamation designating June 20 as Gay and Lesbian Human Rights Day, the first such mayoral proclamation since 1979

» August 19, 1987: Federal Judge Henderson rules in favor of HTG in HTG vs. DISCO lawsuit

» November 1987: At the urging of BAYMEC and the County Task Force on AIDS, the County Board of Supervisors approves an ordinance prohibiting discrimination against people with AIDS

» December 1987: Outlook TV is established at KMVT Studio

in Mountain View

» April 4, 1988: The San Jose Fire Department begins BAY-MEC sponsored training on gay and lesbian issues

» May 21, 1988: BAYMEC holds its first annual dinner at the San Jose Hyatt

» June 7, 1988: Lyndon LaRouche's second AIDS Quarantine Initiative, Proposition 69, is defeated

» June 28, 1988: At the urging of BAYMEC and the Human Relations Committee, the San Jose City Council approves an ordinance prohibiting discrimination against people with HIV/AIDS

» November 1988: The County Board of Supervisors pass an ordinance prohibiting discrimination against people with HIV/AIDS

» November 8, 1988: William Dannemeyer's AIDS/HIV Mandatory Reporting Initiative, Proposition 102, is defeated

» 1989: Imperial Royal Lion Monarchy Court is founded in San Jose

» May 1989: AIDS Memorial Quilt is displayed in San Jose

» July 1989: Documentarian Pam Walton releases *Out in Suburbia*

» April 8, 1990: Ryan White, an 18-year-old hemophiliac who contracted AIDS from a blood transfusion, dies

» 1990: The Silicon Valley Chapter of Log Cabin Republicans is formed by Mark Patrosso

» February 2, 1990: The Ninth Circuit Court reverses HTG vs. DISCO ruling

» August 18, 1990: Congress passes Ryan White CARE Act

» September 16, 1990: First Walk For AIDS in South Bay

» November 4, 1990: Billy DeFrank Center moves to 175 Stockton Avenue

» 1991: BayLands Chapter of FrontRunners is formed by Jay Davidson and Linda Johnson

» January 1991: The Leslie David Burgess Lifetime Achievement Award is created to recognize his work with the HIV community

» April 1991: Loma Prieta Gay and Lesbian Sierrans is founded by Mike Zampiceni and Paul Schoemaker

» June 11, 1991: William Kiley, a gay man living in San Jose, is attacked by his 17-year-old neighbor

» October 10, 1991: Alum Rock School District severs contract with Boy Scouts of America as a result of their policy banning gay Scout leaders

» January 15, 1992: Digital Queers forms, bringing the LGBTQ+ rights movement to high-tech companies

» February 1992: ProLatino is founded with Jamie Alejandro Campos as president and Omar Nunez as vice president

» February 19, 1992: South Bay Queer & Asian forms

» November 3, 1992: Ken Yeager is elected to San Jose/Evergreen Valley Community College Board, the first openly gay elected official in Santa Clara County

» November 7, 1992: The first gay commitment ceremony is published in the wedding section of the San Jose *Mercury News* after initial rejection

» 1993: BAYMEC convinces San Jose City Council to offer bereavement leave for domestic partners

» January 11, 1993: The San Jose/Evergreen Community College Board begins providing health coverage for same-sex domestic partners

» February 23, 1993: The San Jose/Evergreen Community College Board divests from Bank of America due to their contributions to the Boy Scouts

» April 23, 1993: Tonya King leads South Bay delegation to the March on Washington

» June 1993: Supervisor Ron Gonzales Issues first County Lesbian and Gay Pride Week proclamation

» April 12, 1994: San Jose City Council Member Kathy Cole is recalled due to homophobic and racist comments

» July 1994: Bob Sorenson steps down as Executive Director of ARIS; Norm Robinson is hired in his place

» September 1994: First LGBTQ+ Vietnamese Cultural Conference in Northern California is held at the Billy DeFrank Center

» September 12, 1994: SJSU removes ROTC from campus due to anti-gay concerns after 13 years of lobbying

» 1995: Partners for AIDS Care and Education (PACE) Clinic opens

» July 8, 1995: First BayLands FrontRunners Pride Run/Walk is held at Palo Alto Baylands Preserve

» August 2, 1995: President Bill Clinton issues an executive order prohibiting discrimination "On the Basis of Sexual Orientation," reversing the ruling in HTG vs. DISCO to favor HTG again

» September 30, 1995: AIDS Grove is dedicated near Children's Discovery Museum by Assemblyman John Vasconcellos

» December 1995: Santa Clara University bars gay alumni group from forming

» December 5, 1995: Major medical breakthrough with the development of the first protease inhibitor

» 1996: The Rainbow Women's Chorus forms

» January 20, 1996: San Jose native and publicly "out" figure skater Rudy Galindo wins national championship

» September 21, 1996: President Clinton signs the Defense of Marriage Act, which defines marriage as between a man and a woman only, for purposes of federal law

» 1997: Outlet opens for LGBTQ+ youth and young adults in Mid-Peninsula area

» August 23, 1998: First BayLands FrontRunners Run for the Community is held

» September 1998: Protests by SJSU LGBTQ+ Faculty and Staff Association end contract between Spartan Shops and Carl's Jr. due to owner Carl Karcher's reported funding of the 1978 Briggs Initiative that would have banned homosexuals from teaching in California schools

» September 30, 1998: SJSU Gay and Lesbian Faculty and Staff announces scholarship fund in honor of Wiggsy Sivertsen for LGBTQ+ students

» October 12, 1998: Matthew Shepard, who was beaten, tortured, and left to die near Laramie, Wyoming on the night of October 6, dies

» November 1998: Rich Gordon is elected to the San Mateo County Board of Supervisors

» 1999: Governor Pete Wilson appoints Randy Rice to the Santa Clara County Superior Court, making him the first openly LGBTQ+ judge in Santa Clara County

» 1999: The Rainbow Chamber Silicon Valley is established

» December 12, 1999: The Billy DeFrank Center moves to 938 The Alameda

» March 7, 2000: Proposition 22, the Defense of Marriage

Act, passes with 61 percent of the vote

» November 7, 2000: Ken Yeager is elected to the San Jose City Council

» January 2001: Governor Gray Davis appoints Jonathan Karesh to San Mateo County Superior Court

» June 5, 2001: The Rainbow Flag is flown over City Hall by Mayor Ron Gonzales and Councilmember Yeager for the very first time

» October 16, 2001: Councilmember Yeager helps secure $1.8 million from the City of San Jose to remodel the Billy De-Frank Center

» April 23, 2002: The San Jose City Council votes to amend its harassment policy to include protections for gender identity

» October 3, 2002: Teenager Gwen Araujo is brutally murdered by four men after they discover she is transgender

» November 5, 2002: Jamie McLeod wins a seat on the City of Santa Clara Council, making her the first "out" lesbian in the county elected to public office

» November 5, 2002: John Laird is elected to State Assembly

» February 12, 2004: San Francisco begins to issue marriage licenses

» March 4, 2004: San Jose Mayor Gonzales and Councilmember Yeager propose ordinance to recognize same-gender marriages from other jurisdictions so spouses can receive employee benefits

» November 2, 2004: John Linder is elected to the Franklin-McKinley School Board

» March 30, 2006: Danielle R. Castro is honored at the Santa Clara County Human Relations Awards Breakfast for her advocacy and work with the county's transgender residents

» May 2006: Shawna Schwarz is appointed to the Santa Clara County Superior Court by Governor Arnold Schwarzenegger, the first "out" lesbian on the Court

» June 6, 2006: Ken Yeager is elected to the Santa Clara County Board of Supervisors

» November 7, 2006: Evan Low is elected to the Campbell City Council

» 2007: Rodrigo Garcia creates De Ambiente at Outlet, the first leadership program for Spanish-speaking LGBTQ+ youth in Silicon Valley

» June 5, 2007: Supervisor Yeager raises the Rainbow Flag over the County Government Center for the first time

» 2008: Latinos de Ambiente del Area de la Bahia is founded as a Coalition of LGBTQ+ Latinx organizations around the Bay Area

» 2008: Silicon Valley Rainbow Chamber of Commerce holds its first fundraising dinner

» 2008: Silicon Valley/San Francisco LGBTQ+ ERG Alliance holds its first event to raise money for the Billy DeFrank Center

» May 15, 2008: California Supreme Court strikes down Proposition 22

» June 17, 2008: Marriages begin across California; first marriages are performed in Santa Clara County with Supervisor Yeager officiating

» November 4, 2008: California voters pass Proposition 8, enshrining "One-Man, One-Woman" doctrine into California Constitution

» November 2008: Marriage Equality Silicon Valley is founded after Proposition 8 passes

» 2009: LGBTQ+ Youth Space, a safe place for youth ages 13 to 25, opens at the Billy DeFrank Center

» January 10, 2009: Rally to protest the Defense of Marriage Act is organized by Marriage Equality Silicon Valley

» January 12, 2010: Supervisor Yeager serves as the first openly gay president of the County Board of Supervisors

» February 2010: Gov. Arnold Schwarzenegger appoints lesbian Julie Emede to Santa Clara County Superior Court

» October 5, 2010: Jim Unland, a sergeant in the San Jose Police Department, comes "out" as a gay man in a *Mercury News* editorial to criticize San Jose Mayor Reed's endorsement of anti-LGBTQ+ council candidate Larry Pegram

» November 2, 2010: Rich Gordon is elected to State Assembly

» November 2, 2010: Rich Waterman is elected to Campbell City Council

» November 2, 2010: Jordan Eldridge is elected to the Rancho Rinconada Recreation and Park District

» April 2011: San Jose native Judy Rickard writes "Torn Apart" about same-sex couples and U.S. Immigration discrimination

» August 1, 2011: Colectivo Accion Latina de Ambiente, or Colectivo ALA, is founded by Rodrigo Garcia, Omar Nunez, and Hugo Badillo

» August 24, 2011: Tim Cook is named the CEO of Apple, becoming the most prominent openly gay CEO in the nation

» July 2012: Molly O'Neal is appointed by the Board of Supervisors to lead the Public Defender's Office, the first openly LGBTQ+ person to do so

» July 14, 2012: The FAIR Education Act of 2012 is signed

into law, ensuring LGBTQ+ contributions are included in school curriculums

» September 14, 2012: Silicon Valley Marriage Equality, along with Alice Hoagland, whose gay son Mark Bingham died in the 9/11 terrorist attacks, meet with San Jose Mayor Chuck Reed but are not successful in changing his position against same-sex marriage

» November 6, 2012: Chris Clark is elected to Mountain View City Council

» November 6, 2012: Dennis Chiu is elected to the El Camino Hospital Board

» January 29, 2013: President of the County Board Ken Yeager calls for County health assessment of LGBTQ+ community, the first of its kind in the County

» June 28, 2013: Proposition 8 is overturned by the U.S. Supreme Court; same-sex marriage returns only in California. BAYMEC organizes Day of Decision rally in front of San Jose City Hall

» December 20, 2013: The LGBTQ+ Health Assessment is completed, leading to increased funding for health programs and services for the LGBTQ+ community and paving the way for the creation of the Office of LGBTQ+ Affairs

» November 4, 2014: Evan Low is elected to the State Assembly

» November 4, 2014: Omar Torres is elected to the Franklin-McKinley School Board

» November 4, 2014: Daniel Yost is elected to the Woodside City Council

» November 7, 2014: The Health Trust renames and dedicates the Jerry Larson FOODBasket

- » 2015: Teatro Alebrijes is founded, becoming the first LGBTQ+ Latinx theater ensemble

- » March 24, 2015: Supervisor Yeager proposes the creation of an Office of LGBTQ+ Affairs, the first for any county in the U.S.

- » June 2015: Former San Jose Earthquakes player Matt Hatzke comes out as gay

- » June 26, 2015: U.S. Supreme Court allows nationwide same-sex marriages to proceed

- » January 2016: The Office of LGBTQ+ Affairs Officially Opens with Maribel Martinez as director

- » 2016: Valley Transportation Authority (VTA) includes LGBTQ+ -owned businesses as subcontractors as a factor in approving contracts

- » March 2016: The Rainbow Crosswalk is installed near the entrance of the Billy DeFrank Center on The Alameda

- » March 22, 2016: The Transgender Pride Flag flies at County Government Center on the 6th Annual Transgender Day of Visibility

- » June 2016: Santa Clara County allocates $6 million spread over four years for the Getting to Zero Campaign

- » June 2016: Sunnyvale raises the Pride Flag for the first time

- » June 12, 2016: Mass shooting at Pulse Nightclub in Orlando, Florida

- » November 8, 2016: Rene Spring is elected to Morgan Hill City Council

- » March 14, 2017: County approves policy to convert restroom signage at all 430 single-user restrooms in County facilities

- » June 2017: Stonewall Democratic Club of Santa Clara County is formed

» August 8, 2017: Supervisor Yeager proposes expanding Transgender community services and hiring Transgender Services Program Manager

» August 24: 2017: San Jose Police Department becomes first police department in the nation to launch a recruiting campaign featuring SJPD gay and lesbian couples

» September 21, 2017: County celebrates Bisexuality Visibility Week and flies the Bisexual Pride Flag

» October 30, 2017: County is the lead author of a brief filed with U.S. Supreme Court in Masterpiece Cakeshop case

» December 2017: Shay Franco-Clausen is appointed to the Santa Clara Valley Open Space Authority

» June 1, 2018: The City of Milpitas holds its first Pride celebration

» June 2018: The Rainbow Flag flies over Saratoga City Hall for the first time

» June 2018: The City of Campbell lights up a water tower in rainbow colors

» August 2018: Santa Clara County hires program manager for Transgender Services

» August 2018: The Valley Transportation Authority (VTA) wraps a bus in Rainbow Pride

» August 2, 2018: Santa Clara County Fair hosts "Out at the Fair," the first LGBTQ+ inclusive event at the fair

» August 25, 2018: Silicon Valley Pride Hosts Trans and Friends Rally

» September 30, 2018: Assemblymember Evan Low works with SJPD to pass first-in-the-nation LGBTQ+ training law AB2504

» October 2018: Governor Jerry Brown appoints Charles

Adams to the Santa Clara County Superior Court

» October 16, 2018: Supervisor Yeager submits referral for Board of Supervisors to establish an LGBTQ+ Health and Wellness Center

» October 28, 2018: #WontBeErased rally happens at San Jose City Hall to protest the Trump Administration's anti-transgender agenda

» November 6, 2018: Jorge Pacheco, Jr. is elected to the Oak Grove School District Board

» November 6, 2018: Nancy Magee is elected as the San Mateo County Superintendent of Schools

» March 30, 2019: The Billy DeFrank Center hosts Transgender Day of Visibility at San Jose City Hall Rotunda

» April 6, 2019: The County Transgender Health Center has its grand opening in San Jose

» April 9, 2019: BAYMEC successfully lobbies City of San Jose to display Rainbow Pride and Transgender Pride Flags at San Jose Airport in response to opening a Chick-fil-A

» June 3, 2019: First county homeless shelter for LGBTQ+ adults opens in San Jose

» June 21, 2019: The Office of LGBTQ+ Affairs holds its first LGBTQ+ summit

» August 2019: San Jose Police Chief Eddie Garcia raises the Rainbow flag in front of the police headquarters, thought to be the first time any police chief has done so. Since becoming the Dallas chief of police, Garcia has kept up the tradition of raising the flag.

» August 23, 2019: Pride flag flies outside the San Jose Police Department Headquarters

» October 23, 2019: Rotary Club Silicon Valley Rainbow is

chartered

» January 2020: The Santa Clara County Behavioral Health Services Department creates The Q Corner, a peer-run program offering wellness support, resource linkage, community events, and trainings

» June 15, 2020: U.S. Supreme Court rules gay and transgender workers are protected from discrimination under Title VII of the Civil Rights Law of 1964

» June 27, 2020: Black Trans Lives Matter rally is held at the Billy DeFrank Center

» June 29, 2020: Justin Lardinois is appointed to the San Jose Planning Commission

» August 27, 2020: SJPD unveils the Rainbow Patch in support of the LGBTQ+ community

» September 10, 2020: San Jose's LGBTQ+ district Qmunity opens

» November 3, 2020: John Laird is elected to State Senate

» November 3, 2020: Alex Lee is elected to State Assembly

» November 3, 2020: Anthony Becker is elected to the City of Santa Clara City Council

» November 3, 2020: Alysa Cisneros is elected to the Sunnyvale City Council

» November 3, 2020: Ivan Rosales Montes is elected to the Morgan Hill Unified School District

» November 3, 2020: Beija Gonzales is elected to the Oak Grove School District

» November 3, 2020: Carla Hernandez is elected to the Oak Grove School District

» November 3, 2020: Lissette Espinoza-Garnica is elected to

the Redwood City Council

» November 3, 2020: Michael Smith is elected to the Redwood City Council

» November 3, 2020: James Coleman is elected to the South San Francisco City Council

» December 15, 2020: Laura Parmer-Lohan becomes the first out lesbian to serve as mayor of any city in San Mateo or Santa Clara counties

» January 2021: The Q Corner and Gender Health Center launch the Trans Care Coalition, a collaboration of County and community-based staff establishing best practice recommendations to improve services for the trans community

» April 2021: Governor Gavin Newsom appoints Jessica Delgado to Santa Clara County Superior Court

» April 23, 2021: Natalia Smut Lopez, a San Jose Transgender Woman and drag artist, is killed by her boyfriend

» June 4, 2021: LGBTQ+ history exhibit, "Coming Out: 50 Years of Queer Resistance and Resilience in Silicon Valley," opens for a year-long run at History San Jose

» June 4, 2021: The Los Gatos Town Council votes to add rainbow stripes to two crosswalks in front of the Town Hall, leading to protests by hate groups

» November 14, 2021: Chanting "Love, United," thousands of people come together in Los Gatos for a Walk Against Hate to denounce hate speech by a group of MAGA disrupters

» February 25, 2022: Documentary film *Queer Silicon Valley* premieres at Hammer Theater in San Jose

» June 13, 2022: Sera Fernando is appointed as manager of the Office of LGBTQ+ Affairs

» October 22, 2022: The Billy DeFrank Center holds its 40th

Anniversary dinner

» **November** 2022: Ben Geilhufe is hired to create the Specialty Mental Health Gender Affirming Care Clinic

» **November** 8, 2022: Omar Torres is elected to the San Jose City Council

» **November** 8, 2022: J.R. Fruen is elected to the Cupertino City Council

» **November** 8, 2022: Richard Mehlinger is elected to the Sunnyvale City Council

» **November** 8, 2022 Jaria Jaug is elected to the Berryessa Union School Board

» **November** 8, 2022: Chris Sturken is elected to the Redwood City Council

» **November** 19, 2022: Mass shooting at Club Q in Colorado Springs, Colorado

» December 13, 2022: President Biden signs the Respect for Marriage Act, which overturns the Defense of Marriage Act, requiring states to honor marriages from other states, and guarantees federal protection for same-sex and interracial couples

» March 2023: The Q Corner launches The Harm ReduQion Project, a program focused on connecting the LGBTQ+ community with substance overdose prevention and substance use prevention and treatment resources

» March 28, 2023: San Jose City Councilman Omar Torres invites drag queen WooWoo Monroe (aka George Downes) to open the council meeting, a first

» April 14 and 15, 2023: Craig Hella Johnson's *Considering Matthew Shephard* is performed by the Choral Project and SJSU Choraliers at the Hammer Theater

- » April 16, 2023: BAYMEC resumes its annual fundraising brunch with San Diego Mayor Todd Gloria as the guest speaker. Over 500 people attend

- » April 29, 2023: The Billy DeFrank LGBTQ+ Community Center sponsors the Silicon Valley Trans Day of Visibility at the San Jose City Hall Rotunda

- » June 3, 2023: LEAD Filipino holds its annual queer Summit at DeAnza College

- » June 6, 2023: DeAnza Pride holds Queer and Now Conference with activist Honey Mahogany

- » June 6-30: Queer Silicon Valley's traveling museum exhibit is displayed at San Jose City Hall

- » June 9 and 11, 2023: New Museum of Los Gatos hosts historian and author Richard D. Mohr for lectures on Los Gatos artists and life partners Frank Ingerson and George Dennison.

- » June 9-11, 2023: 5th Annual Queer Afro Latin Dance Festival is held in San Jose

- » June 10, 2023: San Mateo County Pride holds its 11th annual festival which includes its first parade

- » June 11, 2023: The Silicon Valley Gay Men's Chorus celebrates its 40-year anniversary at the Hammer Theater in San Jose

- » August 26-27, 2023: Silicon Valley Pride holds its annual Pride parade and festival

APPENDIX B

Four Former County Supervisors Recall the Turbulent Times of Measures A and B

In the back of my mind, there always remained questions as to why the council and supervisors voted for the ordinances when they knew such laws were being defeated across the nation. That is why I thought it would be enlightening to bring the five supervisors together to share their memories of this important part of Silicon Valley history. Four supervisors agreed: Dominic Cortese, Rod Diridon, Dan McCorquodale, and Susanne (Susie) Wilson.

Wilson began with a recollection of her earlier experience with the Religious Right. In her previous position as a San Jose councilmember, conservative church members turned out in force to insist that the council rescind the 1978 vote on the gay pride proclamation. She mentioned the fallout from this vote when she walked door-to-door in her campaign that year for a seat on the board of supervisors. In the end, she was victorious, but she remembered experiencing lots of doors being slammed in her face, something she noted had never happened to her before when campaigning.

McCorquodale commented that discrimination against gays was not a new issue for him. He recounted his anger and helplessness when, as a young Marine, one of his friends was discharged from the Corps for having been seen leaving what was considered a gay bar. There was no due process and no avenue for recourse. He said that he thought his vote on the anti-discrimination ordinance was one of his opportunities to speak out for equality and justice.

Cortese said he considered the vote on the ordinance premature and that it concerned a moral issue to be discussed by the church and not legislated by the government. "In many ways, I still feel that way." He added his thought that "My church has not done enough to open that door." He reminisced, "I was in a learning process. The whole country was in a learning process." He concluded by saying, "I commend my colleagues for moving forward in a very bold manner. We had a very proactive board."

In response to a question concerning what the hearings were like, Diridon said that the calls and letters received by the Board offices numbered at least 10 to 1 in opposition to the ordinance. Still, he didn't believe the opponents reflected the entire community. He commented that anti-gay sentiment was being preached from the pulpits of the conservation churches, as reflected, in part, by the number of calls against the ordinance the board offices received on Monday mornings.

When asked if they saw the referendum coming, Wilson said "no"; Diridon said "yes"; Cortese said he felt the whole controversy was likely to have set back the movement. McCorquodale said he could tell the proponents were in trouble from the very beginning but that rescinding the vote wasn't an option as it would have been much "too disheartening for too many people."

All described the campaign as "brutal."

Diridon recalled leaving the church with his wife and children on one occasion and finding that every car in the church lot had a flyer on the windshield condemning his vote and stating, "Diridon is a false person" and "Actually, he's gay." He subsequently learned that the flyer was distributed to every car in all the church parking lots in his district.

Diridon went on to say that his support for the ordinance was a dominant factor in his losing the Senate election in April 1980. He clearly remembered being told by a state Democratic Party leader, "If he voted for this issue, he was committing suicide." After his vote, he said some state Democratic leaders lost interest in his campaign. However, he concluded, "If you don't vote your conscience, you're not worth a damn."

Wilson said this issue didn't seem to hurt her in her 1982 re-election campaign. Diridon, too, was re-elected to the Board in 1982.

Cortese won the election to a seat in the State Assembly in the November 1980 election. McCorquodale ran unopposed that year for another term on the Board of Supervisors.

However, in McCorquodale's 1982 state senate campaign, his opponent, incumbent Senator Dan O'Keefe, tried to make an issue of the gay rights vote in Stanislaus County, the more conservative part of the district. McCorquodale commented that, while he received adverse reactions from certain individuals, the issue never seemed to gain traction.

When interviewer Terry Christensen asked if the supervisors ever regretted their vote, all said "no." Cortese added that he had been consistent with his votes in support of LGBT issues over his 16 years in the Assembly, although he voted "no" on AB 1 in 1984. Diridon said that it was emancipating to vote his conscience despite the consequences.

APPENDIX C

Names of People Interviewed for the Documentary *Queer Silicon Valley*

Rebecca Obryan

Bennet Marks

Omar Nunez

Liz Burkhouse

Fred Ferrer

Rodrigo Garcia

Lance Moore

Aejaie Franciscus

Dani Castro

Elizabeth Birch

Dr. Dennis Low

Kim Harris

Whayne Herriford

Wiggsy Sivertsen

Gail Chandler-Croll

Jim Michl

Maribel Martinez

Amor Santiago

Diamond John

Sera Fernando

Ken Yeager

Dr. Marty Fenstersheib

Sharon Miller

Appendix D

The Battle Against HIV/AIDS: A Look Back at the First Decades of the Santa Clara County Experience
by Ken Yeager

Introduction

The LGBTQ+ community has made great strides toward civil rights and in the fight against HIV/AIDS. Today does not feel like it did in the 1980s and 90s. It's important to recognize that the decades prior to our recent advancements were ones of hardship and devastating loss of life.

Although the LGBTQ+ community has endured countless hardships, perhaps nothing has cut so deeply as HIV/AIDS. I recognize that no retelling can truly capture the pervasive fear, enormous suffering, and agonizing sorrow this merciless disease inflicted.

I remember losing many friends. In a short period of time, they went from being vibrant and healthy to gone forever. No retelling can fully capture the pervasive fear and sorrow that this disease inflicted during these times.

During these years, hope remained in short supply.

Our entire society is much poorer because of the incredible potential that was taken by these thousands of early, untimely deaths.

Looking back, we find selfless heroes in the battle against

HIV/AIDS. There was amazing tenacity, generosity, and self-sacrifice. I have called attention to a handful of the many Santa Clara County saints. Another entire account could be devoted to the brave and dedicated others.

However, there were also villains who perpetuated bigotry and discrimination for political gain, which greatly exacerbated the suffering and slowed the progress of research and treatment.

I believe that now is the time to remember those years and reflect on the decisions that were made here in Santa Clara County. I have been told by early readers of this manuscript that it was cathartic to recall those grim days, producing tears of sadness but also of joy.

It is my hope that these emotions will be harnessed and focused on the jobs that are yet unfinished. AIDS continues to claim lives, particularly in certain communities. Far too many people are not taking advantage of early and easy testing options and medications.

For those who weren't old enough to experience these early years of the AIDS epidemic, I hope this account will inform you. For those like me, who lived through the darkest days, I hope this serves as a reminder of how far we have come in many aspects of societal changes. For all, I hope it will inspire you to become involved because we can all make a difference.

» Ken Yeager

The Battle Against HIV/AIDS

In 1981, the LGBTQ+ community in Santa Clara County was still in shock following the overwhelming defeats of Measures A and B, which would have established anti-discrimination ordinances for all the unincorporated areas and in the City of San Jose. The political campaigns in favor of the two ordinances had been plagued by disorganization and in-fighting. The community was demoralized and, by all appearances, mostly disinterested in further political action.

With all this, it is not surprising that the first media reports of a new mystery illness affecting gay men did not resonate in the South Bay when they appeared in May and June of that year. The *San Francisco Chronicle* covered the June 5, 1981, announcement by the Centers for Disease Control that five young, previously healthy gay men had come down with a rare lung infection, but the San Jose *Mercury News* did not.

The South Bay's LGBTQ+ newspaper at the time, the *Lambda News*, did not publish its first article about AIDS until December 1982, more than 18 months after the first CDC reports and after it had already been the subject of articles in *Time* and *Newsweek* magazines and a report on ABC's *Good Morning America*.

In his 2002 book "From Closet to Community," Ted Sahl recalled the first case of AIDS in San Jose was reported "in early 1980," affecting a "popular activist in the community." However, his memory of the early 80s was that "life still went on. You never heard any conversation about AIDS, either in bars or at any gay events. The community was in denial for another three years."

My friend Karl Vidt, who would become a prominent HIV/AIDS advocate, including a multi-year term as chair of the Santa Clara County World AIDS Day committee, reflected the prevailing South Bay attitude of the early 1980s. He said during that period, AIDS was "something affecting people in San Francisco."

Dr. Ira Greene knew differently.

In 1981, Greene saw some of the first local AIDS cases when otherwise healthy men began coming down with Kaposi's sarcoma, a rare type of skin cancer. He noticed that these patients also had swollen glands, lethargy, and other symptoms that came to be associated with AIDS.

DR. IRA GREENE:

In 1981, Dr. Ira Greene was already a well-respected and be-loved doctor. As the Chief of Dermatology at Santa Clara Valley Medical Center (VMC), he began seeing an increasing number of patients with Kaposi's sarcoma (KS). At the time, he didn't know that he was treating an illness that would soon grow into an epidemic.

Greene attended medical school at the University of North Carolina, and after initial training as an internist in Arizona, he made his way to Stanford for a residency in dermatology. He eventually became a clinical professor there, in addition to his role at VMC.

The KS cases Greene saw in the early 1980s caught his at-tention because they began appearing in relatively young men. Until then, KS was an extremely rare condition that mostly afflicted elderly patients. Because Greene had experience in internal medicine, he also took note of the strange mix of skin lesions, swollen glands, lethargy, pneumonia, and other symp-toms affecting these patients.

That laundry list of symptoms soon became associated with the syndrome doctors would come to call AIDS. Greene's knowledge and background as a gay healthcare professional made him a logical choice for leading the effort to combat the emerging disease. Alongside Dr. David Stevens, Greene estab-lished a specialty treatment center at VMC that eventually became known as the Partners in AIDS Care and Education (PACE) Clinic. However, it was his empathy and connection to his pa-tients that truly made him the right person for the job.

By 1988, Greene became associate director of Santa Clara County's AIDS program. Even though that leadership role took much of his time, Greene never stopped seeing people with AIDS one-on-one as a primary care physician. His compassion during these often bleak years was steadfast. He did all that he could for his patients, often securing experimental treatments in a last-ditch effort to save the dying.

Friends who knew Greene saw the emotional toll that this work exacted. He developed many close personal ties with patients who ultimately succumbed to the epidemic. Still, he continued to make visits to AIDS patients through the 1990s.

"When you work with dying people, you learn a lot about yourself. You are forced to confront your own feelings about death. You feel very mortal," Greene said in an interview with the San Jose *Mercury News* in the late 1980s.

Tragically, Greene died in 1998 when his Palo Alto home caught fire. It was a shocking loss for the community.

Throughout his life, Greene received numerous professional awards for his work as an inspiring teacher and a skilled physician. Friends and colleagues, though, will most remember him for his kind heart and dedication to treating a community that was desperate for care yet often shunned and misunderstood. Today, the PACE Clinic bears his name, a fitting tribute to a man who made a huge impact on the lives of so many and helped lead this community through the crisis.

In 1981 and 1982, Dr. Marty Fenstersheib, who would later go on to become Santa Clara County's Health Officer and Public Health Director, was living in San Francisco and working part-time at the city's Health Center One, located on 17th Street in the Castro District.

"Guys were coming in, and they had swollen lymph glands. We knew there was this new disease going around, but we didn't have a name for it. There was no etiology; we were calling it GRID," Fenstersheib recounted in a 2017 interview. Gay Related Immune Deficiency was a term used for the disease in its earliest months. By the middle of 1982, it had been replaced by AIDS.

"There was nothing to do for these guys. I remember they came in, and there was nothing, nothing. It was basically people coming in with these strange symptoms. A lot of them were very sick and went right to San Francisco General's Ward 86.

They did not do very well; most of them were dead within nine months," Fenstersheib recalled.

1983: 10 AIDS diagnoses; five deaths

By 1983, AIDS had arrived in Santa Clara County. The Public Health Department reported the county's first confirmed AIDS diagnosis in April.

The South Bay LGBTQ+ publication *Our Paper* published a story on June 29 illustrating the rampant fear at the time regarding contact with AIDS patients. The story reported that two nurses at Santa Clara Valley Medical Center resigned rather than treat someone thought to have AIDS.

Bob Sorenson, later to become executive director of the non-profit group the Aris Project, shared a glimpse into the trauma experienced by persons with AIDS and by those trying to assist them in a presentation in 1983. He emphasized the emotional shock young people felt when told they have a terminal disease, as well as the rejection they experienced from family, friends, and co-workers. As the person became progressively disabled, people around them were having hysterical responses, worried it was contagious.

1983 also saw the formation of the Santa Clara County AIDS/KS Foundation. Many kinds of fundraisers were held to raise money to start a local chapter of the foundation and to support its services. An association of gay bar owners and bartenders raised $5,000. One bar in San Jose, HMS, alone donated more than $1,000. Local volunteer and activist Jeff Barber was instrumental in securing a $3,500 donation from IBM's Fund for Community Service, and donations large and small came from numerous sources.

Organizers of the local chapter began holding weekly meetings at private homes. The meetings were attended by a cross-section of concerned individuals, both gay and non-gay, including medical doctors, science professors, nurse practitioners, counselors, businesspeople, political consultants, and representatives of county agencies and nonprofit organizations.

Their immediate focus was on providing information and referrals through a hotline and drop-in availability at their office. Educational materials were designed to alert people at risk to the danger of AIDS and to dispel hysteria among the public. Support services for people with AIDS, and possibly home care and even housing, were planned as resources permitted. The chapter also organized a legal committee to help with administrative problems and provide advice to patients.

An article in *Our Paper/Your Paper* stated: "The chapter board itself experienced some of the public hysteria when a landlord reneged on an oral agreement for office space in a building on The Alameda. Contacts with other landlords proved unfruitful whenever the term 'AIDS' was mentioned." The chapter finally found a home on North First Street near San Jose's Civic Center.

One of the chapter's first requests was to the County Public Health Department for a nurse to help in teaching about the disease. Millicent Kellogg was selected. She related how difficult it was because of how little was known. "You had to say so often, 'I don't know. We don't know that yet. That doesn't seem to be the case. Well, that's what we understand, but it doesn't sound right,' or 'Yes, that's the way it is.'"

The Santa Clara County Health Department's Public Health Bureau AIDS Program was formed in 1983 to conduct community education. Kellogg and health education specialists David Burgess and Valerie Kegebian were hired. They formed a team led by Fenstersheib, who had been employed as the director of the Santa Clara County Public Health Department Immunization Program. Utilizing a small grant from the state, the team began to educate people in jails, gay bars, and elsewhere. They also distributed condoms. In November, Santa Clara County obtained its first state funding for AIDS. The Public Health Department received $37,545 for AIDS control activities.

On the national scene in 1983, AIDS was first reported among the female partners of men who had the disease, suggesting it could be passed on via heterosexual sex. The first cases of AIDS in children were also reported. Researchers concluded they had probably been directly infected by their mothers before, during, or shortly after birth. By September, the CDC had identified all major routes of transmission and ruled out transmission by casual contact, food, water, air, or surfaces.

By the end of the year, 10 people in the county had been diagnosed with the disease, and five of them had already died. The death toll would continue to increase each year for the next decade. The number more than doubled in 1984 and then doubled again the following year.

1984: 32 HIV diagnoses; 15 new deaths, 20 total deaths; 23 living with HIV/AIDS

Before 1984, education and prevention efforts were hampered because so little was known about the disease. It was not until April of that year that French and American researchers announced that they had jointly discovered the virus that causes AIDS. It was given the name HIV.

In a 1995 interview with Sahl, Fenstersheib recalled what AIDS education was like during these early years: "We would go anywhere, meet with anybody, wherever anybody would listen to us. Sometimes the group would speak to audiences of as few as four people. We would ask, 'How many of you know anything about AIDS?' Over and over again, the response would be the same: 'Nothing.'

"It was an uphill battle all the way," he continued. "Nobody, not even the medical community, recommended testing because they could not offer people anything more than knowledge. On top of that was the discrimination the client might experience and all the other negative things, like family rejection and loss of employment and housing that went along with testing positive for the AIDS virus.

"I remember thinking that we were sending people back out on the street with the knowledge, but there was no place for them to go," Fenstersheib said. "What we really needed was a screening clinic where trained personnel could sit down and talk to clients, ask them how they were doing, and possibly refer them to a medical care facility where they might receive additional help."

DR. MARTY FENSTERSHEIB:

Born in Pittsburgh, Pennsylvania, Dr. Marty Fenstersheib received his BS at Tulane University, MD at Universidad Autonoma de Guadalajara and MPH at U.C. Berkeley. He is Board Certified in Pediatrics and Preventive Medicine. He always craved big challenges. He left his first job in private practice because he found it too easy. He entered U.C. Berkeley's Public Health program and, as a fluent Spanish speaker, was soon working in a Spanish-language clinic in San Francisco's Mission District.

In 1984, he joined Santa Clara County's Public Health Department as director of the immunization program. This was in the early days of the epidemic. "I actually was the first person in the health department that gave results to people that they were HIV positive. The test came out in 1985, and nobody knew what to do, so no one wanted to give the results. So, I did," Fenstersheib said. "It soon became known that if you got the test and I came in the room—it wasn't good news. After that, there was nothing else to tell them."

Fenstersheib achieved national prominence when he pioneered a then-revolutionary AIDS treatment that meshed medical care with education to keep infected patients from spreading the virus. He helped open a County clinic to provide education, referrals, and support. The approach was profiled in the *Journal of the American Medical Association*.

The HIV Early Intervention Clinical Program he started in 1987 became the model for the State of California. More than two dozen similar clinics were subsequently established and funded across the state. When Congress significantly expanded the federal funding for AIDS care in 1990 with the passage of the Ryan White CARE Act, Fenstersheib's program became the national model for AIDS treatment clinics.

Throughout the epidemic, Fenstersheib continued to serve as a hands-on clinician, caring for HIV patients for more than 27 years, even after becoming the County's Public Health Officer and later, after adding the role of the Public Health Department Director.

The epidemic had a profound impact on Fenstersheib personally. His partner was diagnosed as HIV positive in 1984 and died in 1992. In addition, Fenstersheib has sung with the San Francisco Gay Men's Chorus since 1983, and he reflects on the loss of more than 300 members of the chorus who have died of AIDS since the epidemic began.

Meanwhile, Burgess, Kegebian, and Kellogg kept the education program moving forward. Burgess, who was very unabashed, did some of the first safe-sex classes—using a banana to demonstrate the correct method of putting on a condom. Everybody loved him. Kellogg also had a special approach in her delivery—drawing simple pictures and explaining things so well that people really understood what she was talking about.

During this terrifying era of AIDS, many bathhouses were shut down. In October 1984, the San Francisco Public Health Director, Dr. Mervyn Silverman, moved to close San Francisco's gay bathhouses and sex clubs. San Jose's Watergarden was one of only two bathhouses that remained open in the entire Bay Area, largely attributable to Watergarden founder Sal Accardi who pushed for safe sex practices from the beginning. Accardi was one of the first bathhouse owners to work with public health officials to set up a program to stop sexually transmitted diseases. Sadly, he died of AIDS in 1994.

In 1984, the first support group for people with HIV and AIDS began meeting at the Grace Baptist Church in San Jose.

However, when some church members found out and expressed fear of contracting the disease from toilet seats or other surfaces, the meetings moved to the home of community activist Bob Clayton.

This was also the year that I came out publicly in a *Mercury News* op-ed. Within weeks of coming out, I began planning how to politically organize the South Bay's LGBTQ+ community. Discussions with Wiggsy Sivertsen led to our founding of the Bay Area Municipal Elections Committee (BAYMEC) that summer.

While passing civil rights legislation and supporting LGBTQ+ candidates were BAYMEC's primary goals, increased funding for AIDS research and treatment was not far behind. Our first fundraiser was held in October, featuring then-Assemblyman Art Agnos as a speaker. The press announcement said, "Other issues of primary concern to the committee include increased AIDS funding, the Equal Rights Amendment, equal pay for equal work, and the enactment of non-discriminatory government, police, and corporate personnel policies to protect lesbian and gay civil rights."

Also in October, the State Department of Health Services awarded a second grant to Santa Clara County for AIDS-related services. The FY84-85 allocation was $52,905.

1985: 148 HIV diagnoses; 33 new deaths, 53 total deaths; 148 living with HIV/AIDS

There were 33 AIDS deaths reported in the county and 148 people diagnosed with HIV in 1985. At BAYMEC, we were busy trying to grow our new organization and get local elected officials to take us seriously. Still, almost every one of our monthly board meetings included at least one AIDS-related topic.

That year was also when the first HIV test became available, and the Public Health Department opened an HIV testing clinic in San Jose.

Fenstersheib again took on the difficult role of telling people they were HIV positive. In a 2012 *San Jose Business Journal* interview, he recalled the reactions of those earliest patients, "They would run out, bang doors, sometimes they'd cry, sometimes they'd scream. It was horrible."

1985 also saw an explosion of media coverage of the AIDS crisis following movie star Rock Hudson's announcement in July that he had the disease and his subsequent death in October.

Other groups were slowly starting to form that devoted substantial efforts to the battle against AIDS. High Tech Gays (HTG) was founded in 1983 in San Jose by Rick Rudy and several others as a social organization of gays employed in the technology industry. They quickly broadened their scope and, in 1984, gained a high public profile by challenging the U.S. Department of Defense policy that routinely denied necessary security clearances for tech professionals who were known or thought to be homosexual.

By 1985, HTG took on AIDS as a major issue. Their April newsletter reported they had formed a group called Mobilization Against AIDS to provide education and political action on AIDS and AIDS-related issues. "Since its formation only a few months ago, the members have been very active in the Bay Area and Sacramento. The war against AIDS is just beginning. Your help is needed. HTG has joined as a group sponsor in remembrance of Jim Kline. Jim was a member of HTG. He recently passed away, at the age of 34, as a result of AIDS."

RICK RUDY:

Today, the tech industry is hailed as a model of inclusiveness. It is considered to be one of the most LGBTQ+-friendly industries in the U.S. Tim Cook, the CEO of Apple, the world's most valuable tech company, is openly gay.

This reputation did not happen naturally or overnight. It

took years of struggle by LGBTQ+ engineers, programmers, and other tech workers. Rick Rudy played a key role in that struggle.

Rudy was born and raised in New York City. He received his bachelor's and master's degrees in engineering from MIT and afterward began a career in the tech industry that brought him to San Jose in the early 70s.

In June 1982, Rudy was one of a handful of tech industry workers who met in San Jose to form a South Bay chapter of the San Francisco-based Lesbian and Gay Associated Engineers and Scientists. Within months, the organization had separated from San Francisco and was renamed High Tech Gays. Rudy became its first president and helped write the by-laws.

Rudy was a board member of BAYMEC from the very beginning. He hosted some of the earliest meetings at his home, helped write the by-laws, and generated early publicity through the High Tech Gays newsletter.

Rudy made time for BAYMEC when he was busier than ever. He had gotten involved in gay rights at a national level, joining the board of the National Gay and Lesbian Task Force in 1985. This led to interviews both locally in the *Mercury News* and nationally in the *Advocate* and the *Wall Street Journal.*

Rudy's life, however, was filled with much more than just tech and gay politics. He was a theater lover, especially Gilbert and Sullivan. He was a longtime performer with San Jose's Gilbert and Sullivan Society. He also spent a decade as the theater critic for *Our Paper.*

I remember visiting Rudy in O'Connor Hospital. It was good to see him one last time to say goodbye before he died. His life was tragically cut short at age 44. He was one of the more than 2,500 Santa Clara County victims of the AIDS epidemic.

In 1985, Reverend Randy Hill founded a church in San Jose, eventually known as the Hosanna Church of Praise. His background was as a pastor of the Southern Baptist Church in Knoxville, Tennessee. However, he left that position when he felt he couldn't meaningfully serve in that role as a gay man.

Hill's San Jose church emphasized outreach to the homeless and indigent. He relied on donations of clothing, food, and monetary assistance and often found donated items at his front door. With the help of co-founder Gary Givens, this grew into Necessities and More, a group created to help people living with HIV or AIDS. He also started a 24-hour AIDS hotline. Initially operated only with volunteers and donations, these programs both grew as the number of infected people swelled. In the late 1980s, Hill moved his church to the Billy De Frank Lesbian and Gay Community Center on Park Avenue.

In 1985, Yolanda Perez, Raymond Aguilar, Bernie Greer, Toby Nelson, Pat Mayberry, Ed Bilger, and Art Beaten joined together to form the Imperial AIDS Foundation (IAF) in San Jose. Its purpose was to provide personal and financial assistance to people with HIV or AIDS. Grassroots efforts, ranging from spaghetti dinners and stage shows to car washes, provided the funds used to help clients pay rent, utilities, and prescriptions. Of particular value, IAF delivered food to clients who were unable to get out of bed, as well as transportation to medical appointments.

That year also saw the founding of The Aris Project, which would become the major nonprofit group in Santa Clara County focused on providing care, services, and support to people with HIV/AIDS. It was founded in the living room of Santa Clara County Social Services Agency worker Bob Clayton.

Aris is the word for bear used by the Ohlone tribe of Northern California. As such, it is spelled in lowercase until it was changed to an acronym, which is chronicled later. Initially, the group was closely modeled on the San Francisco-based group Shanti Project. Shanti was founded in 1974 to provide services and emotional support for terminal cancer patients. However, it quickly became one of the most important organizations for AIDS patients in San Francisco during the early period of the epidemic.

BOB CLAYTON:

James Robert Clayton, known to everyone as Bob, was born in 1934. He was working for the Social Services Agency in 1981 when a man seeking help walked into his office suffering from a new and unknown malady. The man was one of the first county residents with AIDS. For the rest of his life, Clayton would be at the forefront of the Santa Clara County effort to deal with the disease and care for its patients.

In 1985, Clayton opened his home as the first AIDS residence in the county. In March of that year, he helped form a weekly support group for AIDS patients that initially called itself "Freedom from Fear." By January 1986, that group had incorporated as a nonprofit and become the Aris Project.

In 1994, Clayton received national recognition when he was presented with the Family AIDS Network's National AIDS Caregiver Award. His nomination announcement noted that "Bob cries easily, never afraid to share his grief with other caregivers. Yet, he talks about the pain he carries each day as a 'small price to pay' for the rewards he has found in reaching out to other people in need. Bob talks about each of the people he has been a caregiver for as a proud parent talks about their child – with love and unconditional acceptance."

One of the highlights of his life came in 1996 when he carried the Olympic torch in San Jose as it made its way to Atlanta.

At the time of his death in 2003, Clayton was serving as interim director of ARIS.

Bob Sorenson was a member of the Metropolitan Community Church and volunteered in the same informal AIDS support group as Bob Clayton. His day job at the time was being the administrator of the Santa Clara/Santa Cruz Counties Council of Campfire, providing him with experience managing nonprofit groups. So, when the support group decided they needed to formalize their organization and incorporate, he was the natural person to become the first executive director of Aris. He would hold the job for eight crucial years. During his tenure, the group would grow from volunteers meeting in a living room to one of the leading social service organizations in the county, with annual revenue of more than $1.1 million.

1986: 159 HIV diagnoses; 43 new deaths, 96 total deaths; 264 living with HIV/AIDS

In January, I went before the Santa Clara County Board of Supervisors to present a nine-point proposal for County-provided AIDS services. Representing BAYMEC, our request to the Board was to:

- Provide the Aris Project with $180,000 in funding over the ensuing 18 months.

- Allocate funds to establish a residential care facility for chronically ill AIDS patients.

- Establish a program to educate County employees who may work with AIDS patients, including deputy sheriffs, probation officers, social workers, and health department staff.

- Create a Board-sponsored task force to assess needs and develop a comprehensive AIDS program for the County.

- Allocate additional funds for education and educational materials targeted to high-risk groups.

- Increase staff levels of the AIDS Project in order to provide more proactive outreach to community groups.

- Publicize the County's ability to care for AIDS patients at Valley Medical Center.

- Direct the Mental Health Department to establish a working relationship with the Aris Project to coordinate mental and emotional support for AIDS patients.

The supervisors responded positively to our proposal, embracing the recommendations. Progress was finally being made, albeit in small steps.

The Board gave Aris an immediate cash infusion. This was a major step forward in the fight against AIDS and for the Santa Clara County LGBTQ+ community. No longer was the community solely responsible for raising funds to keep AIDS volunteer programs in operation. The volunteers were now able to devote more time and energy to providing support services to patients and their families.

At that time, the relatively new Aris Project focused on the daily needs of people with AIDS, as well as their emotional health and wellness. Ultimately, it would provide services, including numerous weekly emotional support groups for different communities, transportation services, a monthly food basket program, housing assistance, and HIV prevention education. It dissolved at the end of 2003 following the death of Bob Clayton.

This historic action by the Board was the end result of a long, methodical process. BAYMEC board members had been meeting with individual supervisors before I presented our nine-point proposal. We impressed upon them just how significant a public health crisis the AIDS epidemic was and could become if left unaddressed.

I was honored to be named Chair of the new Santa Clara County AIDS Task Force by Board President Susanne Wilson. We held our first meeting in April. In addition to myself, BAYMEC was represented by Wiggsy Sivertsen and Ron Taylor. The other six members of the task force included Dr. Roger Kennedy from Kaiser Permanente, the largest health care provider in the County; Dr. David Stevens from VMC; Robert Mackler,

Director of the Hospital Conference of Santa Clara County; Sharron Miller of the Visiting Nurses Association; Helen Miramontes of the California Nurses Association; and Campbell City Councilmember John Ashworth.

Unfortunately, while our supervisors saw AIDS for the health crisis that it was, homophobia and misinformation continued to dominate conversations about AIDS in the rest of the state. In July 1986, Republican Governor George Deukmejian vetoed a bill that would have extended anti-discrimination protections to HIV/AIDS patients. Much more disturbingly, conservative gadfly Lyndon LaRouche obtained enough signatures to put a statewide initiative on the November 1986 ballot, Proposition 64, that would have effectively quarantined AIDS patients and anyone diagnosed with HIV.

Fortunately, the campaign against Prop. 64 was enormously successful, with three-quarters of the region's voters rejecting the LaRouche initiative.

After the defeat of Prop. 64, I found myself dealing with more AIDS-related matters. The epidemic, and the lack of adequate government response to it, was becoming the dominant issue in the LGBTQ+ community from the mid-1980s on.

Headlines in the *Mercury News* and throughout the country constantly blared grim news about the disease. A June 1986 conference on AIDS in Paris led to a large front-page headline: Millions may die of AIDS. "Five million to 10 million people worldwide have been infected by the virus believed to cause AIDS, and 3.5 million of them may die in the next five years, the world's AIDS experts have concluded."

Life expectancy from diagnosis to death was around two years. People got sick and died so fast. I remember a friend learning he had AIDS and was dead five months later. His family didn't even know he was gay. In the course of the epidemic, tens of thousands of families learned for the first time that their sons were gay only after they became sick. Often parents had to simultaneously come to grips with their son's sexuality and their deaths.

Against this backdrop, during the 11 months after its formation in February 1986, the Santa Clara County AIDS Task Force worked extremely hard and accomplished numerous objectives. We assisted in the development of an AIDS policy handbook for County employees, investigated the Sheriff Department's medical unit policy on AIDS, and reviewed the need for anti-discrimination ordinances for people with HIV or AIDS.

The battle against AIDS was moving into a new phase, both nationally and in the South Bay. In October, Surgeon General C. Everett Koop shocked the political and public health worlds by issuing a report on the AIDS epidemic that forthrightly talked about how the disease was transmitted and strongly advocated for increased sex education in public schools and the widespread use of condoms to prevent the spread of the virus.

Locally, the LGBTQ+ community no longer felt like we were fighting the epidemic on our own. The Board of Supervisors adopted all of the Task Force's recommendations, and even as the County was facing tight budget times, they were committing critical dollars to AIDS services.

BOB REED:

Bob Reed moved to the South Bay from Idaho in 1982, the year before Santa Clara County's first HIV infections and AIDS deaths were recorded. He first read about the infection that became known as AIDS in 1981. Even though he was a nurse, Reed continued to have unprotected sex and embrace an "eat, drink, and be merry lifestyle," as he describes it, for the first half of the 1980s.

By 1986, he knew he had HIV. That was confirmed during a terse phone call from his doctor after he got tested. He recalls the doctor saying only, You're HIV-positive," and then following that with, "You're a nurse, so you know what that means. Call me if you need anything," and then hanging up. The entire call lasted less than two minutes.

271

Reed recalls even then, five years into the epidemic and the year after Rock Hudson's death, there was still a tremendous amount of ignorance about HIV and AIDS in the county.

His doctor told him he would be dead within six months. His apartment manager worried that he might infect other tenants just by living in the same building. In a hospital lobby, he helped himself to a bowl of popcorn put out for patients but was then reprimanded for contaminating it and making it unsafe for others.

Like many HIV/AIDS patients, Reed internalized a tremendous amount of self-loathing and felt at the time that he deserved a certain amount of this mistreatment.

A turning point came when he began receiving services from the County's Early Intervention Program. Under the leadership of Fenstersheib, it was one of the few dedicated HIV/AIDS clinics in the nation at that time. It did not do a significant amount of advertising. He learned about it the way most patients did, through word of mouth. He described its services as "life-saving."

Ultimately, Reed would spend three years working as a nurse at the clinic. His personal experience as someone living with HIV made him especially effective. This was particularly true in the years before the AIDS cocktail became widely available when an HIV diagnosis was considered akin to a death sentence. Reed provided an example for so many others in those years just by living his life and doing his job.

In 2004, Reed became a member of the County's HIV/AIDS Planning Council for Prevention and Care, now known as the Santa Clara County HIV Commission. He has been elected co-chair of the commission on two separate occasions.

Overall, Reed says Santa Clara County is an "exemplary" place to live for the LGBTQ+ community, and the County's response to the HIV/AIDS crisis was one of the best in the nation. "I've lived here since '82, and I've stayed here because there are no villains."

1987: 235 HIV diagnoses; 76 new deaths, 172 total deaths; 423 living with HIV/AIDS

While things were changing on the political front, the epidemic continued to grow rapidly. This was the first year that more than 200 people were diagnosed with HIV in a single year in Santa Clara County. It was also the first year that the County recorded more than 100 AIDS-related deaths. The infection rate would continue to grow every year until 1993. The death rate did not stop increasing until 1995.

In the first years of the epidemic, getting information from the County Public Health Department was often difficult. Questions about the effectiveness of current programs, new programs in development, and funding sources for educational programs went unanswered far too frequently. However, that started to change in 1987. The department became more open about how it was addressing the epidemic, and it formed a committee of people and organizations involved in the fight against AIDS to exchange information and coordinate and combine resources. It was a very welcome step.

The County was also getting a little more financial help from Sacramento. In the summer of 1987, the State of California Health Services Department increased its annual allocation for Santa Clara County to $90,000 for AIDS services for the 1987-88 fiscal year.

The Task Force issued a 12-page final report in March that contained multiple recommendations in the areas of medical needs, education, social services, mental health, housing, AIDS policies in the jails, and needed County legislation. We also concluded that the Task Force should remain in existence in order to oversee the successful accomplishment of the recommendations in our final report.

Over time, the County made steady progress in implementing the recommendations. However, continual pressure by BAYMEC on the Board of Supervisors and other local elected officials was required. As the organization approached its third anniversary, its vital role in the LGBTQ+ community was becoming clearer.

I remember 1987 as being a year when persons living with HIV/AIDS were being discriminated against out of fear of contracting AIDS. This was the basis of an article I wrote for the Task Force about the discrimination that was happening in Santa Clara County.

"Because AIDS is not spread by casual contact, a person with AIDS or ARC (AIDS-Related Complex) poses no health threat to the general public. However, in Santa Clara County, there are reports that certain services have been unnecessarily denied to patients with AIDS. Based on our projections, the number of AIDS cases in Santa Clara County will increase almost geometrically over the next five years. With increasing numbers of individuals with AIDS and ARC, increased cases of discrimination are anticipated.

"The Task Force does not know the full extent of current discrimination. We do know that certain publicly supported groups turn away AIDS patients. In the past, the prominent United Way agency refused to provide services to AIDS patients. To our knowledge, all long-term care facilities (i.e., nursing homes and convalescent hospitals) have not allowed admission to AIDS patients.

"While paramedic services appear to be available, AIDS patients are charged an additional fee of $50 to 'sterilize' the ambulance after usage. Similar fees are not applied to other patients. The Sheriff's Department routinely isolates individuals testing HIV-positive.

"Families and friends of AIDS patients also face discrimination. Helen Miramontes, President of the California Nurses Association and a member of the Task Force, reported a case in Santa Clara County where the fear of AIDS led one employer to fire the husband of an AIDS patient.

"Unfortunately, certain political and religious groups have

taken advantage of the AIDS epidemic and have morally condemned the victims. Without the force of law to stop this bigotry, these individuals can perpetuate the myth that AIDS patients must be separated from the community. Fortunately, the defeat of the LaRouche-sponsored AIDS initiative indicates that a large majority of the voters in Santa Clara County believe that AIDS patients do not pose an undue threat to the community."

BAYMEC again demonstrated its effectiveness in November when the supervisors unanimously passed an ordinance prohibiting discrimination against people with HIV/AIDS. The ordinance made it illegal to refuse housing, employment, property loans, medical care, or business services to anyone solely because they had AIDS or a high risk of developing AIDS. It also mandated that agencies or businesses that receive County funding could not discriminate against people with HIV/AIDS.

This ordinance had been one of BAYMEC's main priorities for the year. I spent many hours talking with individual supervisors and other County officials about it. This was the first time that elected officials in Santa Clara County approved a non-discrimination ordinance championed by the LGBTQ+ community since the defeats of Measures A and B in 1980. The County ordinance had a limited impact because it only applied to unincorporated areas, but it set a precedent that we intended to use in 1988 to convince cities in the South Bay, especially San Jose, to adopt their own ordinances.

I stepped down as chair of the County AIDS Task Force at the end of 1987 as I began working on my Doctorate in Education at Stanford. I was extremely gratified with what the Task Force accomplished in my almost two years as chair. Overall, I was hopeful as we headed into the late 1980s. I wrote to BAYMEC members that spring that we were moving towards a future where "instead of two steps back for each step forward, it will be two steps forward, one step back."

One big step forward in 1987 was the release of the first AIDS treatment drug, Azidothymidine, or AZT.

Researchers have been trying to find a treatment or vaccine for AIDS ever since the HIV retrovirus was identified as the cause of the disease in 1984. At the National Cancer Institute, Dr. Sam Broder and colleagues Hiroaki Mitsuya and Robert Yarchoan began testing already developed drugs to see if they would be effective against HIV.

AZT was originally synthesized in 1964 as a possible cancer treatment. It was shelved shortly after development when it proved to be ineffective in tests with mice. A decade later, a researcher in West Germany found that AZT could halt the replication of the retrovirus that caused a type of leukemia in mice. However, this attracted little further attention from the scientific or medical community because, in 1974, there were no known human diseases caused by retroviruses.

Broder and his colleagues pulled AZT off the shelf and, in February 1985, began testing it against HIV. They got positive results almost immediately. In June, the NCI and drug maker Burroughs Wellcome, now known as GlaxoSmithKline, applied to the Food and Drug Administration for permission to begin testing AZT on human patients. That permission was granted in seven days. On July 3, 1985, the first patient enrolled in the AZT clinical trials in Bethesda, MD.

In September 1986, the second phase of AZT clinical trials was halted after preliminary results showed that patients treated with AZT had a significantly higher survival rate than the placebo group (1 death in 145 vs. 19 of 137). By mid-October, the FDA was making AZT available to physicians treating AIDS patients who requested the drug, even though it was still unlicensed. In March 1987, the FDA approved AZT as the first drug to treat AIDS. The time between the first demonstration of AZT's effectiveness against HIV and its approval by the FDA was just 25 months, the shortest approval period in recent history.

Sadly, the hope generated by AZT was short-lived because HIV proved to be a very hardy retrovirus. It had the ability to quickly mutate and develop resistance to the drug. It would be almost another decade before researchers found a way to finally contain HIV. Far from perfect and somewhat controversial, at least there was finally some medication to treat HIV.

On May 1, 1987, President Ronald Reagan delivered his first speech on AIDS and called for widespread testing. However, this was after 36,058 people had already been diagnosed in the U.S., and 20,849 had died. Not only that, but he quipped: "When it comes to preventing AIDS, don't medicine and morality teach the same lessons?"

The health, science, and environment editor at the *Washington Post* wrote, "Reagan was silent at a time when silence equaled death. His cowardice in the face of the crisis will forever tarnish his legacy."

1988: 281 HIV diagnoses; 93 new deaths, 265 total deaths; 611 people living with HIV/AIDS

As the debate over the effectiveness of AZT grew, the number of deaths continued to increase. With more individuals being diagnosed and falling ill, there was a growing demand for beds to treat the patients. In January, the Santa Clara County Senior Care Commission took under consideration the difficulty in finding beds in nursing care facilities for people with AIDS.

In order to reduce the burden on hospitals and provide needed services for individuals suffering from complications due to AIDS, the Department of Health recommended funding a Visiting Nurse Association program for in-home treatment of people with AIDS.

Norm Robinson, who would become Aris director in 1994, remembers how fearless the nurses were. He recalls how they had no hesitancy to work with people with AIDS and would aggressively intervene when patients were not being properly cared for in their nursing homes or hospice situations. "There was nothing they hadn't seen or heard before. Nothing phased them. They were wonderfully caring," he added.

However, despite the epidemic being years old at this point, little had been done in schools to inform the public about the importance of testing or how to prevent the disease. A *Mercury News* story in February reported that "nearly two years after the U.S. Surgeon General began urging AIDS education for students of all ages, only a handful of Santa Clara County's 37 school districts are teaching students how to avoid the deadly disease."

In May, the U.S. Surgeon General mailed an eight-page report to all 107 million households in the United States, marking the first federal authority to provide explicit advice to citizens on how to protect themselves from AIDS.

BAYMEC continued lobbying cities to adopt an anti-discrimination ordinance similar to what the Board of Supervisors did in 1987. When the City of San José put one up for a vote in June, the Religious Right came out in opposition, much like they did for Measures A and B at the beginning of the decade. Rev. Stewart Smith of the Los Gatos Christian Church cited numerous Bible verses, including, "The Lord said to Moses 'Command the people of Israel that they put out of the camp every leper...'"

Mercury News columnist Joanne Jacobs published a brilliant response to that sentiment in her September 8 column: "If HIV-antibody testing is a way to decide who's a leper and who can live and work in our society, then AIDS will go underground. It will not go away."

In that same September column, she illustrated how stark the anxiety and paranoia about HIV had become in the general public's mind. Her daughter had to get tested for HIV because of a blood transfusion several years earlier, and Jacobs fretted over how much to tell people, especially the parents of her daughter's friends. "Don't say it's a blood test. She might ask what for, and then you'll have to say AIDS, and then she won't want her kid to play with Allison. She'll be mad at you for not warning her. Don't tell her it's AIDS."

Jacobs was a strong ally in the fight against AIDS, regularly writing about the need for more funding for research and treatment. In the column, she described the argument she had with herself about her daughter's test. "The other half of my brain was saying, 'Don't be ridiculous. This is an intelligent woman. Why are you acting like she's a fool? Why are *you* acting like a fool?...' AIDS does that. It makes people act stupidly."

Ultimately, Jacobs decided to get her daughter tested. "Allison tested negative. She isn't an AIDS leper. Nobody should be."

Despite the opposition from the Religious Right, the San Jose City Council approved the non-discrimination ordinance in a 9-2 vote. Of the dissenting votes, Councilwoman Lu Ryden was a religious conservative who was offended when Councilwoman Susan Hammer used the Bible verse "love thy neighbor as thyself" in support of the ordinance. The other no-vote was Councilman Bob Putnam, who gave a 15-minute speech that only proved he didn't know anything about how AIDS was spread.

Unfortunately, all that lobbying might have been fruitless if a new ballot initiative in California passed because it would only further such discrimination.

Proposition 102 was scheduled to be placed on the November ballot. It would have "required doctors, blood banks, and others, to report patients and blood donors, whom they reasonably believe in having been infected by or tested positive for AIDS virus, to local health officials."

It would have permitted insurance agencies and businesses to require HIV testing results to qualify for health insurance or employment. Additionally, it would have endedall confidentiality or anonymity when receiving the test by requiring your name to be attached to the results. It went even further, mandating that health professionals report positive test results to the government, insurers, employers, and the courts. It even required the mandatory contact tracing of sex partners by the government.

Needless to say, this would have been a huge step backward for AIDS patients and the LGBTQ+ community. We couldn't match the campaign funding available from the insurance industry or the Religious Right, but at BAYMEC, we were determined to leverage all our resources to defeat the proposition.

Ultimately, we were successful; the proposition overwhelmingly failed, with 69.6 percent voting no across the state. We were extremely proud of Santa Clara and San Mateo Counties, where our lobbying had the most influence, achieving 71.2 percent and 73.4 percent no votes, respectively.

Another initiative, Proposition 96, which mandated testing for victims of sex crimes and emergency services workers where bodily fluids may have been exchanged, passed with 62.4 percent of the vote. Thankfully Prop 102 prevented the reporting requirement of positive test results.

This was also the year World AIDS Day was created by the United Nations. It was designed as a celebration of victories in the AIDS movement, such as increased access to treatment and prevention services. The day lives on, serving as a day of remembrance to commemorate those we have lost to HIV/AIDS and to continue to build awareness until we eradicate the disease. It takes place annually on December 1.

1989: 340 HIV diagnoses; 124 new deaths, 296 total deaths; 827 living with HIV/AIDS

As the 1980s came to a close, the death toll from AIDS continued to rise, easily crossing the 100 mark in Santa Clara County in 1989. Even with AZT now on the market, so many people continued to die so quickly.

One moment of light was inspired by the darkness of all the deaths: The AIDS Memorial Quilt. San Francisco LGBTQ+ activist Cleve Jones conceived of the quilt in 1985. While planning the annual candlelight march in San Francisco to commemorate the assassinations of Supervisor Harvey Milk and

Mayor George Moscone, he learned that more than 1,000 people in the city had already died from AIDS. He asked marchers to write the names of friends and loved ones who had died on placards, and at the end of the event, all of the placards were taped to the walls of the federal building in San Francisco, making it look like a patchwork quilt.

Jones and some friends made plans for a much larger permanent memorial. He made the first quilt panel in memory of his friend Marvin Feldman who had died in October 1986 after a two-year battle with AIDS.

The response to the quilt idea was immediate and enthusiastic. Panels were sent in from all over the country. By the time it was first publicly displayed in October 1987 at the National Mall in Washington, DC, the quilt contained almost 2,000 panels and covered a space larger than a football field. More than 500,000 people visited the quilt during its first weekend on display.

In May, part of the quilt came to San Jose as part of a nationwide tour. Panels were laid out on the floor of the San Jose Convention Center. Among the many visitors who came to see the quilt was Congressman Norm Mineta. Less than five years earlier, when BAYMEC was first formed, Mineta was one of the many elected officials reluctant to meet with us or to publicly support our issues. However, times had changed, and Mineta became a strong supporter of the LGBTQ+ community. He attended our annual dinners frequently and supported federal legislation protecting the rights of the LGBTQ+ community.

In August, Aris began offering housing for Santa Clara County low-income AIDS patients. Back in December 1987, an Aris task force had concluded that there were dozens of local AIDS patients who were in unstable housing situations. However, it took almost two years to secure funding and find a suitable location before Aris could open its first residential housing. The initial funding came from three sources: the County of Santa Clara, the State of California, and the United Way.

One of the big stories that year was the increasing militancy of some activists in the fight against AIDS. Playwright Larry Kramer founded the AIDS Coalition To Unleash Power, ACT UP, in New York in 1987. The group used direct action and civil disobedience to draw attention to the lack of government funding for AIDS research and services and to the high prices that drug maker Burroughs Wellcome, now known as GlaxoSmithKline, was charging for AZT, as much as $10,000 a year.

In 1988, ACT UP activists managed to shut down the Washington, DC, headquarters of the Food and Drug Administration for a day. In October, seven ACT UP activists chained themselves inside the New York Stock Exchange to protest Burroughs Wellcome.

In the Bay Area, activists from ACT UP and other groups closed the Golden Gate Bridge during rush hour in January 1989, and in September, they crashed the opening of the San Francisco Opera season, traditionally one of the highest profile events among the society page crowd in the city.

While I understood the anger and passion behind these direct-action efforts, I told the *Mercury News* in October that those types of tactics were not something that BAYMEC took part in because we were having success at the local level by working through more traditional channels.

In the federal fiscal year that began on October 1, 1989, the County's Health Department received $250,000, its largest federal grant to date, for community AIDS planning services.

1990: 337 HIV diagnoses; 137 new deaths, 433 total deaths; 1,027 living with HIV/AIDS

The early 1990s were some of the darkest times of the AIDS epidemic. Death tolls continued to increase locally and nationally. The highest number of deaths were in 1993 and 1994: 219 in 1993 and 220 in 1994. Aris and other community organizations were strained to capacity with the sick and the dying.

More volunteers were needed as caregivers, and it turned out they came from within the LGBTQ+ community.

Over the decades, gay men and lesbians have often kept to their own communities, but AIDS changed that. As Wiggsy Sivertsen noted, "The AIDS crisis brought lesbians and gay men together because women knew how to take care of people. That's what we are trained to do as women. We all had to work together, and it evolved into a more cooperative group of relationships than used to exist."

HIV had proven to be a cagey and deadly virus, evolving at a rapid enough rate to negate much of the effectiveness of AZT. The hope that I and many others felt upon the drug's release was slowly extinguished as months and years went by, and the death toll continued to rise.

One particular death in early 1990 did galvanize the public and lead to some notable progress in treating the epidemic. Indiana teen Ryan White was a hemophiliac who was diagnosed with AIDS in December 1984 following a blood transfusion. He was one of the first children and the first hemophiliac to come down with the disease. He gained national attention and became a symbol of the misinformation surrounding AIDS and the discrimination sufferers faced. When his local school district tried to prevent him from attending classes, his parents sued.

White was initially given a maximum of six months to live, but he surprised his doctors and survived for more than five years after his diagnosis, dying in April, one month before his high school graduation.

In August, Congress passed, and President George H.W. Bush signed into law the Ryan White Comprehensive AIDS Resources Emergency, or CARE Act. It provided funding for health care and other services for low-income, uninsured, and underinsured AIDS victims and their families. It was the largest federally funded program in the country for people living with HIV/AIDS, and it quickly became the third largest federal healthcare program after Medicare and Medicaid.

Also in 1990, the Board of Supervisors formed an AIDS Planning Advisory Committee to help formulate an expanded HIV/AIDS services plan. The committee included community representatives, service providers, industry and nonprofit representatives, and HIV/AIDS patients.

Although there had been successful Walks for AIDS in major cities across the country, there was never one held for the Peninsula, East Bay, South Bay, or coastal communities. On September 16, the first four-county Walk for AIDS took place to benefit AIDS service organizations within Santa Clara, San Mateo, Alameda, and Santa Cruz counties. The goal was to raise $400,000 for 29 nonprofit AIDS organizations.

1991: 335 HIV diagnoses; 171 new deaths, 604 total deaths; 1,191 living with HIV/AIDS

A November *Mercury News* article, "AIDS Program to Get $1.3 Million Boost," reported, "The federal government has promised Santa Clara County $1.3 million to expand its much-admired services for people who have just learned of their infection with the AIDS virus. The money, part of a nationwide dispersal of funds under the Ryan White Act, which Congress approved last year, will be distributed over a three-year period. Since 1986, the 'early intervention' program has offered counseling, information, lab tests, and medical exams."

KARL VIDT:

Karl Vidt moved to Santa Clara County in 1969. When the AIDS epidemic began in the early 1980s, he did not pay much attention to it, believing it was "something affecting people in San Francisco."

Vidt became much more aware of the disease and the toll it was taking in 1985 when he joined the board of the Metropolitan Community Church, one of the first denominations in the

South Bay to provide a welcoming and inclusive atmosphere for the LGBTQ+ community. Coincidentally, the church became the original home of the Aris Project the same year that Vidt joined its board.

Despite his work with the church, Vidt did not get tested until 1989, when he learned that he was HIV positive. He remembers being "just numb" after getting the news. He says that the tester who told him he was positive, Sandy Gudino, was kind and spent more than an hour with him answering questions and giving him information.

Vidt told only a few people about his diagnosis. "I just picked up and went on." However, by 1991 he had gotten sick and was taking regular medications. In the fall of 1992, he came down with Pneumocystis carinii, the strain of pneumonia that had been closely associated with the AIDS epidemic since the early 80s.

In 1993, he developed an infection in his eyes that eventually led to his blindness in December 1996.

Throughout the early 90s, Vidt survived with virtually no T-cells whatsoever. Luckily, by the mid-90s, his T-cell count began to grow with the introduction of new medications. This led to an overall improvement in his health.

He got his first guide dog in 1999, which significantly improved his self-sufficiency and mobility. He was able to play an active role in the community again and continued working at Metropolitan Community Church as the half-time church administrator.

Vidt also threw himself into the thick of the fight against HIV/AIDS in the South Bay. He joined the Santa Clara County HIV Planning Council for Prevention and Care in 2002. He spent multiple years as chair of its Care and Treatment Committee. He also served a stint as the chair of its Planning and Resources Committee. In addition to his HIV Planning Council service, Vidt also served on the City of San Jose's Disability Advisory Commission and spent four years as chair of the Santa

Clara County World AIDS Day Committee.

Vidt says all of the volunteer services are just his way of contributing to the health care system that he believes has taken such good care of him since his diagnosis. "There was a time when I thought my parents would have to care for me. Who would have guessed that now I am taking care of my mom," he said.

In 2008 I was honored to present to Vidt the Leslie David Burgess Lifetime Achievement Award. It was well-deserved recognition for a man who has not just provided countless hours of service to HIV/AIDS prevention and care. He is also an inspiring example of how to live a full life even after coming down with some of the worst illnesses associated with HIV and AIDS.

1992: 309 HIV diagnoses; 172 new deaths, 776 total deaths; 1,328 living with HIV/AIDS

In late 1991, basketball star Magic Johnson announced he was HIV positive, once again reinforcing the fact that HIV/AIDS could strike anyone. The idea of AIDS as a strictly "gay disease" was finally starting to recede in the minds of the general public. Thankfully, more than a quarter of a century after his announcement, Magic is alive and healthy, still a major public figure. His health is a testament to the rapid progress in AIDS treatment that would come in the 1990s.

The first major medical treatment breakthrough occurred in 1992 when combination drug therapies were introduced. They proved much more effective than AZT alone in controlling HIV and slowing the virus's mutations and development of drug resistance. However, it would still be a couple of years before the AIDS "cocktail" would come into its own and dramatically change the trajectory of the epidemic.

By the end of 1992, Aris's housing program had expanded to four houses with 18 bedrooms. "They are intended for independent living. We do not have live-in staff at those houses, but it does provide a place where primarily the Visiting Nurses Association comes in and provides in-home nursing care and case management services for those people who are at least on disability income and otherwise are, for other reasons, homeless. Some of those reasons include being rejected by family or living in roommate situations where their HIV status is not acceptable to their friends and family," said Aris Executive Director Sorenson on a panel before the Santa Clara County Medical Association in January 1993.

1993: 265 HIV diagnoses; 219 new deaths, 995 total deaths; 1,374 living with HIV/AIDS

In 1993, AIDS became the number one cause of death for Americans between the ages of 25 and 44. "A lot of my friends died in the spring of 1993. There were about one every two weeks. That was a tough time," said Aris volunteer Pat Duffy.

The local fight against HIV/AIDS continued to experience periods when the momentum either stalled out or seemed to shift dramatically into reverse. The larger economic trends of the early 1990s led to local government budget cuts. The end of the Cold War devastated California's defense and aerospace industries, resulting in a significant drop in tax revenue. This hit Santa Clara County especially hard as defense contractor Lockheed was the region's largest employer for much of the 80s.

In 1993, this situation threatened almost a decade's worth of progress on AIDS care in Santa Clara County.

The Director of Public Health, Delia Alvarez, proposed cutting nearly $1 million from the County's AIDS programs. This included the elimination of the County's five-member HIV education program; $173,000 or 18 percent of the Aris funding; four staff members in the early intervention program clinic, which provided medical treatment and counseling to 1,200 recently diagnosed patients; and five of 14 employees in the family planning unit, which was part of the AIDS program.

Everyone was stunned.

As I wrote in a March BAYMEC newsletter, "Any cuts to the budget for fighting an exponentially growing epidemic could be construed as inappropriate, but Alvarez's budget strikes deep at the heart of the individuals and groups which are on the front lines."

I explained that the proposed budget called for the elimination of all County-funded HIV educators, cuts in testing site services, and cuts to the Aris Project for housing and services for people with AIDS. However, little money was being cut for County administrative expenses. "The cuts would take the County's commitment to AIDS back to the level of 1985 when the County first funded AIDS services," I added.

With a broad coalition of organizations and support from several supervisors, we were able to prevent the cuts from taking place. Alvarez eventually resigned from her post because of the fallout from this budget proposal. However, I knew that unless we kept up the pressure to continue having services funded, we would always be vulnerable to budget cuts.

With public dollars being threatened, fundraising for AIDS services took on a new urgency. One effort in San Jose got some high-profile help in 1993. While the four-county AIDS Walks were raising much-needed dollars, there was some controversy over how money was being distributed to organizations and whether it was better for each county to have its own walk. Thus, in October, the fourth annual Walk for AIDS was held in downtown San Jose with singer-songwriter Joan Baez participating.

According to the *Mercury News*, Baez, who lived in Woodside, said she would be at the march not only to support fighting AIDS but to be with her cousin, local AIDS activist Peter Baez. Organizers hoped to raise $275,000 for Aris and other local groups.

PETER JOHNSON:

Days after the walk, the *Mercury News* ran an article illustrating just how devastating the epidemic was in those years.

"As the fourth annual Walk for AIDS drew near, every visitor to the bedside of Peter Johnson had to make a pledge. 'He was dying, and he was asking people to sponsor him,' said his mother, Helen Johnson.

"On Monday, Peter Johnson, down to 100 pounds from his normal 150, 6-foot-1, confided to his friend Bob Clayton: 'It'll be a chair-athon for me on Sunday.' Bob replied, 'Fine. We'll all push.'"

Regrettably, Peter Johnson didn't make it to the annual fundraising walk for the disease. He died of AIDS on October 13, 1993, just under two months after his 30th birthday.

Throughout his illness, Johnson drew strength from the support of his family. His mother, Helen, volunteered at Aris alongside him and walked in the AIDS Walk with him every year. She continued to walk for many years after Johnson's death.

Johnson graduated from Overfelt High School in 1981. He was diagnosed with HIV at the end of the 80s and shortly afterward began volunteering with Aris. By early 1991, he was a member of the Aris board, with the group's executive director Bob Sorenson telling the *Mercury News* that Peter was "one of our best interpersonal ambassadors."

In 1992, he was appointed to the County AIDS Commission. He attended every commission meeting, even those where there was not a quorum present. Sadly, his time on the commission was too short.

I still see his parents at events every World AIDS Day. They have kept boxes of documents and articles about his life and about AIDS, some of which helped me in the writing of this history. When I saw them recently, I sensed they miss their son very much, even after all these years.

That year also saw efforts begin for one of the first permanent memorials to victims of the epidemic in San Jose: the

AIDS Grove. The nonprofit group, Our City Forest, assembled a coalition of AIDS service organizations to plan a permanent memorial grove. More than $10,000 was raised privately. After an extensive search, a site near the Children's Discovery Museum in Downtown San Jose was selected in December 1994.

In September 1995, volunteers planted 30 Chinese pistache trees on the site. The pistache were chosen for the grove because they are deciduous and renew themselves every year. They also thrive when planted in groups where their branches can intertwine. The grove was dedicated on September 30 by then-Assemblyman John Vasconcellos.

1994: 228 HIV diagnoses; 220 new deaths, 1,215 total deaths; 1,382 living with HIV/AIDS

Despite the challenging budgets and cutbacks of the early 90s, the Board of Supervisors did not shy away from embracing new programs for dealing with HIV/AIDS in this period.

In September 1994, the Board declared a state of local emergency "due to extreme peril to the safety of persons caused by the significant risk of HIV infection among injection drug users in the county, their sexual partners, and offspring."

At the same time, the Board also approved the establishment of a countywide needle and syringe exchange program. Santa Clara County became only the fourth jurisdiction in California to initiate a needle exchange program. However, the County was the only jurisdiction that used public funds and government employees from the Public Health Department to provide people who inject drugs with clean needles.

It was hugely controversial at the time. I was a vocal advocate for it as a member of the County's AIDS Task Force. In 1994, more than 11 percent percent of HIV/AIDS patients were people who injected drugs, and that percentage had increased every year for the preceding decade.

The needle exchange program would help stop not only the

spread of HIV/AIDS but also other potentially deadly blood-borne pathogens such as Hepatitis B and C. The program also gave health workers the opportunity to interact with people who inject drugs and offer them information and referrals to substance abuse programs and other services.

The program would remain controversial for a number of years. In 1996, California's then Attorney General, Republican Dan Lungren, forced it to shut down after threatening to sue the County. The County would continue to grant money to nonprofit groups that operated needle exchanges, but the professionals from the Public Health Department would not be directly involved again until 2000 when Governor Gray Davis signed legislation that effectively legalized needle exchanges.

Norm Robinson, who became director of Aris in January 1995, remembers what a turbulent time it was. "We had everyone involved: San Jose Police Department, District Attorney's Office, Public Health, outreach workers at the sites," he said. "We had a rule of exchange: One needle for one needle. SJPD told their sergeants not to hassle any of the participants. The City and the County were incredibly supportive," he added.

The effectiveness of the County's needle exchange program has been well-established since 1994. A study that looked at the first 16 years of the program found that it prevented an average of eight new HIV infections each year in the County and saved an estimated $21 million in avoided treatment costs. That worked out to approximately six dollars saved for every dollar spent on the program.

AIDS patients continued to die in a relatively short time span. At the end of 1994, the Public Health Department produced an analysis of the first 10 years of the AIDS epidemic in the county. It revealed that in all but the most recent four years, more than 90 percent of individuals diagnosed with AIDS had died within the same year. In both 1983 and 1986, every single individual in Santa Clara County died the same year they were diagnosed with AIDS.

Thankfully, 1995 would bring some hope for HIV/AIDS sufferers. A medical breakthrough dramatically transformed an AIDS diagnosis from a likely death sentence to a serious but manageable health condition.

1995: 183 HIV diagnoses; 187 new deaths, 1,402 total deaths; 1,378 living with HIV/AIDS

In 1995, progress was finally being made in the fight against AIDS in Santa Clara County. One significant step was the establishment of the Santa Clara County HIV Health Services Planning Council by the Board of Supervisors. The council became the body that would apply for and designate the local uses of federal Ryan White CARE Act funds. It included 24 members, with more than a quarter of the council slots reserved for people who were living with HIV/AIDS. In that first year, the council secured $2.8 million in federal Ryan White funding for Santa Clara County.

There have been a number of mergers and name changes over the years. The council is now known as the Santa Clara County HIV Commission, but the work continues. The HIV Commission is one of the key bodies responsible for implementing the Getting to Zero initiative.

HELEN MIRAMONTES:

Miramontes' nursing career began in 1972 in Kaiser Santa Clara's critical care unit. It later continued at Valley Medical Center, where she worked for 20 years, ultimately as a nurse supervisor.

Her involvement with AIDS policy and services came about because of her family. In the 1980s, one of her sons was openly gay and suffering from alcoholism. "In the beginning, she sort of got into it because she needed to know what this is about because (my parents) thought I was going to get sick," said her son David Miramontes during an interview with me in October 2018.

David's twin brother, Jonathan, was also gay but still in the closet at that time. He would ultimately die of AIDS in 2006.

The epidemic was not the first time that Helen had gotten involved in a cause. "My mother was involved in the civil rights movement, the Vietnam War movement, and the migrant farm worker movement in the 60s. I remember being next to her with my siblings, all six of us, listening to Cesar Chavez," said David Miramontes. "She always said that social work helped her really get started doing AIDS work."

She developed one of the first train-the-trainer programs that addressed the need for cultural competency in HIV/AIDS care. The course provided nurses with straightforward information, focusing on the role of stigma, ignorance, misconceptions, and intolerance in undermining treatment and research toward a cure. She explained the course's direct approach by saying, "You don't change attitudes with slides and didactic lectures."

As she became nursing's "go-to" person about HIV/AIDS, she also served on a host of committees and boards, including Santa Clara County's AIDS Task Force. As chair of the task force, I got to know her and saw firsthand the dedication and passion she brought to her work.

In 1993, Miramontes became an Associate Clinical Professor at UCSF School of Nursing's Department of Community Health Systems. She taught and mentored faculty and students and was involved in the UCSF AIDS Research Institute. She continued her public service on numerous local, national, and international boards. In 1995, she was appointed to President Clinton's Advisory Council on HIV/AIDS, serving on both the research subcommittee and executive subcommittee on international issues.

Miramontes retired from UCSF in 2000 as a Full Clinical Professor and relocated to be closer to her children in the Las Vegas area. Her activism continued there. During this time, she also cared for her son Jonathan. She died in May 2016, six days shy of her 85th birthday. Her name, and Jonathan's, have been inscribed on the Circle of Names at the AIDS Memorial Grove in San Francisco's Golden Gate Park.

The second significant event at the county level in 1995 was the opening of the PACE Clinic, or Partners in AIDS Care and Education. PACE was the combination of the early intervention clinic that Fenstersheib began operating in the 1980s for people with AIDS that was profiled in the *Journal of the American Medical Association* and the hospital clinic for AIDS care that Greene was running at VMC.

PACE offers patients at all stages of HIV infection state-of-the-art primary care in a friendly and compassionate environment. It stressed a holistic approach with comprehensive services ranging from primary care to nutrition and psychotherapy. Clinic workers also made a special effort to ensure that ethnicity, gender, gender identity, language, culture, residency status, and economic level were not barriers to care.

There were also big changes at Aris in 1995. After building the organization from scratch, Bob Sorenson stepped down as the group's executive director in July 1994 for other pursuits. The group spent four months searching for a new leader before hiring Norm Robinson from Stanford University.

In an interview with me, Robinson remembers that one of the first actions that he took was to call for a board retreat to develop a new strategic plan. The issue of the name "Aris" came up. The public was aware of the name, but there was always confusion over what it meant. "The bear just wasn't cutting it anymore," he said. "In the early days, you couldn't have the word 'AIDS' in your name, but we didn't want to buy into that." Fortunately, the letters in 'Aris' ended up being a good acronym. Now capitalized, ARIS stood for AIDS Resources, Information, and Services.

However, the biggest HIV/AIDS-related developments in 1995 occurred not on the local stage but globally. There was a major scientific breakthrough in treatment with the development and testing of the first protease inhibitor.

Protease is a type of protein that the HIV virus needs in order to replicate itself. It was identified in 1985 by researcher Steve Oroszlan at the National Cancer Institute. Scientists quickly realized that inhibiting protease could be a way to slow or stop the spread of the HIV virus in the body. Teams at several pharmaceutical companies, as well as at universities and the National Institutes of Health, began racing to see who could be the first to develop a protease inhibitor drug.

By the early 1990s, research had progressed enough that study results began appearing in scientific journals, and the first human testing began. Public pressure and the growing death toll from AIDS led the Food and Drug Administration to approve the protease inhibitor Saquinavir for use outside of clinical trials in June. Six months later, on December 6, the FDA approved Saquinavir for use in combination with other AIDS treatment drugs. The era of the AIDS cocktail had begun.

The official name for the new treatment name was Highly Active Antiretroviral Therapy or HAART. It would not become widely used in the U.S. until 1996, but the earliest results were extremely promising. Perhaps not coincidentally, 1995 was the first year in which the number of AIDS deaths declined in Santa Clara County.

1996: 178 HIV diagnoses; 124 new deaths, 1,526 total deaths; 1,432 living with HIV/AIDS

AIDS deaths in Santa Clara County declined for the second straight year in 1996. Nationally, the Ryan White CARE Act was reauthorized by Congress through the year 2000, ensuring that there would be a steady stream of federal funds for HIV/AIDS programs for several years.

The FDA also approved the Home Access HIV-1 Test System, the first home HIV test. Taking this test was not a simple process. It required a blood sample, most often from a finger prick, and the sample had to be mailed to a lab. Still, the results were generally available one business day after the lab received the sample. This was a big change from the two weeks I had to wait for results when I got tested in the 80s. The home test was also important because of its anonymity. People were much more likely to get tested if they did not have to make multiple trips to a public clinic.

The effectiveness of HAART, popularly known as the "cocktail," started showing up in national statistics. AIDS deaths declined in the U.S. that year for the first time since the epidemic began. HIV/AIDS also was no longer the leading cause of death for Americans between the ages of 25 and 44.

RUDY GALINDO:

In 1996, San Jose was the site of one of the biggest upsets in American figure skating history when Rudy Galindo became the oldest male national champion of the modern era at age 26. Galindo was also the first openly gay figure skating champion, having come out before the competition began.

Galindo was raised in a trailer home in East San Jose with his sister Jess. He began figure skating at an early age, and his career took off when he began skating pairs with Fremont native Kristi Yamaguchi. As a team, Galindo and Yamaguchi won three U.S. national championships. However, after 1990 Yamaguchi retired from pairs competition to focus on individual skating.

The AIDS epidemic had a major impact on Galindo's personal and professional life. His and Yamaguchi's first coach, Jim Hulick, died of AIDS in 1989. In 1994, Galindo lost both his brother George and another coach Rick Inglesi to AIDS.

Despite those hardships, Galindo won the men's singles champion title in front of a hometown crowd as the U.S. Figure Skating Championships were held at the San Jose Arena in 1996. In the competition, he was the only male competitor to land combination triple jumps. After his performance, Rudy chanted the names Jess, George, Jim, and Rick, who had all helped him to achieve victory.

His championship defied the norms of the U.S. Figure Skating Association. Galindo later said he feared being an out skater might lower his score because of some judge's discomfort with his identity.

In 1997, he released his autobiography *Icebreaker*. Proceeds from the book were donated towards funding the expansion of the San Jose Public Library's Biblioteca Latinoamericana.

In 2000, Galindo announced he was HIV positive. Today, he coaches figure skating at Sharks Ice in San Jose. He was inducted into the San Jose Sports Hall of Fame in 2011 and the U.S. Figure Skating Hall of Fame in 2013. He has set the path for numerous LGBT and HIV-positive athletes to be themselves.

1997: 188 HIV diagnoses; 67 new deaths, 1,593 total deaths; 1,553 living with HIV/AIDS

By 1997 the full effects of the "cocktail" were becoming apparent to public health officials in Santa Clara County as the year-end statistics showed that only 67 people died of AIDS-related causes. That is a drop of almost 50 percent compared to the previous year. The same declines were showing up across the U.S. as federal health officials reported that AIDS-related deaths dropped nationally by 47 percent.

However, while more people living with HIV or AIDS were finding that the disease could be managed with new drug therapies, the spread of the virus continued.

In Santa Clara County, it was becoming evident that a disparity had developed in HIV transmission rates, with African American and Hispanic communities getting infected at higher rates. While the percentage of AIDS cases among white MSM had been steadily declining, from 66 percent in 1985 to 36 percent in 1997, the AIDS incidence among African American and Hispanic demographics had increased. The rate among

African Americans rose from 10 percent in 1990 to 17 percent. Rates among Hispanics increased during the same period from 20 percent in 1990 to 27 percent.

DR. GEORGE KENT:

By 2022, Dr. George Kent has cared for people at Santa Clara County's AIDS clinic for over 33 years. He has seen the disease evolve from one that was untreatable and incurable to what is now a chronic condition.

As someone who has treated patients since the early days of the epidemic, he remembers how difficult it was. "People my age were dying in the prime of their lives. Many were gay and estranged from their families. There was a social stigma. It was a terrible time."

The Stanford and Case Western Reserve graduate came to the HIV field after a Family Medicine residency at the UCSF-affiliated program in Santa Rosa, followed by training at the CDC as a medical epidemiologist, then returning to San Jose and completing an HIV mini-residency with the AIDS Education and Training Center at UCSF.

Afterward, he looked around San Jose to see who cared for HIV patients. One day he went to the Santa Clara Valley Medical Center.

"The clinic was in this little corner in the outpatient department; there were a few exam rooms. A person I met there was Dr. Ira Greene, a dermatologist and a wonderful guy. We hit it off. After he got to know me and checked me out a bit, I said, 'Ira, you need some help.' He said, 'sure, you can join us.'"

Kent reflected on some of the difficulties in the early days. "We felt a little like a MASH Unit. At one point, we were in a flimsy little trailer in a parking lot. It was hot in the summer and cold in the winter. It made us more cohesive because we really did feel like it was us against the world."

The PACE Clinic assembled an interdisciplinary team from

the beginning. "You had oncologists, you had infectious disease, you had internal medicine, you had primary care, and you had dermatology because a lot of these conditions manifested with skin problems."

Working with HIV was the ultimate medical education for Kent. The virus was a multifaceted issue that impacted family relationships, societal attitudes, and the whole LGBTQ+ community when it first hit the United States. There were concerns over confidentiality and end-of-life planning that just did not exist when it came to other terminal illnesses.

"It certainly has made me a better doctor," Kent said of caring for his patients.

In the PACE Clinic, the staff kept a whiteboard where they recorded the names of the people that died each month. "At the end of the month, we'd have a service. We would all get in a circle and say something about each person that died. We'd light a candle and have a memorial service, and then we'd have to erase the whiteboard and start over the next month."

Witnessing the deaths of so many young people took a toll on Kent, and he needed time to cope with the stress and burnout. "I took two months off during the height of it," he said.

Things started looking up for HIV patients in the early nineties, more than a decade after the first cases were discovered in the United States. With protease inhibitors and other medical therapies, the virus no longer claimed the lives of the majority of people in Kent's care. "People just came back to life."

Some of those individuals are still alive today. "I have these 25-year relationships with these patients who were basically at death's door."

Although Kent recognizes the magnitude of his work back in the early years of the AIDS crisis, he doesn't want to glorify it. "We were all there on the front lines, and we felt like we were doing something important and meaningful."

1998: 153 HIV diagnoses; 53 new deaths, 1,646 total deaths; 1,653 living with HIV/AIDS

Santa Clara County health officials tried to address the disparity in African American HIV infection rates in 1998 by hiring an African American physician at the PACE Clinic. They also developed a partnership with a leading African American community service provider for a significant outreach and educational effort in that community.

The County also made efforts to increase the reach of its HIV/AIDS services in other underserved communities. The PACE Clinic served monolingual and limited-English-proficient clients through eleven bilingual employees and one fluent in sign language. Outreach and case management services were established for Spanish-speaking clients by a community health-care provider primarily focused on the Latino community. The County also expanded HIV/AIDS services in the geographically isolated, underserved, and heavily minority-populated South County area. Services for women were also expanded with risk reduction activities for women who have sex with women, the production of a women-focused HIV/AIDS video, and a new women's clinic.

PACE patients were able to obtain their medications at an on-site pharmacy or at any of the seven other County public health pharmacies, all of which dispensed AIDS Drug Assistance Program (ADAP) drugs.

The clinic had a hospital liaison who worked closely with VMC medical staff, case managers, and discharge planners to coordinate the treatment of current and potential patients. Upon hospital admission, the liaison reviewed charts and contacted the patient's primary care physician, as well as other relevant departments, to share information crucial to the patient's treatment. At the time of discharge, the patient's case manager and discharge planner were also contacted by the liaison.

In addition, the County was collaborating with Chaboya Dental. Health officials recognized that common conditions such as tooth decay and gingivitis contributed to weight loss and general physical deterioration in HIV/AIDS patients.

The County's HIV/AIDS programs have grown so much since the early years of the epidemic. They now included confidential HIV outreach, testing, and prevention services in both fixed and mobile facilities, client care coordination and case management, home health care, hospice services, respite care, mental health therapy and counseling, nutritional services, substance abuse treatment and counseling, transportation, client advocacy, housing assistance, direct emergency financial assistance, and alternative therapies.

The mobile service bus program was a good example of what the collaboration between the PACE Clinic and the Public Health Department had achieved. The bus traveled throughout the county, targeting migrant populations, the homeless, needle exchange programs, gay and lesbian community centers, etc. It made approximately 1,500 outreach or testing contacts per year, spending time on eight college campuses and stopping at special events such as the Pride Festival, African-American Juneteenth Celebration, and the Gay Rodeo.

The changing demographics of the epidemic were readily apparent to those working on the front lines of treatment and social services in Santa Clara County, as ARIS Director of Volunteer Resources Pat Duffy told me during an interview in 2018.

"The kind of clients we had at ARIS evolved over the years. When ARIS first started, it was mostly gay white men, mostly in their 20s, 30s, and 40s, and kind of easy to relate to," said Duffy.

"As the disease dragged on, as people were starting to live a little longer than six months, or 12 months, or 18 months, the people we started getting and retaining as clients were people who had other issues as well as HIV. So, they had been in the system for most of their lives. They had been in the correction system. They had substance abuse issues. So, there were other flowers in that bouquet besides AIDS."

One area where ARIS continued to see a lot of demand was housing. By the end of 1998, the group was providing housing for 55 people at multiple facilities throughout the county. There were 25 beds of supportive, shared housing at six residences in Gilroy and San Jose, 24 studio apartments at Casa de Los Amigos in San Jose, and a six-bed residence on Thornton Way in San Jose for those needing around-the-clock care and supervision. Despite all of these beds, the waiting list had 110 names on it by the end of that year.

1999: 143 HIV diagnoses; 49 new deaths, 1,695 total deaths; 1,747 living with HIV/AIDS

In 1999, the number of HIV/AIDS patients admitted to VMC was a little more than half the previous year's total: 38 compared to 61. Cumulative HIV/AIDS patient days at VMC also dropped significantly from 465 to 328. Clearly, the plague days of the 1980s and early 90s were now behind us.

Acknowledgments

The Battle Against AIDS was written as a booklet in 2018 and published by Santa Clara County. Many people assisted me in this endeavor. I would like to thank my staff at the Board of Supervisors: Bryan Aubineau, Jason Bennert, Michelle Collins, Brian Darrow, Alexis Fields, Nolan Golden, Yvonne Jimenez, Baltazar Lopez, Mario Lopez, Daniel Vainish, and Jim Weston.

From the County of Santa Clara, I would like to thank Benny O'Hara, Valerie Altham, Laurel Anderson, Dr. Sara Cody, Dr. Sarah Lewis, Linlin Li, Wen Lin, Jim McPherson, and Dr. Jeff Smith.

Many people graciously shared their time and memories of the years 1981 to 1999 with me, including Jeff Barber, Mark Bonine, Denny Carroll, Pat Duffy, Dr. Marty Fenstersheib, Helen and Ted Johnson, Dr. George Kent, Dr. Denny McShane, David Miramontes, Bob Reed, Norm Robinson, Bob Sorenson, and Karl Vidt.

APPENDIX E

BAYMEC's Important Work Continues

By the mid-1990s, I was busy with teaching, writing my first book, and running for office, so I stepped down from the BAYMEC board. Throughout the years, Wiggsy has stayed on the board—her institutional memory and extensive political network remaining one of the organization's greatest assets. Many members have rotated on and off, each bringing their own energy and fresh ideas to the table.

For the most part, BAYMEC has been able to help elect progressive candidates to local office. One exception was Chuck Reed, who served as mayor of San Jose from 2007 to 2015. Never a friend of our community, he was the only councilmember who voted against my 2003 proposal to grant spouses of same-sex City employees equal benefits. He also refused to take a stand against Proposition 8, the 2008 California constitutional amendment that restricted marriages to "one man and one woman" only.

The 2010 election resurrected a former Republican councilman, Larry Pegram. He was a longtime vocal opponent of LGBTQ+ rights and the co-founder and president of the Values Advocacy Council, a group he called "a voice for Judeo-Christian values in policy making in Silicon Valley." He worked on an aborted effort to recall Mayor Ron Gonzales due to his vote on spousal benefits for LGBTQ+ City employees. In a San Jose

Metro article, he is quoted as saying, "If you're disabled, female, or African-American, those are things you can't change. But gays and lesbians are not born that way; it's a decision they made."

BAYMEC sprang into action, opposing and organizing against Pegram. They found an unlikely partner in the San Jose Police Union. The union's president, Jim Unland, and board member James Gonzales were not "out" on the force, although Gonzales served on the BAYMEC board. Unland became the first openly gay San Jose police officer when he came out in an opinion piece for the *Mercury News* criticizing Reed for his endorsement of Pegram.[134]

Support soon coalesced around Don Rocha, whom I had long known to be an ally and who actively sought BAYMEC's endorsement. I was so concerned about Pegram serving on the Council that I made Rocha's campaign my top priority. I did all I could to recruit volunteers, walk precincts, and raise money for him, as did other BAYMEC board members. Thankfully, Rocha went on to defeat Pegram. If an organization like BAYMEC had not been around to draw attention to the race, speak to the press, and shine a spotlight on Pegram's positions, he likely would have won.

Efforts to get Reed to change his position on same-sex marriage continued, especially after the passage of Proposition 8. A grassroots group called Marriage Equality Silicon Valley was formed to educate people about gay marriage, should there be a future ballot measure. The group, along with Los Gatos resident Alice Hoagland—the mother of Mark Bingham, a gay man who lost his life on 9/11 when he joined other passengers wrestling terrorists to take back control of Flight 93—met with Reed. They both grew up in the Midwest, and in Hoagland's former life as a practicing Mormon, had opposed gay marriage, too. She spoke about how her thinking had evolved and

----

134   Jim Unland. "San Jose council candidate's beliefs invite discrimination against gays." *San Jose Mercury News*. October 10, 2010.

encouraged him to keep an open mind. I remember being so impressed by her compassion, hoping that if anyone could persuade Reed to change his mind, it would be her. Unfortunately, it was all for naught.

The following year, I became president of the Board of Supervisors. To help foster better communication between the city and the county, a tradition was established to have the city's mayor and the County's president meet quarterly. As the day of the first meeting approached, I felt my anger toward Reed rising. I decided I couldn't just sit across a table from someone who didn't think I deserved the same basic rights as him. I wrote Reed a short note telling him that, adding that the Board's vice-president would be our representative that year.

Fast forward to 2016. Another Family Advocacy Council candidate, Steve Brown, ran for city council with the endorsement of now-former Mayor Reed. BAYMEC discovered Brown's anti-gay stance on a Family Values Advocacy Council questionnaire that was posted online, where he indicated that he believed businesses had the right to refuse service to LGBTQ+ people based on their religious beliefs, similar to the infamous Hobby Lobby position. Brown had received the endorsement from the San Jose Chamber of Commerce political action committee, a close ally of current mayor Sam Liccardo, who BAYMEC believed was close to endorsing Brown.

James Gonzales, who was now BAYMEC president and police union vice-president, quickly organized a rally in front of the Billy DeFrank LGBTQ+ Community Center on The Alameda. Assemblymembers Evan Low and Ash Kalra, along with Labor Union leader Ben Field, myself, and other LGBTQ+ elected officials, spoke at the press conference. To our surprise, Brown showed up, walked straight to the podium, and began speaking to the cameras. After reluctantly leaving the podium, he heckled from the audience, coming across as unstable. At that point, between the press coverage and his own actions, Brown's campaign had effectively sunk, making way for BAYMEC's endorsed candidate in the race, public defender investigator Sergio Jimenez, to easily win the election.

All Hell Breaks Loose in the Town of Los Gatos

The Town of Los Gatos, nestled beneath the Santa Cruz Mountains, is generally seen as a quiet, upper middle class enclave. However, when BAYMEC board members asked if the Town Council could raise the Rainbow flag in front of the Town Hall for Pride, they were told that no such flag policy existed, nor was there time to create one. Instead, Town staff proposed to add rainbow stripes to the two crosswalks on East Main Street in front of the Town Hall. On June 4, 2021, the action was unanimously approved by the Council.

Then all hell broke loose. A group of MAGA Republicans (who were regularly protesting the results of the 2016 presidential election) had been speaking out at Council meetings against critical race theory, Black Lives Matter, vaccine mandates, and the LGBTQ+ community. Upon hearing about the rainbow stripes, the group became completely unhinged. They began constantly disrupting Council meetings and threatening councilmembers. To make matters worse, since these were public meetings, the Town didn't have the authority to eject them.

MAGA activists started heavily targeting Los Gatos Mayor Marico Sayoc. They went so far as to stalk her teenage son online, posing as another teenager and ultimately revealing what they believed to be his sexual orientation. This information was brought up against his will during the public comment at a Town Council meeting, intentionally outing the teenager. The incident so infuriated the mayor's husband, who was listening to the meeting at home, that he ran all the way from their house to the Town Hall and confronted the bigots.

Town leaders were unsure of what to do. They had never

encountered anything like this before in their gentile town. Seeing that help was needed, BAYMEC immediately organized, providing legal and political advice. They mobilized people to attend the next Council meeting to support the mayor and condemn the actions of the extremists.

One resident who strongly supported the Council was Rob Moore. He regularly spoke against the MAGA extremists at the meetings, even when hostilities reached an all-time high. He co-organized a United Against Hate walk on November 14, 2021, where thousands of people came together in Los Gatos to walk for love and peace. It sent a strong message that the vast majority of Los Gatos residents *were* in support of the Council's actions related to diversity and acceptance. It was seen as a turning point in the controversy.

After things calmed down, it was apparent that state law had to be changed to deal with people who only wanted to cause chaos at meetings. Inspired by Mayor Sayoc's experience, state Senator David Cortese and Assemblyman Evan Low introduced SB 1100, which increased protection for government officials and employees who face threats, intimidation, or harassment as a result of their public service. The bill was signed by Governor Newsom in August 2022.

As for Moore, he would announce his run for Town Council the following year. This led to flyers being distributed around town that included the wording, "We want to preserve our historical presence, wholesome traditions, family community, and continue to be a desirable place to live. Just say NO MOORE." On the list of "No Moore" things they wanted were rainbow crosswalks.

As it turned out, they got more "Moore" than they bargained for. In November 2022, he won the election with the highest number of votes. And, at just 24, he is the youngest councilmember in the Town's history.

BAYMEC Galas

BAYMEC continued to hold their annual dinners and brunches over the years. They were able to consistently bring in big-name state politicians as the keynote speakers, such as California Senate Pro-Temp Toni Atkins, Assembly Speaker John Perez, state Attorney General Rob Bonta, and gay Warriors President Rick Welts.

In 2013, the U.S. Supreme Court's decision to overturn Proposition 8 happened only months before the BAYMEC gala brunch. The board knew this overlap was an opportunity for straight people to experience the significance of such an advancement in equality. So, it was decided that there would be a surprise wedding held during the event. Julie Adiutori had recently started a gay wedding business to show support for her gay son helped plan the event, and we brought in two same-sex couples who were willing to be married in front of a large crowd of people. I was asked to officiate, which I gladly accepted.

We hired Frenchie, a queer singer and recent American Idol reality show winner, to perform the first dance. As the lights dimmed in the grand ballroom of the Fairmont Hotel, spotlights shone on opposite ends of the room. The two grooms and two brides walked down the aisle towards me, while "Somewhere Over the Rainbow" played sweetly in the background.

For the 500 people in attendance, many of whom were straight allies, it was their first chance to witness a gay wedding. There was great joy and teary eyes from everyone in the room. Following the brief ceremony, Frenchie delivered a powerful ballad that brought the house down. BAYMEC galas were always wonderful events, but this one was truly unforgettable.

After a three-year hiatus due to COVID, BAYMEC resumed Sunday brunches in 2023 as its main fundraising event. Board members were anxious because no one knew if the LGBTQ+ community would still be able to support such an event, especially at $200 a ticket. It turned out there was no need to worry;

nearly 500 people attended. As per BAYMEC tradition, all the elected officials and candidates—about 100 of them—formed a conga line and walked on stage to introduce themselves. Openly gay San Diego Mayor Todd Gloria gave an inspiring keynote speech. Together $140,000 was raised.

Ever since its first spaghetti dinner in 1986, BAYMEC has recognized individuals who exemplify true leadership. For 2023, Los Gatos Mayor Marico Sayoc received the BAYMEC Profile in Courage Award. In her presentation, Congresswoman Anna Eshoo talked about hostilities aimed at Sayoc in meetings and at her home. "None of our public servants—no, none of us *period*—should have to endure what Marico did. Still, she has stood up to hate and intolerance with unwavering determination."

Eshoo ended with these words: "For her extraordinary bravery and dedication to defending the rights of all members of her community, Marico Sayoc is a deserving recipient of an award of courage. Her unwavering commitment to justice and equality serves as an inspiration to us all, and we are honored to recognize her."

Rob Moore was also acknowledged with the Stan Hajduk BAYMEC Ally of the Year Award "for his courage in fighting against hatred in Los Gatos and standing unapologetically with the LGBTQ+ community." It was presented by San Jose Councilwoman Pam Foley, who was the last recipient of the award.

Also receiving awards were Tyller Williamson, the openly gay mayor of Monterey, and Lance Moore, the founder of the Silicon Valley Trans Day of Visibility.

It was a privilege to be present for the brunch to see these four individuals receive their well-deserved recognition.

As the brunch came to an end, I felt such pride knowing that a clear message had been sent to all locally elected officials: the queer community was as strong as ever, and we could be relied upon to support our friends and fight our enemies—which was exactly what Wiggsy and I set out to do 39 years ago.

ACKNOWLEDGMENTS

Writing this book has been a large undertaking, mainly due to its many components. Because it is part history book, much research needed to be done. Some of this early work was completed when I wrote two history booklets while serving on the Santa Clara County Board of Supervisors. Foremost among the people who helped were Jim Weston, Jason Bennert, Brian Darrow, and Brian Aubineau. Jim has been kind enough to continue assisting me well after I left political office.

Other staff members who helped catalog my government papers were John Mills, Megan Doyle, John Myers, Laura Jones, Tony Filice, Mitchell Nelson, and Michelle Runyon.

Working closely with me on the *Queer Silicon Valley* history project, as well as any task assigned to him, was one of my best SJSU students Steven Peck. His assistance with numerous details of the book was invaluable.

Don Cecil, another outstanding student, helped immensely in making the chapter on running for office even more comprehensive and valuable. James Gonzales was helpful with writing about current BAYMEC activities.

Michael Haberecht, Terry Christensen, Jean McCorquordale, Arlene Rusche, and Leslee Hamilton were kind enough to read various chapters of the book and provide feedback. BE Allatt and Chloe Siennah also made helpful edits.

All the staff at History San Jose, especially Bill Schroh, Ken Middlebrook, and Monica Lock, were indispensable in assisting with the exhibition, as was Amy Cohen, the exhibition developer from Exhibit Envoy.

Bob Gliner directed the excellent documentary; it was wonderful working with him.

Thanks go out to Dan DiVittorio for designing the book cover as well as for suggesting the title. Luis Castillo, who always makes me look better than I am, took the cover photo. Thanks, too, to everyone at Atmosphere Press.

To be particularly thanked is my colleague at San Jose State University, Dr. Ken Peter who, after I gave a lecture about my LGBTQ+ activism to his American Government class, encouraged me to write a book about my life. He also gave astute editing suggestions.

I would be remiss if I didn't do a shout-out to the editorial page editors of the *San Jose Mercury News*. They were always agreeable to printing my op-ed pieces, starting with my "coming out" piece in 1984 and ending with the one about the opening of the *Queer Silicon Valley* exhibition in 2021, with a dozen pieces in between. This platform allowed me to tell stories about the LGBTQ+ community to a greater audience for close to 40 years.

Throughout this endeavor, I could sense my mother looking over my shoulder, and just as she did after reading each chapter I sent her from my first book, she would respond back to me, "Oh, Ken, that's my favorite chapter so far."

ABOUT ATMOSPHERE PRESS

Founded in 2015, Atmosphere Press was built on the principles of Honesty, Transparency, Professionalism, Kindness, and Making Your Book Awesome. As an ethical and author-friendly hybrid press, we stay true to that founding mission today.

If you're a reader, enter our giveaway for a free book here:

SCAN TO ENTER
BOOK GIVEAWAY

If you're a writer, submit your manuscript for consideration here:

SCAN TO SUBMIT
MANUSCRIPT

And always feel free to visit Atmosphere Press and our authors online at atmospherepress.com. See you there soon!

About the Author

KEN YEAGER received his bachelor's degree in Political Science from San Jose State University and his Ph.D. in Education from Stanford University. In 1984 he co-founded BAYMEC, a political action committee in the Bay Area that is still active today. In 1992, he was elected to the community college board, becoming the first openly gay official in Santa Clara County. He subsequently won election to the San Jose City Council and the Santa Clara County Board of Supervisors. A long-time lecturer at SJSU, he returned to teaching in 2019. He and his partner Michael are proud dads to their Yellow Labrador, Hank.

Made in the USA
Las Vegas, NV
03 April 2024

88194922R00177